The House on Dream Street

The House on Dream Street

Memoir of an American Woman
in Vietnam

by

Dana Sachs

ALGONQUIN BOOKS OF CHAPEL HILL
2000

Published by Algonquin Books of Chapel Hill
Post Office Box 2225
Chapel Hill, North Carolina 27515-2225

a division of
Workman Publishing
708 Broadway
New York, New York 10003

Parts of chapter 13, "Firecrackers on Dream Street," appeared in a different form as
"Tet" in the January/February 1995 issue of *Destination: Vietnam* magazine.

Library of Congress Cataloging-in-Publication Data
Sachs, Dana.
    The house on Dream Street : memoir of an American woman in Vietnam /
by Dana Sachs.
        p. cm.
    ISBN 1-56512-291-7
        1. Hanoi (Vietnam)—Description and travel. 2. Hanoi (Vietnam)—Social
life and customs. 3. Sachs, Dana—Journeys—Vietnam—Hanoi. I. Title.
DS559 93.H36 S23 2000
959.7—dc21   00-044191

10 9 8 7 6 5 4 3 2 1
First Edition

To my friends in Vietnam,
for inviting me into their
lives and encouraging me to
write about it; and to Todd
and Jesse, for everything

In memory of Leah Melnick

Contents

Ếch ngồi đáy giếng coi trời bằng vung.

A frog that sits at the bottom of a well

thinks that the whole sky

is only as big as the lid of a pot.

— VIETNAMESE PROVERB

*T*HIS IS A STORY ABOUT VIETNAM, but it's not about the war there. It is a story about Vietnam much later, and about one American woman's life in that country. It's the story of a love affair with a place, a love affair that I never would have predicted.

I was born in 1962, and when I was a kid, the words "Vietnam" and "war" were interchangeable. People asked questions like, "When will Vietnam be over?" and, for me at least, such a question didn't sound strange at all. I'd never heard of "Vietnam" except as war, and the place itself conjured nothing in my mind but dust and blood and wailing faces.

Of course the war did end, finally, after more than twenty years, and the deaths of fifty-eight thousand Americans and nearly two million Vietnamese. After North Vietnamese tanks crashed through the gates of Saigon's Presidential Palace on April 30, 1975, Vietnam became one nation, then it shut itself off from the Western world.

Nothing that had happened during the war in Vietnam had caused my family to suffer. My father had been too old for the draft. The people we knew who had served in the war hadn't died, thank goodness, or even been injured. And now that it was over, Vietnam receded into history for me, which amounted to the few bits of information I absorbed when my harried American history teacher compressed all of Vietnam and Watergate into the last week of eleventh grade.

Nothing in my background hinted at the possibility of my falling in love with Vietnam. Then in 1989, when I was twenty-six and working as a journalist in San Francisco, a friend and I decided to quit our jobs and go backpacking through Asia. In Thailand a few months later, we found out that Vietnam, for the first time since the war ended, was offering tourist visas to Americans. We were hungry to go to a place that hadn't been transformed by tourism (and travelers like us), and so we went.

Realistically, I knew no bombs would drop during that visit, but my imagination couldn't get past television images of my childhood: screaming women in black pajamas, military jeeps roving city streets, and bomb-shocked children begging for food. Instead, I was confronted by a world in the midst of regenerating itself. I saw lush vegetation growing out of the broken carcasses of airplanes, and I met passionate, stubborn, intensely engaging people who, far from being beaten down by their past, focused limitless energy on constructing for themselves a less troubled future. We traversed the country during that month, from Ho Chi Minh City to Hanoi, and in a way that no other place I'd ever visited had done, the country seemed to open its soul to me. I stood on busy sidewalks as teary-eyed young mothers held my hands and told me stories of their lives. I spent happy evenings laughing and guzzling beer with cranky old men, and lazy afternoons riding bicycles along quiet country roads with foreign language students who collected hip English phrases as obsessively as American teenagers collect CDs. I fell in love with Vietnam during that visit.

I spent most of the 1990s either living in Vietnam or figuring out how I could go back. I held a number of different jobs: I taught English, wrote a newspaper column, edited English-language radio broadcasts, led tours. More often, I worked for Hanoians, and my wages came in the ten- or twenty-dollar bundles for which my employers had scrimped and saved. Once, I contributed the voice-over narration for a documentary on the production of silk. For that, I earned a few dollars and a pale peach blouse.

I never made more than what I needed to pay the rent. But I kept returning. It was memories, and moments, that drew me back: the feel of my rickety one-speed bike careering through the streets of Hanoi; the rich, woody smell of freshly steamed rice; my friend Huong and the way a smile appeared, like sun after rain, across her face. I missed the green, crashing summer storms and the way they managed to break the heat. I missed carrying home lunch wrapped in a banana leaf and a few recycled pages of some child's homework. I missed sitting in cafés and drinking sweet sugarcane juice with Phai, the Hanoi man I would come to love. Over the course of all these years, some part of my soul reserved itself for Vietnam. When I went there, it became alive again. And when I left, it retreated.

Not surprisingly, my personal life changed enormously over the next eight years. In 1995, I got married, and in 1997, I had a baby. I no longer had the luxury to take off by myself for Vietnam. I'd like to say that it didn't matter, that, over the course of those years, my passion for the place had finally waned. But it hadn't. I still wrote about Vietnam. Read about Vietnam. I still dreamed about it. Regularly.

In May of 1998, I went back, this time with my husband and son. The journey was long and complicated, demanding nearly thirty hours, crossing twelve time zones, and changing planes three times. Still, I forgot my fatigue when the jet finally touched down on the tarmac of Hanoi's Noi Bai Airport. As the other passengers on the plane hurried to pull their belongings down from the overhead racks, I held my son in my arms and turned toward the window, straining for a glimpse of what I knew lay

outside: deep green fields stretching off toward the hazy silhou-
ette of Ba Vi Mountain. And there it was, just as I'd remembered, a view spread out before me beneath a rice-colored sky.

I had not always felt so sure of this place. Six years earlier,
on a blustery day in early March of 1992, the view outside the
window of the plane looked barren and uninviting. Staring out
across the rice fields toward that unknown mountain, I'd felt
alone and quite terrified. My plan to come here, which had once
sounded like great adventure, now seemed foolish, like a game
of pretend that I'd taken too far. I had nothing except a backpack
and a wavering determination to build a life for myself in this
place. Just those two things. And one address.

1 Through the Green Gate

THE CYCLO PULLED TO A STOP in front of an enormous
green gate. I turned around and looked at the driver, but he only
gave me a smug smile from his seat on the pedicab. "This is number four," he said, gesturing toward the address beside the gate.
I glanced at the number, then at the address in my hand, then
glared at him. When he had first approached me as I stepped off
the bus in central Hanoi, he had insisted that my destination was
ten kilometers away and that he, in turn, deserved a hefty fee for
pedaling me there. But we had traveled less than a kilometer and
arrived in five minutes.

"Stay here," I said as sternly as I could in my miserable
Vietnamese. I clambered over my backpack and out of the bas-
ketlike passenger seat, unwilling to pay him before I knew if
this place was, indeed, the home of the only person I knew in
Hanoi. The cyclo driver shrugged, then twisted around on his
bicycle seat and immediately leapt into a discussion with the
people gathered around a sidewalk tea stall across the narrow
street. "She's an American. Came here to study Vietnamese.
Twenty-nine years old. Not married yet," he told them, mak-

ing quick work of all the information I had given him on the ride over.

I stood for a moment, looking around. I remembered Hanoi from my previous visit, in the late winter two years before, and much that I saw around me now felt familiar. Today's sky was the same impermeable gray, the color of the rice porridge I'd watched people swallow quickly on their way to work. The air had the same chilly moistness, carrying hints of motorbike exhaust, overripe fruit, and chicken broth simmering all day over tiny charcoal stoves. Across the road, a group of pale-faced old women sat at the tea stall. They wore scarves around their heads and held tiny cups of Hanoi tea between their fingers. I remembered that tea as well. In Saigon, people had drunk endless glasses of iced tea. At restaurants and sidewalk food stalls, every order, even coffee, came with tea. But Saigon tea was weak as water, barely yellow. The copper-colored Hanoi tea was a different drink entirely, whiskey strong and drunk in shots. On my first trip to Hanoi, I had sipped it and gagged.

I could remember a lot about Hanoi, but I felt shaky anyway. My earlier visit to Vietnam had lasted only a month. Now, I was moving here. The difference between visiting and living in Vietnam felt immense, and very scary. I'd had big dreams to come back to this country to live. But now, I only felt small and fragile and very foreign. I couldn't satisfy myself with a quick jaunt through the famous sites and then a taxi ride back to the airport. I had to find a job. A home. Some friends.

From across the road, the tea drinkers stared at me with speculative interest. Pulling my scarf tighter against the wind, I wished I could take a little break, maybe just sleep in my own bed tonight in San Francisco, then try Hanoi again tomorrow. But the tea drinkers didn't disappear. One of them, perched on a stool with her knees tightly folded against her chest, lifted a hand

and briskly waved me toward the gate. Her face, as infinitely lined as cracked porcelain, broke into a great, wide grin, revealing two rows of deeply red, betel-nut stained teeth. I looked at her for a moment, forcing my mouth into a smile of its own. Then, mustering all my courage, I turned around, walked over to the doorbell, and rang. I'd come all this way. It was too late to change my mind.

After a minute, I heard a shuffling behind the gate. A latch turned and a husky, pale-skinned teenage girl appeared in the doorway. She looked out at me in shock. I stammered in Vietnamese, "Uh. Is Tra here? I want to meet Nguyen Thi Tra."

The expression on her face did not change. "Nguyen Thi Tra!" yelled the cyclo driver from behind me. The girl's mouth twitched in some form of recognition, and she disappeared again behind the gate.

I had met Nguyen Thi Tra less than a year before, when she taught Vietnamese at a summer-long intensive language course I'd attended in upstate New York. All the students adored her, not because she was such a fine language teacher—she was actually an economist drafted for a job outside her field—but because she had that rare and very lucky quality of being completely attractive. She was less than five feet tall, but maintained an energy that, even compressed inside that tiny body, could expand to fill a room.

Although Tra was Vietnamese, she was not an easy person to imagine living in Vietnam. I had only known her as a resident of the States, where she had been studying business at the University of Michigan for the past three years. America suited her well. There, she had guzzled diet Cokes, developed a preference for poppy-seed bagels, and become a jogger who worried about her weight. The only thing that tied her to Vietnam, it had seemed to me, was that she had a husband and young son who still lived there. I was anxious to see how this fiery spirit, so thrilled by America, would appear in Hanoi, an ancient city of crumbling colonial mansions and wizened old ladies who could make an afternoon out of staring at a foreigner.

I heard a squeal on the other side of the wall. The teenager pulled back the gate to reveal a young woman bounding toward me. She was wearing a burly white sweater, Day-Glo aquamarine biker shorts, and brand new Nike sneakers. With her hair pulled back into a high ponytail, she looked more like a college gymnastics star than a Hanoi wife and mother. I smiled. It was Tra.

We passed the next minutes in a frenzy of loud, American-style greetings. The neighbors, the cyclo driver, and the teenage girl watched us as if we were enacting the reunion of long-lost sisters in a traditional folk play. "Don't just stand there," Tra said, finally, ready to drag me by the hand into her house. I paid the cyclo driver and grabbed my backpack. As the gate slammed shut behind us, I felt, for a moment at least, that I was safe.

The yellow, two-story house curled around the sides of a courtyard. The older section at the left looked over the high wall into the street outside and had the elegant symmetry of French colonial architecture. Behind it sat a more modern U-shaped addition, a utilitarian two-story structure with a balcony running the length of the second floor. Together in its two parts, Tra's house looked like a stately Paris mansion run up against a Motel 6.

The two of us stood in the blue fluorescent glow of the kitchen. We'd spent an hour or two catching up over tea and candy and now I'd offered to help cook dinner. Tra was planning to serve rice pancakes wrapped around grilled pork, a sort of Vietnamese version of the burrito. To accompany the dish, she was preparing a platter of rice noodles, lettuce, bean sprouts, sliced lemons, hot chilis, and a variety of herbs. Tra pushed a bowl of herbs in my direction.

"This is what you do," she said, the tone in her voice reminding me of the way she used to beat the blackboard with a nub of chalk while trying to explain some complicated rule of Vietnamese grammar. Today's lesson centered on a sprig of basil, from which she plucked off the smooth green leaves. "What do you call this vegetable in English?" she suddenly paused mid-demonstration to ask. Tra believed that her chances for success in the world outside of Vietnam were directly related to her aptitude in English. "Basil" was a word she needed to know.

"You should learn to say these things in Vietnamese, too," Tra said, after I had carefully pronounced "basil," "cilantro," and "mint" for her. Slowly, she said each word for me in Vietnamese, adding the names for several mysterious-looking herbs that sat before us on the table. The one called *tía tô* was maple-shaped, green on one side and royal purple on the other. Chewing the leaves, Tra said, would cure a sore throat. The *rau răm* had long, thin leaves and a spicy smell. Tra held it up and looked at me with one of her wicked grins, the kind of expression that she would describe as meaning, "I have something in my sleeves." *Rau răm,* she whispered now, "is for the monks to eat, so they won't want to have the sex." Then she dissolved into laughter.

I tried to pronounce the new words correctly, but I couldn't absorb a thing. At this point, I could hardly recall the Vietnamese for "eat" or "buy." Meanwhile, Tra stood next to me, slicing cucumbers and repeating "basil," "cilantro," and "mint" to herself as if she were trying to remember the recipe for some complicated salad.

I moved slowly through the bowl of basil. Back in the States, I might have rushed to finish such a task, but here I took my time. I didn't have anywhere else to go. Tra had described some possible rooms for rent, but nothing sounded promising. My great secret hope had been dashed when she told me that she didn't have government permission to house a foreigner. At this moment, Tra and her house felt like my only refuge. I picked through the basil carefully, hoping that if I were a good enough guest at least she'd invite me back.

A hinge creaked and I looked up to see the husky teenage girl peek in through the door of the kitchen, then disappear again.

"Tra, who is that girl?" I asked.

"That's Lua," Tra said. "She's from the countryside. Her family's very poor, so she came here to work for us."

"The Vietnamese government lets people have servants?" I tried to place this in the context of Marxism.

"Of course," said Tra. "We could always have servants." She explained that, in the past, if a family had servants the government would consider it an exploitation of labor, but as the economy started to pick up, no one cared as much.

The girl was back, eyeing me again through the doorway. Lua was taller than average, with a physique that in another decade might have hiked the length of the Ho Chi Minh Trail, one more able body in the intricate network that supplied the Communist forces down south. Now, her family probably spent its days bent double in the rice fields, backs burning in the sun. Lua had managed to get away from all that, taking up the less strenuous life of a servant in the city. She didn't look like either a fighter or a farmer. No famous black pajamas. No conical hat. She had on pink pastel pants and a frilly yellow top. Perhaps she was wondering why I wasn't wearing a pith helmet and a flak jacket.

I pulled together a few words in Vietnamese. "My name is Dana," I said to Lua. She giggled and ran away. I looked at Tra quizzically.

Tra dumped the last handful of cucumber slices into a bowl. Wiping her forehead with the back of her hand, she said, "She's never been so close to a foreigner before. She's scared."

"What can I do?" I asked.

"You can't do anything. People from the countryside, they don't know anything about foreigners." Tra gave a wave of her hand that showed her impatience with Lua's lack of sophistication, then she looked at me for a moment. "I was thinking about something the other day. What is the word in English for a person with a nice face, so nice that it means good luck for their children?"

I thought about it. "I guess we would say a nice face."

"No. It's more than that. In Vietnamese we say *phúc hậu,* a face that means good destiny."

"I don't think we have a word for that in English," I said.

Dissatisfied, Tra pulled a handful of greens from my bowl and began to tear them apart impatiently. Despite her years in the States, she hadn't realized that the concept of destiny is not as important to Americans as it is to Vietnamese. Tra took destiny, and the role it played in people's lives, for granted. I, on the other hand, never thought of destiny at all. It wouldn't be long before I began to realize how fundamental it was in Vietnam.

I couldn't sleep at Tra's, but her neighbor across the street, Nhung, had permission to rent rooms to foreigners. Nhung's place was clean and convenient, but I didn't fancy the brand-new carved wood furniture inlaid with mother-of-pearl, or the price, which seemed to reflect the cost of the opulent surroundings. On the bedside table, perhaps to entice me to stay longer, I found a plate of bananas and oranges with a little note that said, in simple Vietnamese, "Enjoy! All of this fruit is a gift for you, and you don't have to pay for it." For a long while, I lay sideways across the imperial bed, eating a banana and staring at the ceiling. I'd lived in Hanoi for more than eight hours, and so far, I reminded myself, things were going just fine. On the other hand, I'd spent seven of those hours cloistered inside Tra's house, and my hour-long journey from the airport had felt a bit dicey. I considered the fact that, for as long as I lived in Vietnam, I would always stand out in a crowd—bigger, paler, and richer than everyone else.

Maybe I was a little out of my league as an independent traveler. I doubt that Paul Theroux or Graham Greene got shaky every time a group of old women stared at them from across the street. Eric Hansen, author of *Stranger in the Forest,* trekked through the jungles of Borneo—facing wild animals, debilitating ailments, and the constant danger of getting lost—and then he turned around and trekked right back. A guy like that wasn't likely to quake when a cyclo driver demanded a better price.

But women and men, in general, experience travel in very different ways. A man carries a certain cachet in international society. He's the explorer, and although locals might question his behavior, they're not likely to question his very right to travel. When women venture into foreign societies, we often throw ourselves up against the hard surfaces of traditions that aren't flexible enough to accept us there. Simply by daring to go, we break a taboo. Many local men regard breaking one taboo as license to break another, or so I had learned from a hotel bellboy in Thailand, who sat down on my bed, expecting sex as a tip, and from the tour guide who couldn't keep his hand off my thigh, and from the sweet older man in North India who suddenly grabbed me from behind and tried to kiss me. Women travelers have to move through the world very carefully.

Sure, I'd heard about the woman who rode a camel by herself across Australia, but I didn't know any women (or men, for that matter) like her. Most of the women I knew who traveled had to overcome huge obstacles in their own psyches before they even packed their bags. Growing up, I'd always considered myself a physical weakling. When I started to travel, I realized I had to either find my own strength or stay home. One of my most exhilarating experiences had been a very mundane one. It was my first day alone in Asia and I was terrified. My backpack felt like a small child hanging from my shoulders. At the airport bus stop, someone pointed out the bus I needed to go to Bangkok. I watched the vehicle pull alongside the curb and slow down and then realized it was never going to come to a full stop. With my pack bumping along behind me, I jogged to the open door, grabbed the metal bar at the side of it, and pulled myself up. I was still hanging over the side when the bus sped away. For one eternal moment, my arm muscles competed against the weight of the backpack and I knew that I could either pull myself into the bus or allow myself to come crashing down onto the street. With a strength I didn't know I had—a powerful combination of desire and fear of disaster—I pulled myself into the bus.

For me, success in travel had always depended on that mix of desire and fear. Desire got me to buy the ticket, and fear of failure kept me from cashing it in. Coming to Hanoi was no different, except that the stakes were higher. My desire to live in Vietnam was so absolute that I could not imagine any other way to spend the next great chunk of my life. Fear, on the other hand, made me think that if I failed at this I'd have to take it as a general sign of failure in life. I pictured Eric Hansen, setting off into the wilds of Borneo, confronting the challenge of nature. But I wasn't Eric Hansen.

It was nearly midnight. I rolled my banana peel into a little ball, tossed it onto the bedside table, and switched off the light. Upstairs, I could hear the landlady's family watching TV. A dog in the house next door let out a whiny howl. I calculated the time difference between Hanoi and San Francisco—fifteen hours —and fell asleep.

2 *The House on Dream Street*

I HAD VISIONS OF RENTING A LITTLE GARRET in an old villa built by the French. I didn't want anything big, and I could live with creaky doors and peeling paint, as long as I had a view of a tree or two. I pictured renting a room from a big family full of wise grandmothers and cooing babies. I would help them celebrate their weddings, and if someone died I would be with them to share their grief. This house would be my entry point into the culture and customs of Vietnam, and at the end of each eventful day, I would climb the stairs to my quiet little garret, where I would look out at my tree and reflect on what I had learned.

Unfortunately, this was not to be. Garrets, Tra explained, were hard to come by in Hanoi and seldom rented out to foreigners. Though the city had many villas, most were decrepit tenements that lacked such amenities as indoor plumbing. The families lucky enough to have government permission to rent rooms to foreigners were generally the people building the shiny new houses springing up all over town. I might have to make do with something a bit less quaint, Tra told me, but I'd be happier with the plumbing.

We went to look at a townhouse around the corner. The building was four stories high, towering over every other structure in the neighborhood, and so new that I was looking at it through a haze of construction dust. Its most prominent feature, aside from its startling gawkiness, was a strange hull-shaped trellis covering its roof.

"I designed the house myself," said the owner, a man about my age named Tung, who had come outside to meet us. "I didn't need an architect."

"What's that thing up on the roof?" I whispered to Tra in English. "It looks like a boat."

"That's the Hanoi style," she said.

We followed Tung into the ground floor room of the house, which was bare, except for a brand-new gray sofa and matching gray armchair, both covered in clear plastic. Tung stopped and pointed to an empty place on the wall, then said something to Tra.

"He's going to have a telephone," she told me, obviously impressed. Tra's family had a private phone, but they were among the few Hanoi families that had one. Tung explained that his name was at the top of the waiting list for private phones in the city and that he expected to have it installed any day. "We're number three three four seven one," he said proudly, and his future telephone number was the first thing he said in Vietnamese that I could understand.

We followed Tung up a flight of stairs to a second floor back door, which opened on to an exterior stairway leading to the rooms above. Behind the house sat an old French villa, built decades earlier at a stately distance from the road. Now its front and side yards served as real estate for newer buildings—stone cottages and concrete one-room homes cluttered together in such density that, except for a narrow bicycle path, the mansion was completely cut off from the street. From the second-floor landing of Tung's house, I gazed down at the villa with vague longing. Wouldn't I be more likely to find my dream family in that villa than in this tall, skinny townhouse with a nautical trellis on its roof?

Tra and I struggled to climb the stairs. The landlord may have been able to design his own trellis, but he clearly didn't understand how to build a simple staircase. The staircase was not only uneven, it was also excessively steep, and I nearly tripped over one sudden change in the elevation. Tung, meanwhile, was talking nonstop as he climbed the stairs in front of me. I understood few of his words, but it wasn't hard to recognize the intonation and body language of a salesman. He was a modern guy, a Vietnamese Burt Reynolds, possessed of a thick mustache and that easy self-confidence that comes with good looks and financial security. Judging from his shiny loafers and well-tailored pants, I decided he wasn't the kind of fellow who would take an interest in teaching me the old and honored customs of traditional Vietnam.

After climbing three flights, Tra and I were breathless when we finally reached the room. As Tung continued talking about the house, and Tra nodded politely, I looked around. It was large and airy, with a Western-style bathroom adjoining it and double doors at the far end that opened to a balcony overlooking the street. The color scheme was inconsistent enough to seem random —brown-and-orange tiled floor, yellow walls, a ceiling painted in two shades of baby blue, a pink coverlet for the bed, dark green curtains, and a pair of reddish-orange Naugahyde armchairs. Tapestry scenes of deer grazing in green mountain meadows (Vietnam?) hung on two walls, and at various spots around the room dangled the shiny metal balls I'd always thought of as Christmas tree ornaments. The room contained enough furniture to fill a small house. In addition to the bed, desk, couch, coffee table, three-piece wardrobe, armchairs, and folding chairs, there was a Barbie-style mirrored vanity with matching red leather stool. I walked over to the faux-rosewood wardrobe and looked in at the contents of its tinted glass shelves: a pair of small porcelain ballet dancers, a green inflatable clown, a vase of synthetic-fabric flowers, a conch shell polished to a shade of pale peach, a small plastic reindeer, and a toy motorcycle. Tung carefully opened the cabinet, and Tra, who looked beguiled, reached inside to get a closer look at the reindeer. In the United States, such furniture would serve as a substitute— those who couldn't afford real rosewood or mahogany could at least enjoy a laminated facsimile of the real thing. But here in Vietnam, where "rich" meant access to a few thousand dollars, the ability to buy a sumptuous fake was itself a sign of wealth. Here, most families both slept and ate their meals on the same mat-covered wooden platform.

My house in San Francisco was decorated with Indonesian woven baskets, Indian embroideries, and lacquer boxes I had carried back from Burma. Vietnam has its own highly developed traditions of lacquer painting, wood carving, and silk weaving, but just as I didn't buy La-Z-Boy recliners, not all Vietnamese valued their local handicrafts. Tra handed me the tiny plastic reindeer, and as I turned it over in my hand I realized the decor made the place familiar and comforting. The pearl-inlaid lacquer furniture at Nhung's seemed sterile in comparison. I glanced at the satin-fringed harlequin-doll lamp sitting on the vanity. Okay, so some of the furnishings were excessive, but the profusion of objects showed somebody's careful attempt to turn a bare room into a pleasing home. Tung didn't seem like a kindred spirit, or even someone I might choose as a friend. He was a businessman determined to rent out a room. But his face also betrayed an expression of deep pride in this house and in having built it. It was that private look of satisfaction that made me want to live there.

The door creaked open and a little boy squealed and leapt into the room. "This my son," said Tung, speaking in English for the first time. "His name Viet." The child couldn't have been more than five years old, and he was robustly skinny in that way that only healthy children can be—with limitless energy and absolutely no need for extra bulk. He stared at me with such intensity that, if his father had not held him firmly by the shoulders, I felt sure he would have tried to leap on top of me. I gave him an uncertain smile, and the boy, like a visitor to the zoo delighted to see that monkeys can put their toes in their mouths, began to laugh. It wasn't the sweet tinkling giggle one might expect from an innocent young boy, but a deep, gravelly chuckle, the laughter of a child who had smoked too many cigars.

"Viet!" a voice hissed across the room. We looked up to see a young woman half hiding behind the door.

"This my wife. His name Huong," Tung said, motioning for her to come inside.

I nodded at the woman as she gazed in my direction. She was rather tall for a Vietnamese, but thin and pale, with eyes that took in everything while revealing nothing. I would never have guessed that she was married to this businessman. The two seemed as mismatched as the clothes she was wearing: a lace-embroidered, mud-red shirt topping a pair of orange-flowered pants. (As I would later learn, Huong had a fashion sense that was quite common in Hanoi, one that was reminiscent of the leaner days of socialism, when personal style was dependent on the availability of products, not on choice between them.) Only her hair, which bore the unmistakable frizz of a perm, gave any indication that she had an interest in the modern fashions that so obviously delighted her husband.

The couple stood looking at me. He seemed anxious to hear my decision. She hovered behind him, exhibiting a shyness that would have been more understandable in the little boy now straining to touch me. It seemed to take all the effort she could muster simply to look me in the face and smile limply. I glanced over at Tra in her smart slacks and oxford-cloth shirt. Had I not known, I would have taken my friend Tra for the landlord's wife. I tried to smile at Huong.

Tra said something to Tung and Huong that made them laugh.

"Duyen," said Tung. "Yes, good."

Tra looked at me. "I told them to call you Duyen. You should use your Vietnamese name, you know." Tra herself had given me the name Duyen when I began to study Vietnamese back in the States. It meant "charming," and Tra had chosen it not because of any particular attributes of my own personality (she had nothing to go on but a class roster when she picked it) but because, like Dana, it began with the letter *D*.

"Duyen," my future landlord said. He tapped his index finger against his chest. "I. Three years. Deutschland."

"You lived in Germany?" I asked.

Tung nodded, beaming. "I speaks Germany. Germany no good." He gave a little shrug and held his empty palms up. "I want study English." Robbed of his smooth sales ability in Vietnamese, he didn't seem as slick.

"I like your house," I said slowly, in English, pausing between each word.

He nodded happily. "Yes, I want study English." Tra looked at me and giggled.

Later, I counted. From my front door to Tra's took ninety-three steps.

• • •

The backpack I brought to Hanoi contained a few changes of clothes, a sampler of antibiotics, an armful of thick novels, a twenty-pack of black Uni-Ball pens, and a six-month supply of tampons, which were not yet available in Hanoi. I had so few things of my own that I felt grateful for the green plastic inflatable clown, the pair of porcelain dancers, and all the other knickknacks in my new room. Even if those weren't *my* things, at least they were things.

As soon as I moved in, Huong started bringing me more. A few minutes after she saw me walk upstairs carrying a bouquet of flowers, she knocked on my door with a bright purple and orange ceramic vase. The next morning, she knocked again, this time to hand me a pair of pink rubber sandals to wear in the bathroom. A day later, after our new phone was installed, she brought me a copy of the Hanoi phone book, as if I would actually have numbers I needed to look up. None of these offerings led to conversation between us. I wanted to talk to her, but my Vietnamese was not comprehensible. Each time I uttered a word, Huong's face froze in concentration. Sometimes, she'd nod as if she understood, but mostly she was just being gracious. After a moment of silence, she would simply smile, then turn and walk back down the stairs. Shutting my door, I would think back over everything I'd said, trying to figure out where I'd gone wrong.

A few nights after I moved in, Tung and Huong invited me to have dinner with them. When I came down, I found Tung sitting in the living room with two other men. He was holding the new telephone in his lap as if it were a prized cat.

"Sit down," he told me. "Drink Johnnie."

Vietnamese is a language that seldom gets bogged down by excess words, but, with me particularly, Tung made sure to speak even more simply, which only made me feel worse. Despite ten weeks of intensive language study in the States, I was only able to understand Tung because he pointed to an empty stool and held up a bottle of Johnnie Walker so that I could see it.

I sat down. All three men were looking at me, but in very different ways. Tung was leaning forward, eagerly pouring the whiskey and grinning hospitably, as if he were trying to make up in facial gestures what he lacked in ability to converse. The man sitting next to him, a ruddy-faced fellow in his forties, was smiling broadly and openly staring. The third man perched on a stool, not so much with us as halfway between where we were sitting and the door, as if he'd just stopped by and meant to leave at any moment. He was younger than the other two, about my age, with fine features, honey-colored skin, and hair that fell in thick waves across his forehead. Unlike Tung and the other man, both of whom were wearing new jeans and bright, freshly pressed shirts, this man wore black cotton work pants and a wrinkled white shirt stained with something that looked like automotive grease. He didn't look at me directly. Rather, he rested his elbows on his knees, staring at the cigarette dangling between his fingers, and glanced up at me every few seconds before looking down again.

I managed to endure this scrutiny for about ninety seconds. Then I heard the clatter of pots in the kitchen. Pointing in that direction, I made an apologetic smile and escaped.

The kitchen was tiny. Huong and another woman were squatting on the only available floor space, hovering over large wooden cutting boards. Huong merely smiled when I appeared, but the other woman's entire face lit up. "Duyen," she exclaimed, as if she'd been waiting years for me to show up. She stood, rubbed bits of Chinese broccoli off her hands, then pointed her index finger to herself, said, "Nga!" and broke into laughter.

Huong watched the two of us and grinned, then turned her eyes back to the large fish she was in the midst of gutting.

"*Chào, Nga,*" I said. Hello, Nga.

Nga had long, wavy hair, a curvaceous body, and a face that, were she just a few years younger, might have adorned the glossy photo calendars I'd seen for sale at the post office. She pointed to Huong and said, "*Em,*" then pointed to herself and said, "*Chị,*" then back to Huong—"*Em*"—and back to herself—"*Chị.*" For once, my intensive Vietnamese course did me justice because I understood that Nga was telling me she was Huong's older sister. I felt like I'd cracked a secret code.

The Vietnamese system of pronouns feels immensely complicated to Americans. The language has no simple word for "you," and, despite a Communist-era effort to promote the word "*tôi*" as an all-purpose, egalitarian "I," most people still rely on the ancient system of pronouns, which honors age and status. To put it simply, in Vietnamese one must modify the words for "I" and "you" depending on one's own identity and that of the person with whom one is speaking. Thus, a thirty-year-old woman would call herself "little sister" when speaking to someone ten years older than herself and "niece" or "daughter" if she were speaking to someone even older. With a child, she'd call herself "aunt," with a younger friend, she'd be "older sister." With a dear friend, she'd use her given name, and with a colleague, she'd call herself "friend." In a culture less concerned with personal individuality than with one's relationship to others, identity itself was relative in Vietnamese. Who you were depended on whom you were with.

Once I figured out that Huong and Nga were "younger sister" and "older sister" in a literal rather than figurative way, I must have looked shocked. It wasn't the fact that the two looked so different, but that their personalities were so completely dissimilar. Nga was such an extrovert. Huong was so laconic that I had my doubts she and I would ever have much of a conversation, even if I did manage to learn Vietnamese.

Nga pulled me through the door and back into the living room. The younger, dark-skinned man had disappeared. I couldn't remember—actually, I didn't know—if Tung had introduced him to me or not, and I had no idea who he was or where he'd gone. Now Nga seemed intent on introducing me to the other man. He was still sitting with Tung, drinking whiskey. "*Chồng! Nga,*" she announced, pointing to him.

For a moment I was at a loss, trying to remember if *chồng* meant "brother" or not. Then Tung helped me. "His husband," he announced in English, and then Nga, apparently satisfied, dragged me back into the kitchen.

Over the next twenty minutes, the two sisters managed to prepare a four-course dinner in a space no bigger than the average American bathtub. I watched them for a few minutes from the doorway, then pulled a knife from the dish rack and pointed to myself. Huong and Nga both shook their heads so violently that they might have feared I was planning to kill myself. I put the knife down and said, "I. Like," in Vietnamese, then couldn't remember how to say "cook." They burst out laughing.

Nevertheless, Nga tried even harder to converse with me. While Huong cooked, Nga and I used mime and my few words of Vietnamese to commiserate over the plight of women in Vietnam and the United States. Nga didn't speak a word of English, but she had the range of a fine actress when it came to communicating the arduous nature of cooking, scrubbing, and, most convincingly of all, delivering a baby. Huong, frying the fish, only smiled at us occasionally, like an indulgent mother. For the first time, she didn't seem timid so much as self-contained. I began to think of *her* as a hard-to-please older sister.

When dinner was ready, Huong directed Nga to take the plates out to the living room. Nga, grinning as if we shared a secret, finally indulged my need to help by handing me something to carry by myself. I looked down into the bowl; it was filled with sprigs of fresh basil and mint. If only I'd paid attention when Tra had tried to teach me my herbs. Maybe Huong would have been impressed.

Vietnamese didn't seem like a new language as much as a new medium of communication. It had tones, which were as important to the meaning of words as spelling or the pronunciation of consonants and vowels. I thought of the tones as little devils sabotaging my attempts to simply remember the spelling of words. Sometimes, I boycotted them altogether. It didn't help. After one particularly disastrous effort—I had thought I was saying "my feet hurt," but I said, "I'm sick of living" —Tra got serious. She tried reasoning, drawing me a diagram of the word *ma,* for example, which, depending on which of the six tones one used, could mean "ghost," "mother," "but," "grave," "horse," or "rice seedling." When reasoning didn't work, she tried scare tactics, explaining that if I used the wrong tone for *dai,* instead of saying "tough," I'd end up saying "penis." That worked. I began to concentrate so hard on trying to get the tones right that they started to develop their own little personalities, like Snow White's seven dwarves: the flat tone was Boring; the rising tone was Panicked; the falling tone was Depressed; the falling-and-then-rising tone was Curious; the rising-and-then-falling tone was Choking; and, lastly, the abrupt tone was Angry. Unlike the dwarves, however, these guys were not my friends, and they never stuck with me. I'd begin each sentence with my brain cells completely focused on pronouncing every word with the right tone, and by the time I got halfway through, my words would dissolve into flatness and my listener would stare at me in total confusion.

For some reason, Tung had less trouble than his wife in comprehending the garble of sounds coming out of my mouth, and, because he could speak a bit of English, we were much better fit to converse. He'd often come up to my room to chat, bringing along two lists, one of words he wanted to learn in English and another of words he thought I should know in Vietnamese. He was so serious that he made me feel hopeful. To a certain degree, we succeeded. Over the first few weeks, Tung taught me the Vietnamese for "enough," "Please repeat that," and "I'm leaving." At the same time, he learned "Fantastic!" "It's up to you," and "Pay in advance." While Huong and I struggled with pantomime, Tung and I switched back and forth between the two languages, developing a skeletal little Vietnamenglish of our own. After a while the two of us were spending so many hours poring over our dictionaries that one might have assumed we actually had something important to say.

Now that I was getting to know Tung better, I could see what an operator he really was. He always had a plan, and those plans regularly involved getting something out of me. With Tra translating to make sure that none of our misunderstandings were ever linguistic, he presented me with a new request almost every week. His eyes would open, wide and slightly nervous, like a child angling for more candy he knew he shouldn't get. We'd long before agreed on the cost of my rent, which was two hundred dollars a month—a price that would have been impossible for a Vietnamese to pay, but which was pretty standard for foreigners at officially sanctioned guesthouses. Then, only two weeks after I moved in, he wanted to increase it by twenty dollars, saying the addition would cover the electricity my air conditioner used in the summer. A week later, he took the couch out of my room, replacing it with a second bed. Tung needed to find a space for the thing, and so he did his best to convince me that a second bed would really make me happy. Most of the time, I let him do what he wanted. I liked my room and didn't want any tension with my landlords. Besides, the difference in rent was negligible, and I had so much furniture already that I didn't really care if one piece was a couch or an extra bed. The only thing that bothered me was the fact that, because I couldn't understand Vietnamese, Tung assumed I couldn't recognize manipulation.

Both of my landlords regularly came up to my room, Tung to practice conversation and Huong to clean, or water the plants, or bring me some new little item to add to the decor. I could always tell which one of them was knocking at the door. Huong tapped so lightly that the door merely rattled its hinges, like the wind bumping it at night. A loud bang on the glass, smack in the center of the door frame, could only be Tung. He had no sense of privacy, and if I didn't bolt the lock, I knew he would open the door and walk right in. One night when I heard his bang I glanced at the clock. It was nearly ten o'clock and I was tired. I straightened my sweater, then opened the latch. Tung walked in with two men I'd never seen before.

"*Ngồi đi! Ngồi đi!*" Sit down! Sit down! Tung said, as if it were perfectly normal to invite strangers into his tenant's room at bedtime. Now that I was couchless, the visitors pulled up chairs and sat around one side of the coffee table, which was next to my bed. I perched on the edge of my mattress. The two men were giving me that new-acquisition-in-the-zoo look, and I knew that Tung had brought them upstairs with the sole purpose of showing off his American renter. As if I weren't having a hard enough time with people staring at me out in the street, now I had to deal with them in my room.

I had thought that Tung understood my predicament. At least, he'd given me reason to think he did. People were pounding on the doors, quite literally, to get me to teach them English.

One woman and her daughter had essentially camped out on my doorstep to convince me to help the girl get a scholarship to Harvard. Tung, sensing my despair, had finally drawn the line. The next time the Harvard wannabees appeared at my house, he had told them, flatly, to go away and not come back. But now here he was.

I glared at him, but he smiled back placidly, as if he didn't notice. Switching into English, he said, "This my brother," gesturing toward one of his guests, a younger, skinnier version of himself. Then he turned toward the other man and said, "This my mother brother son."

Tung's mother brother son, who was dressed in a business suit, looked over at Tung and sighed aggressively. Then he leaned back in his chair, crossed his legs, and adjusted his tie. "He means that I am his cousin," he said in perfect English.

"Cousin," Tung nodded. He stared at the ceiling, consigning the new term to memory. Then he pulled a pack of cigarettes out of his shirt pocket and passed it around to his guests. Not only was he bringing people to my room, but now he was acting like it was *his* room.

On the coffee table sat a bowl of mandarin oranges I had bought that morning. I picked one up, scored the skin into quarters with my fingernail, and folded it back from the fruit like the petals of a flower. This was a hostess trick Tra had taught me. The men gasped, impressed that a foreigner could be so accomplished. I smiled. They were my guests now.

"I can tell that you're becoming a real Vietnamese lady," said the cousin, inspecting the orange flower I offered to him. His baby-round cheeks made him look like a toddler in a business suit. He held the orange in his palm, admiring it. "This is very lovely," he said.

"Oh, I don't think so," I responded demurely. This Vietnamese way of hedging compliments was another trick I'd picked up—not from Tra, who wasn't that good at it, but from her older sister. The men nodded approvingly. Tung looked proud, which irritated me even more.

The cousin was a lawyer. The extent of my knowledge of Vietnam's legal system lay in a conversation I'd had with a former South Vietnamese army officer I'd met two years earlier in Saigon. After the war, the man had spent ten years in re-education camps and, for obvious reasons, his opinion of the present government was less than favorable. Vietnam's leaders couldn't understand the rule of law, he had complained, and they chose to operate under the same brutal system they'd developed during their underground years as revolutionaries. He'd called it "Jungle Law."

"What kind of law do you practice?" I asked the plump-cheeked attorney.

He gave a ponderous pull to his tie. "I work for the Ministry of Justice," he said. "I've been involved in a large number of significant cases concerning vital issues related to important international law." I waited for specifics, but he looked around the room as if he'd finished.

During the ensuing pause, the younger brother tried out his language skills. "Excuse me. I would like to introduce to you a few things about myself," he said. He told me that he was studying English at the Foreign Language College, that he lived with his parents, that he was twenty years old. Then, he added, "Excuse me, may I now ask you some questions about yourself?"

"Sure," I said, handing him another orange. I'd only been in Vietnam two weeks, but I'd had a dozen such conversations already. The cousin watched us both indulgently. Tung, who couldn't follow the conversation at all, was simultaneously puffing on a cigarette and picking at his orange.

Tung's brother cleared his throat and leaned forward. "I would like to know something about your chosen profession," he said.

I told him that I was a journalist and that I had worked as an editor for a community newspaper in San Francisco that catered to the city's Southeast Asian immigrant population. "That's where I made my first Vietnamese friends," I said.

"And why did you decide to come to Vietnam?" he asked.

Despite so many similar conversations, no one had asked me exactly that. Tra knew so many Americans fascinated by Vietnam that she took it as a matter of course that I would come. And Tung and Huong never would have questioned why an American would move to their city. I looked at Tung's brother. "Well, I traveled here as a tourist in 1990," I began, and then the cousin cut me off.

"Did you travel in the south?" he asked.

"Yes," I told him. "I traveled to many cities in the south." It was in Saigon that I had first realized how much I could learn in Vietnam, and how much I actually had in common with these people. But in Hanoi people had kept me at a distance, and, though I'd thought their city beautiful, with its lakes and tree-lined streets and elegant French colonial architecture, I hadn't found it friendly. When I'd made plans to come back to Vietnam, I'd had every intention of moving to the south. Then, when I studied Vietnamese in the States, I met a professor from the Institute of Linguistics in Hanoi who told me he could arrange a long-term visa for me to continue my studies in his city. Securing long-term visas in Vietnam was no easy thing for an American to do, so I'd decided to give the north of Vietnam another chance. I'd met Tra by then, and she'd promised to help me.

Now, after almost a month here, I was making progress in Hanoi, but I often wondered if I would have had a smoother acclimation had I lived in Saigon.

I looked at the lawyer and smiled. "I really loved Saigon," I said.

The expression on the lawyer's face hardened. "Excuse me," he said, "we haven't called it Saigon since we reunited the country in 1975. We Vietnamese call it Ho Chi Minh City now."

I felt my stomach tense. On my first visit to Vietnam, I'd been determined to use the name Ho Chi Minh City, proving that I, for one, was an American who recognized the legitimacy of the Hanoi government. But the local people insisted that I refer to their city by its original, prerevolutionary name, Saigon. I might have attributed this behavior to linguistic dissent were it not for the fact that, even in Hanoi, I seldom heard anyone use the name Ho Chi Minh City. Even Tra, whose father had fought in the revolution alongside Ho Chi Minh, always called the place Saigon. After much thought, I had finally decided it was both more prudent and more convenient to use the term Saigon.

The lawyer was staring at me like the cherubic baby doll in a monster movie, suddenly possessed with the dazzling pinwheel eyes of the devil. Clearly, the "everybody else calls it Saigon" argument would not do here. I was an American. "Ho Chi Minh City," I mumbled. With a sense of surrender, I gazed down at my orange. "Sorry," I added.

Suddenly I felt overcome with exhaustion. I had come to Hanoi to discover some other Vietnam, a Vietnam that wasn't exploding bombs and burning villages and screaming babies. I had come with a belief that by learning about the country at peace, even learning such silly things as a new way to peel an orange, I could develop an understanding of this place that was broader and deeper than what my country had learned during so many years of war. But now I saw that Americans weren't the only ones who could reduce an entire nation to their own country's experience with it. Here was a Vietnamese who believed he could judge my political opinions by my choice of a proper noun.

Tung seemed aware that the conversation had taken a turn for the worse. He suddenly stood up and said, "We'll go downstairs now."

Tung didn't follow the other two down the stairs immediately. Instead, he stood for a moment on the landing outside my door. Behind his head, the lines of the rooftops zigzagged across the dark horizon. I looked in his eyes and I saw something I'd never seen before, concern. "*Ngủ đi,*" Go to sleep, he finally said, adding with a gentle smile, "*lo nhiều quá.*" You worry too much.

After Tung went downstairs, I stood on the landing for a long time, the loneliness seeping into me like dampness through the porous walls of this house. I had felt alone almost every minute since I'd gotten here, but it was always simple homesickness mixed with the uncertainty of finding my bearings in a foreign place. What bothered me now was not the pain of physical distance so much as the absolute sense of mental isolation. My relationship with Hanoi had to be more complicated than my relationship with Saigon. After all, the United States had bombed this city. Maybe no one would ever completely trust me here. Maybe I wouldn't trust anyone myself. In the space of ten minutes, Hanoi had switched back to "Hanoi," the totalitarian, eternally frowning center of a Communist dictatorship. The war wasn't some show that I'd seen on TV as a kid, and I wasn't even sure that it was over yet.

I stood outside for a long time. One by one, the lights went out in the nearby windows. In the distance, I could see a lone pine tree towering like a great leader against the sky. I leaned on the railing of the stairway and took a deep breath of enemy air.

I tried to remind myself that I was making progress. I'd even started to do something I never would have expected from myself: I was using a bicycle to get around Hanoi. For another American, riding a bike in Vietnam might not have been such a big deal. But I was always the kind of rider who rode on the sidewalk, then stopped and walked whenever I had to cross a street. I wasn't very brave. I wouldn't have been crushed to learn I'd never ride a bike again. But in Hanoi, I didn't have a choice. My other options were worse. Cyclo drivers not only demanded exorbitant prices of foreigners, but they also had the confounding habit of insisting, once we reached our destination, that I pay them even more. An American lawyer who lived in Vietnam later explained this phenomenon to me in terms of cultural differences in contract theory. While Westerners consider contracts the final phase of business negotiations, Vietnamese view them as a starting point, a basis for further discussion. Thus, when I agreed to pay a cyclo driver five thousand dong, I expected to pay five thousand dong. The driver, however, would, after completing the trip, take into consideration the difficulty of the route, his fatigue, and the estimated size of my wallet, then give me an updated price. The extended process of negotiation may have made sense to him, but after a while I couldn't bear it. I couldn't rely on walking, either. Central Hanoi didn't cover a lot of territory, but on foot I would have had to spend two or three hours a day making my way across it.

The obvious solution was a bicycle, but I was nervous. A few days after I first moved into my house, I had spent a morning on my balcony. Observed from above, rush hour alone was enough to give me a terror of riding a bike. Set against a symphony of noise, with motorcycle horns supplying melody and mufflerless engines carrying an insistent beat, my street was a stage for an anarchic dance of buses, trucks, cars, bicycles, cyclos, and motorbikes, each vying for its precious meter on that narrow space of road. I had watched a boy on a bike glide in a casual diagonal across the street, moving out of the path of a honking bus a split second before it flattened him. A tiny orange Honda Chaly motorbike, carrying a sandwich of three teenage boys, swerved around a slow-moving cyclo, drifted into the opposite lane of traffic, then, after nearly colliding with an oncoming truck, carelessly slid back to its own side of the road. It looked like the death-defying circus act of a trapeze family that, with each progressive trick, moved closer to disaster. I knew that, eventually, someone would miss, and a fractional miscalculation of speed or distance would leave some sad soul sprawled and bloody in the middle of the street. General Westmoreland's much-criticized comment about Vietnam that "the Oriental doesn't value life the way we do in the West" had begun to sound less like a racist slur and more like a clear-eyed assessment of fact.

I had tried to explain my fears to Tra, but she wouldn't listen. In one of my earliest encounters with bossiness, a quality I would find endemic in Vietnam, Tra insisted that I had to ride a bike. One morning, standing in the courtyard of her house, she pushed one in my direction. "If you want to live in Hanoi, you have to ride it," she'd said. When I refused to take it from her, she walked it out to the street herself. Then, pointing at the passing traffic—a grandfather wheeling a small child to school, two teenage girls riding side by side, holding hands—she asked, "Does that look dangerous to you?" It *did* look dangerous, but I had to admit that she was right. I sighed, defeated, then put my hands on the handlebars, my legs on the pedals, and shoved off.

My first collision occurred only a few blocks from the house. Few Hanoi intersections have traffic lights, or even stop signs, so vehicles cross without stopping, just slowing down or speeding up to propel themselves through without hitting one another.

Not knowing that the fundamental rule is "Keep going," I wavered at the sight of a cyclo crossing in front of me. Had I simply slowed down, I could have put my bike into holding position, treaded water while the cyclo passed, and continued on my way. As it was, I swerved to avoid the cyclo and was rammed by a motorbike coming up from behind me.

The crash threw me off the pedals, but I caught my balance. I turned to look at the motorbike driver, a young man in a business suit. Before I could say a word to apologize, he sneered at me, jerked his front wheel out of the spokes of my bike, and sped off. Now I was stuck alone in the intersection, and when I looked up I saw a large army truck barreling toward me. At that moment, another bicycle was moving slowly past in the same direction I was going. I jumped back on my bike and, maintaining the exact speed of the other cyclist, managed both to let that rider run interference between myself and the truck and to rely on her experience in making the split-second decisions required to cross the street.

My second collision came about a half mile farther down the road, also at an intersection. When a motorbike seemed about to cut across the path in front of me, I tried the treading-water maneuver to let it pass. Unfortunately, I hadn't yet perfected the technique of slowing the bike and pedaling in place, and so I lost my balance. This time, I swerved into the rear end of a large Caucasian pedestrian, who extricated his legs from the front wheel while yelling what sounded like obscenities in German. My pleas of "I'm sorry!" did not move him and, as his anger showed no sign of abating, I opted for the less intimate dangers of the street and plunged back into traffic.

By the time I got back to Tra's house, my entire body was shaking and I was desperate to tell her about my brushes with death. But, apparently unconcerned about my fate, she'd already gone out for the day. I took the bike and slowly began to walk it toward my house.

Maneuvering a bicycle between Tra's house and my own wasn't a simple task, given the peculiar geography of Hanoi. Over the centuries, Hanoi's commercial streets had developed a tradition of specialization. In the city's Old Quarter, for example, the merchants on Silk Street sold silk and the ones on Silver Street ran jewelry stores. Not every establishment on Cha Ca Street sold the famous fried fish specialty *chả cá,* but if you wanted to eat that dish, you only had to name the street and any Hanoian would know your destination. Though the Old Quarter streets were the ones famous for carrying the names of what was sold there, the entire city followed a similar organizing principal. Shopping in Hanoi was like navigating oneself through a citywide department store. You'd go to one street to buy paint, another for toys, and another one if you were in the market for a Western-style toilet.

Although my street, Tran Phu, was named in honor of one of Vietnam's famous revolutionary martyrs (who was, incidentally, a relative of Tra's), I called it Dream Street because of all the Honda Dream motorbikes cluttering its sidewalks. Of course, there were other kinds of bikes parked there as well: lots of Honda 50 and 70ccs, Chalys, and Russian Minsks. But Dreams were the coveted vehicle of the day, the bike to buy if you had money. Unlike the clunky-looking older-model Hondas, the Dream was sleek and elegant. One long smooth line glided back from the handlebars to the rear edge of the black leather seat. It was the Hanoi equivalent of a BMW or a Lexus. On Tran Phu, you could usually spot a lot of Dreams, because Tran Phu specialized in washing and repairing motorbikes. On my side of the block alone, there were nine places to wash motorbikes and three to repair them.

Wheeling a bicycle the ninety-three steps from Tra's house to my front door was, given the layout of Dream Street, no easy prospect. French-colonial-era city planners probably conceived of the wide, shady sidewalk that ran along my street as a pedestrian thoroughfare, but, even on the quietest of days, walking along it required dodging whipping water hoses and stepping around wandering vendors hawking boiled sweet potatoes. At first glance, the scene appeared chaotic. Like every other open space in the city, however, this expanse of sidewalk was actually a highly organized commercial district. At the edge closest to the road, lottery-ticket sellers displayed their brightly colored tickets to passing traffic. Just behind them, motorbike mechanics squatted in front of flat tires and broken-down engines, their tools spread in wide arcs on the sidewalk surrounding them. Rarely did mechanics work alone. Instead, they squatted in groups of two or three, cigarettes dangling from their lips, pointing and poking, discussing transmissions and carburetors like a surgical team intent on probing the cause of a particularly mysterious ailment. The remainder of the street's commercial life was dominated by the motorbike washing establishments, teams of four or five people who competed with one another for business by employing someone, usually a big, bellowing woman, to stand out in the street trying to wave down passing motorists.

On Dream Street, it didn't matter if I was going into my house, stepping outside, or bending over to tie my sneakers; I was the only foreigner on the block, and people always watched me with the scrutiny of scientific observation. Usually, I pretended to ignore them, which wasn't that hard, considering that I had to devote most of my concentration simply to keeping from tripping over a pile of tires or a mechanic squatting in front of a broken Dream. Today, maneuvering my way along the sidewalk with a bicycle was even trickier than normal, but I was so relieved to be back on my feet and still alive that when people stared at me, I stared right back. Their expressions were as unfriendly as ever.

After a moment, I saw Tung up ahead, squatting on the front steps of the house. The sight of a familiar face filled me with relief. I imagined describing to him my debacle on the bike, even if I had to use more pantomime than Vietnamese. I didn't even care if he found my ineptitude laughable. As I walked toward him, the stares of all these strangers seemed less oppressive. I wasn't entirely on my own here, I thought. Up ahead was a person who would, at the very least, smile at me. As I got closer, Tung spotted me and waved, but when he lifted his arm, I saw that someone else was sitting beside him on the steps. It was the young guy who'd been drinking whiskey with Tung the night I'd eaten downstairs—not Nga's husband, but the other one, the one who had glanced at me between drags on his cigarette, then disappeared before dinner. Now he was looking at me with the same blank stare that I got from everyone else on the block. I lost all my will. When I reached the house, I gave Tung a quick hello, locked the bike, and hurried upstairs.

3 Navigation

THOSE FIRST FEW WEEKS IN HANOI were blank days. I couldn't get used to the weather. Absent of snow or frost, the only thing that told me it was winter was the chill that would enter my body with the force of a blizzard. This place was hardly the sweaty tropics I'd seen in *Platoon*. I was freezing. Every morning, I'd force myself out of bed, look out the window at the concrete wall of sky, and contemplate another faceless day. San Francisco mornings often had that same chalky grayness to them, but by noon the fog would lift, revealing a brilliant sun. In Hanoi, I had to remind myself that the sun existed. Whenever I had a chance, I'd take a long ride through the city. I'd wrap myself in a T-shirt, sweatshirt, sweater, and huge scarf and then pull my bike out the front door and into the street. Then I'd summon my courage and launch myself one more time into the flood of traffic. After a while, I could ride without staring straight in front of me, teeth clenched, knuckles turning white with their grip on the handlebars. If I sneezed while I pedaled, I no longer expected to disappear beneath the wheels of oncoming traffic.

I spent a lot of time thinking over a conversation I'd had with an American teacher who'd been living in Hanoi for the past two years. Jack had come to Hanoi as one of the first three teachers —two men and a woman—sent to Vietnam by the New York–based organization Volunteers Around the World. After two years here, he spoke excellent Vietnamese and could use the latest slang to flirt with the women and banter with the men. He walked down the crowded Hanoi streets like an American politician—shaking hands, cooing over babies, and pulling crabby grandmothers off their little wooden stools to make them dance with him. If I had any lingering doubts that an American could be accepted here, Jack dispelled them. And he wasn't the only American to have done well for himself in Hanoi. The other man from Volunteers Around the World had slid into Hanoi life as easily as Jack had. The woman, however, had problems. "Here was this young, pretty American woman walking down the street," Jack had told me. "People couldn't take their eyes off her. They'd tease her, try to touch her, follow her. I don't think they were physically threatening, but they wouldn't leave her alone, either."

Jack was carrying me home from dinner on his little Honda 250cc. With the wind slamming against my face, I clutched the leather seat with both hands, trying to hang on and listen to his story at the same time. "Laura had a hard time from the beginning," Jack yelled back through the sputtering of the engine. "She couldn't stand all the attention every time she walked outside. She didn't feel safe. She didn't make friends. She wouldn't do anything but go to school to teach her classes. Then she even stopped doing that. After a while, she refused to leave her room. She just sat there, all alone, and we had to bring her food or she wouldn't eat. Then one day, she just packed her bags and left." Jack laughed a little, not because the story was funny, but because he found it so perplexing. I laughed, too, as if I couldn't believe anyone could be scared away like that. The truth, though, was that I understood completely. All those eyes could make you crazy.

And so I pushed myself to leave the house, to ride that bike, to become a part of the world here. I discovered lakes I'd never seen before, and instead of pedaling nervously past them, I made myself pull up to park benches, get off, and allow the curious passersby to crowd around me and look. I rode past schoolyards full of uniformed children yelling chants and doing jumping jacks, and when they waved at me through the gaps in the fence, I waved right back. I hated the men who slowed their motorbikes down beside me to stare. I hated the women who tried to grab me in the market, as if by doing so they could force me to buy. But most of all, I hated the specter of the American teacher, so traumatized by all this unwanted attention that she had had to escape.

Sometimes, I was so worn down by the city that I hid in my room for entire days. But, despite those low points, I became convinced that I would stay here. All I had to do was leave the house in order to remind myself of how deeply I wanted to be here, no matter how much the city could overwhelm me. Hanoi was still so new to me that every day brought fresh discoveries. I had arrived not long after the Lunar New Year celebrations of Tet, which also marked the beginning of Hanoi's busiest wedding season. Despite the fact that I often felt distant from everything taking place around me, I was able to sense the feeling of joy that seemed to permeate the city during those cold winter days. Hanoians, conscious of astrology and the predictions of the fortune tellers, considered certain dates most fortuitous for weddings. Riding my bike through the city, I'd pass dozens of wedding buses. They were covered with flowers and large red paper cutouts of the ancient Chinese character for "double hap-

piness." (Though Vietnamese now write their language in a ro-
manized script, ancient Chinese characters continue to play a
role in the religious and spiritual life of the nation.) The wedding buses were always full of people, and when they looked out
the window and saw me, the foreign woman, pedaling along on
her bike, they would sometimes smile and wave. I was still on
the outside of Vietnam, but on days like those I could begin to
believe that the walls weren't so high, that I would someday
scramble over them.

One morning, the clouds receded for a few hours and revealed a sky so blue it seemed artificial. I took a bike ride down
Duong Giai Phong, Liberation Street, named in commemoration
of Liberation Day—April 30, 1975—the date of the "Liberation of Saigon," as most Vietnamese called it, or the "Fall of
Saigon," as most Americans called it. Liberation Street led toward the southern edge of Hanoi and, eventually, became Route
1, which continued south all the way to Ho Chi Minh City. From
Liberation Street, I turned west, crossed the tracks of the south-
bound railway, and entered a neighborhood of enormous Soviet-
style housing blocks, three- and four-story monoliths mildewing
and crumbling before their time. Judging by the architecture, I
guessed that this neighborhood represented some Socialist attempt to "modernize" the ancient city. It seemed ugly and de-
pressing in comparison to the cramped but lively neighborhoods
in the unreconstructed sections of the town.

If I had known my history, I might have looked at the map
and figured out that I was riding through the Kham Thien neighborhood, which suffered some of the worst effects of the 1972
"Christmas bombing" of Hanoi. In an effort to force concessions
out of the Vietnamese, Richard Nixon sent American B-52s on
bombing runs over a sixty-mile stretch of a highly populated area
in North Vietnam. The campaign, known officially as Operation

Linebacker II, destroyed not only much of Kham Thien, but also a large part of the nearby Bach Mai Hospital. More than thirteen hundred people died in Hanoi and another three hundred in the nearby city of Haiphong.

If I had been ten years older, these facts might have been familiar to me. I would have remembered the bombing of Hanoi and the name Bach Mai Hospital, which became a rallying point among anti-war activists, might have still sent shivers down my spine. But I was only ten years old during the Christmas bombing, and I didn't remember it at all. I had understood almost nothing about what was happening in Vietnam, except that people were dying there. I was terrified by death, and so I began to pay attention to Vietnam. I reacted to the war by drawing rainbows of peace signs on my denim-covered notebook, hoping that these flimsy Magic Marker symbols could somehow lessen the violence I saw on TV. For me, that jungly ever-exploding backdrop to dinner was the televised version of death itself.

I was lucky. No one I cared about went to the war. The closest I ever came to knowing someone lost in Vietnam was the POW/MIA bracelet I wore around my wrist that bore the name of a missing soldier and the date he disappeared. Among the elementary school set, the bracelets began as fashion statements, but, for many of us, they became our most powerful connection to what was taking place in Southeast Asia. Like me, my MIA, Captain Raymond Stacks, had grown up in Memphis. This hometown connection, combined with what I considered an astonishing similarity in our last names, gave me a strange sense of knowing the man already. I came to think of him as my unlucky missing uncle and became convinced that I might somehow bring him home myself through the sheer power of focusing with utter concentration on the metal band hanging on my wrist. The only effect of these efforts was that I squeezed my bracelet too hard and eventually broke it. My captain never made it home. Years after the war ended, I happened to see a newspaper article about his parents and how they had lived with their loss. I felt guilty, not simply because I had failed in my mission to rescue their son, but because I had forgotten him altogether.

During those first few weeks in Hanoi, the thing that surprised me most about Vietnam was how little I saw around me that still related to the war. Sure, I had seen the old airplanes in the courtyard of the Army Museum near my house, but in other contexts the influence of the war seemed negligible. Nearly twenty years after the conflict ended, I was living in Hanoi, the one-time enemy capital, and, had anyone asked me, I would have described the defining characteristics of this city as motorbikes, commerce, lakes, and trees. I knew that the war had left scars on this city, but I didn't recognize them yet. And I mistook the reconstruction of a devastated neighborhood for an inept attempt at urban renewal.

After a while, I pulled my bike over to the side of the road and stopped to consult my map. I was determined to take a new route home. On the map, I found a small road that seemed like it would get me back to the center of town. I pedaled back and forth looking for it, then discovered a gap between two buildings, a concrete-paved lane hardly wider than a footpath from which a line of bicycles and motorbikes poured in and out with as much nonchalance as I would have had driving up the on ramp to a freeway.

I sat motionless for a moment. I didn't even like to admit to myself the kinds of things that scared me here, but this little lane was one of them. Until now, I'd stuck to the big roads, where I could maintain distance between myself and everyone else. If I rode my bike down this tiny lane, I would lose that tiny amount of privacy. At the same time, though, to ride home the way I'd come would amount to a failure of nerve. Would Jack have given a moment's pause to a little lane like this one? For a few seconds, I strained my eyes to see where it was leading. Then I killed some time fussing with my map. Finally, as if the route itself were a dare, I took it.

A few feet past the entrance, it was already too late to turn back. The road was paved like a sidewalk, its great slabs of cracked and broken concrete betraying a history of heavy use and official neglect. Every thirty yards or so, the path made a ninety degree turn, veering left at some points, right at others, as if each bend were a concession to a building that predated the road. There was just enough room for a lane of two-wheeled traffic to flow in each direction. Nobody looked at me. They couldn't. Like me, all the motorbikers and bicyclists were too busy maneuvering their vehicles to pay attention to anything else. Smashing into another rider meant facing the embarrassment and aggravation of putting a halt to all the traffic in both directions.

Despite the exertion required just to keep my bike upright, I realized that I had discovered something. One simple turn onto that narrow road had brought me into another Hanoi. Away from the crowded anonymity of the rest of the city, I had entered the intimate realm of the urban village. Instead of the sidewalk, bushes, trees, and closed front doors that sectionalized other parts of Hanoi, here nothing divided those of us passing through from the people who called this address home. A woman leaned out a window and dumped her dishwater onto the pavement, barely missing the shoulder of the bicyclist in front of me. Two teenage girls stood in the doorway of a house, painting their fingernails. Three little boys treated the road like a playground, hurling their sandals into the traffic, then making hysterical attempts to grab them from between the wheels of passing vehi-

cles. An older man pulled his motorbike out of the gate of his
house and, during the ensuing pause, I glanced through an open
window and spotted an ancient woman standing before a cere-
monial altar, eyes closed, waving sticks of incense in a slow circle in the air. I had come upon a different side of the crowded,
crumbly, mildew-speckled city, and for that brief instant, at
least, I felt part of it.

Just as I was beginning to wonder if I were riding in a circle,
I saw in the distance a main road. I pedaled a few more yards and
then, spotting a small tea table just before the intersection, I
jumped off my bike and quickly pulled it out of the flow of traffic. I was famished. The food stand was nothing more than a
bench and an old wooden table set into a small empty space between two buildings. The proprietor, a middle-aged woman in
spectacles, looked at me placidly, as if Americans regularly
stopped by. "*Cô muốn gì?*" she asked. What would you like, miss?

I had a craving for *bánh bao,* the steamed meat-and-egg filled
roll that was both tasty and unchallenging. I didn't eat red meat
in the States, but following such a regimen had come to seem fu-
tile here in Hanoi. Northern Vietnamese considered meat a del-
icacy. Since arriving, I'd been offered pig's feet, cow's tongue,
dog meat, and the roasted heads of tiny birds. All of these things
I'd managed to avoid, but when it came to basic dishes with
chicken, pork, or beef, I'd chosen to eat rather than argue with
my hosts, who invariably couldn't understand why I would skip
the best part of the meal. Just in case I found myself face to face
with something I absolutely could not eat, Tra had taught me the
Vietnamese way to avoid anything unappealing. "Just say, '*Không
biết ăn,*' she instructed: I don't know how to eat it.

I didn't see any *bánh bao* at this tea table, so I pointed my finger at a bowl of hard-boiled eggs. The proprietor nodded and
handed me a cup of tea. I accepted it gratefully. The bike ride

had chilled me, and soon, after taking the first bitter sip, I could feel the liquid spread its heat through my stomach. Holding the warm cup against my cheek, I looked around. On the other side of the lane, a young mother squatted on her front stoop, trying to get her distracted toddler to take a bite of rice. The notes of *Swan Lake* floated out the front door of the house, and the little boy was too busy dancing to pay attention to his mother. "Child! Child!" the woman coaxed, following her son back and forth across the stoop. Finally, the little boy stopped long enough to take a bite, then instantly spit it out. The rice sprayed the leg of a passing cyclist. The little boy cried, "Hot!" His mother nodded, slid a spoonful into her own mouth, held it there for a moment to cool it for her son, then spit it back out onto the spoon. "Child!" she said again. The boy opened his mouth like a little bird and let his mother slide the rice on in. Then he stood on his tiptoes, lifted his arms into the air, and pirouetted like a swan.

"Miss!" said the tea stall proprietor. I turned around, took the small bowl from her hands, and looked inside it. This was not a hard-boiled egg. It was a half-formed, embryonic chicken. I might have been looking down at the results of an abortion.

It would be more dramatic to say that my first major crisis in Vietnam occurred when I was accosted by a gang of drunken war veterans, or when I was suddenly overcome by a life-threatening disease, but it didn't happen that way. This small and nonthreatening confrontation with a tiny, semi-developed bird felt like disaster in my mind, and my newfound sense of oneness with Hanoi suddenly shattered. I held the small pottery bowl in my hands, paralyzed.

The proprietor saw the look of horror on my face. "It's delicious," she said. "Try it." I stared into the bowl. It was now clear to me why the yolk of a hard-boiled egg is the same color as a live chick.

The young mother picked up her son and crossed the lane. She sat down next to me to watch. "Try it. It's delicious," she said, as if at any moment she might put a spoonful in her mouth and cool it down for me to eat.

I shook my head. "I've never eaten it before," I said.

"Try it," both women coaxed.

"I don't know how to eat it!" I wailed.

The mother looked at the proprietor. "She doesn't know how to eat it," she said. The proprietor nodded.

I knew that if I didn't get back on my bike, I'd start to cry. I offered the bowl to the little boy. His eyes lit up and he reached to take it. His mother laughed. "It's so delicious," she said.

I walked my bike up to the main road and started pedaling toward home. Although the day was still clear, the city streets were a blur to me, as if I were gazing at them through a car window in the pouring rain. Back at my house, I lay down on the bed and stayed there for hours. If something as insignificant as an unborn chicken bothered me, how would I react to something really bad? The very thing that had drawn me to this place, its foreignness, seemed repulsive to me now. How bad had it gotten for the American teacher before she left?

The sky was dark when I finally left the house again, to walk over to Tra's for dinner. She laughed when she heard about the chicken egg. "That wasn't a chicken," she said. "That was a duck. It's the best thing you can eat. So many vitamins. Vietnamese women eat that dish when they're pregnant. You should try it. It's so delicious."

"I don't know how to eat it," I told her. I felt a lump in my throat.

Tra nodded. Now she understood. "That's happened to me in the States, too," she said, putting her hand on mine. "People try to get me to eat something disgusting. It's awful. I tell them I don't know how to eat it, but they still don't understand."

I tried to imagine which American dish the gristle-loving Tra would find impossible to eat. And how could anything be worse than an embryonic baby duck?

"Mashed potatoes," Tra said. "All that butter and cream— disgusting! How can people eat that?"

Once, after I'd been in Vietnam for almost a year, I went to see a play by a local playwright, the setting of which was in a Hanoi neighborhood not unlike my own. If I were to write a play about my own life in Hanoi, it would take place on a set like that one. Almost all the action would occur in the downstairs living room of Tung and Huong's house and on the sidewalk right in front of it. Every morning, Tung would pull open the folding front doors, exposing the entire width of the living room. It was hard to know where the inside stopped and the outside world began. The street had a ceiling of dark green leaves and the living room had a ceiling of plastic tiles. The sidewalk had a layer of dust. The linoleum floor of our house also had a layer of dust. Outside, the ladies who ran tea stalls whacked the ground smooth with their feather-soft straw brooms. Inside, Huong swept the dust into pieces of newspaper and dumped it out in the gutter of the road for the street sweepers to gather on their nightly rounds. The food vendors and wandering beggars passed through both domains, walking hunched, palms open, eyes fastened now on the ladies selling tea, now on the customers drinking it, now on Huong sitting inside on her couch. The only difference between inside and outside was that outside was constant motion. Inside, we rarely moved. We formed the Greek chorus to the drama in front of us. Every day I spent in Hanoi my knowledge and understanding of Vietnam expanded, while every day the central focus of it constricted, until it seemed like the whole universe centered on this little living room and the sidewalk in front of it.

The living room of the house was always crowded, and I had to develop tricks to remember who the players were. The sweet-faced older man who rode the rickety bicycle was Tung's father. Huong's father wore a black beret and spoke to me in French. Tung's mother was bony and cheerful. Huong's mother was round and sullen. Two of Huong's brothers looked like twins, but the one with the Vietnamese flag tattooed to his forearm was the older one, who had driven a supply truck during the war, and the one who wore the flashy shirts was younger and would have barely reached puberty by the time the war ended. Huong had three sisters-in-law, and, because of the limited number of Vietnamese given names, two of them were also called Huong. Thus, I had the advantage of greeting all of them with, "Hello, Huong," and being fairly certain I was right.

Then there was Huong and Tung's five-year-old boy, Viet, the wild child. Sometimes I'd sit down on the couch and he'd jump onto my lap, throw his arms around my neck, and let out blissful coos. At other times, he'd lure me with the promise of a kiss and punch me in the mouth. One night I brought home a flower-covered chocolate cake for Viet. He took one look at it, breathed deeply, then plunged his whole face into the middle. Viet could hold nearly a whole bowl of rice in his mouth and eat it while singing a song and standing balanced on the seat of his father's Honda Dream.

The family drifted in and out of conversation as easily as one drifts in and out of sleep. At first, I kept wondering why they didn't get bored. We Americans are always searching for distractions, even at those moments that demand we do nothing but stare at whatever's right there in front of us. We read while sitting on the toilet, thumb through magazines in supermarket checkout lines, and listen to the radio while driving to work. Even "relaxing" involves some action verb: eating, watching TV, going for a walk. Now I found myself in a place where people could sit for hours observing the relentless monotony of traffic. Only Tung had trouble. He could only last for a few minutes before he'd start to fidget, jump out of his chair, light a cigarette, comb his hair, walk into the kitchen, walk back out, make a phone call, then sit down again, finally ready for another stint at it. Everyone else could last forever, silently staring out the front door.

In the beginning, when I spent a lot of time downstairs, I wondered what I was missing. I'd only walked by the Army Museum, and I wasn't even sure where the History and Fine Arts museums were yet. Maybe something major was happening in this city while I sat on a plastic-covered sofa watching traffic. Maybe revolution was fermenting in Hanoi and I didn't even know it. But ever so slowly I became completely absorbed by the life of this house, and my American compunction to "use my time wisely" disintegrated. Whole hours passed unaccounted for, marked only by the steady rise and fall of noise. Time started to pass in a different way, not so much in the turn of the clock as in the change in the light, the growling of my stomach, Viet's ecstatic return from school, or the smell of Huong's cooking.

If someone had told me, even a month before, that I would spend so many hours hanging out on a couch with a native Hanoian, I still might have doubted it. It was hard to believe that I could feel so relaxed around a woman like Huong, who wasn't Westernized and who had never had a chance, as Tra had, to make peace with America. About the time I was polishing my

POW/MIA bracelet back home in Memphis, Huong was hiding out in the countryside, avoiding the bombs the United States was dropping on her city. But here we were, twenty years later, sitting on the couch together, not only not discussing the past, but—on my part and I believe hers as well—not even thinking about it.

Something was finally shifting between myself and Huong. I couldn't mark any exact moment that had caused the change, but each time we passed each other on the stairs, each time she came into my room to water my plants, our smiles became more relaxed, our exchanges easier. I don't know that my Vietnamese tones had gotten any better, but she had gotten much better at understanding them. The more time I spent with her, the more I realized how smart she was, and the more incomprehensible became my initial reaction to her as a timid young wife cowering behind her husband's back. That image seemed laughable now, as I watched her directing Tung through his daily chores like a factory boss. She spoke to her older brothers with a voice of authority, and they listened to her. I don't think I was the only one intimidated by her.

Huong had not only never shown an interest in why I came to Vietnam, she never asked me anything at all about my past. Her world was compact, as tightly woven as the finest straw basket, leaving no space to contemplate my existence in America. She acted as though the span of my life began at that moment I'd first stepped through her front door. I think this assumption accounted for how, although I was actually a year older than she was, she treated me like her innocent younger sister. As our conversation became easier, she took to giving me advice on everything from my love life to how I washed my towels. On quiet mornings, she rested her hand comfortably on my knee, just as she rested it on her sister Nga's knee, and taught me new words, all the while keeping her eyes out for passing vendors hawking something she might like to cook for lunch.

One day, Huong was trying to explain to me all the Vietnamese words for rice. She found it incomprehensible that I could use the same term for the plant growing in the fields, the uncooked grain sold in the market, and the food we ate for dinner. To prove to me that these were in fact three very different things, she opened the cabinet under the glass coffee table and pulled out the Vietnamese-English dictionary. I leaned back on the sofa and prepared to wait. I had already found out, during any number of dictionary-aided conversations with Huong, that, like many Vietnamese, she didn't know the system of alphabetical order. Every time she wanted to find a word, she did a random search for the first letter, then slowly scanned the rows until she finally found the word for which she was looking. It could take her fifteen minutes to find a single word, and by that time I'd nearly forgotten what we were talking about. But Huong hadn't. She was patient. The two of us experienced time in completely different ways. Sometimes I tried to imagine what kind of person she'd be if she were an American. I could see Tung wrangling his little deals in New York or Dallas as easily as here in Hanoi. But Huong's pace, the steady and absolutely certain way she moved through her days, was an exact mirror of her surroundings. She was rooted to this place in the same way that a tree is rooted to the soil. I sensed that if she were ever torn away from this house, this street, this city, she might not survive.

I was waiting for Huong to find the third of her rice words when, suddenly, from out of the normal roar of traffic, we heard the sounds of screaming. Both of us jumped up and ran outside. A crowd of thirty or more people was forming at the edge of the street. Passing motorbikes, bicycles, and even a couple of cars had stopped to look at whatever was going on in the middle of the road. This is it, I told myself. Our neighborhood's collective karma had been used up. Now, instead of another near miss, we'd had the real thing. "Viet! Viet!" Huong shouted. My stomach turned, but then I saw him trying to nose his little body into the middle of the crowd. Huong dragged him out by his shirt. The three of us stood at the edge of the mass of people trying to figure out if anyone had gotten hurt.

In the middle of the crowd, an angry cyclo driver was arguing with a tall, muscular teenager who, judging by his rubber boots, was one of our street's motorbike washers. The teenager pointed at a woman standing next to them. She had on a smart pea green business suit and high heels. She was leaning over her Dream, investigating a broken headlight. The teenager's voice rose, and he began to stomp his foot for emphasis.

I felt as though I were watching a foreign film without the subtitles. "What's going on?" I finally asked Huong.

"The cyclo driver hit that woman's motorbike, and the teenager's mad because the cyclo driver won't say he's sorry." Though I couldn't get all her Vietnamese, Huong's hand motions and facial expression told the story perfectly well.

The shouting escalated. The cyclo driver jumped off his seat, then the teenager moved toward him. Drawing his fist back in the air, the teenager looked like a cartoon character going through the stylized motions of a fight. He was fast and his fist went flying.

Before the blow hit its mark, two other men grabbed the teenager and pulled him back. One of the men let go of him, then walked over to the cyclo driver. He was smaller and less intimidating than either the burly teenager or the tough-looking driver, but, with a few words, he managed to appease them both. I realized that this peacemaker was someone I recognized.

I nudged Huong. "That's Tung's friend."

She nodded. "Phai. He's a motorbike mechanic."

The crowd was silent, everybody straining to hear Phai, whose voice was as quiet and steady as the swish of the street sweepers' brooms I heard when I lay in bed at night. The cyclo driver's eyes were focused on his fingernail, but he, too, was listening. Finally, he looked up and said something to the owner of the Dream. She shrugged, then got on her motorbike and kicked it into gear.

"Doesn't he have to buy her a new one of those things?" I asked. I didn't know the word for headlight.

Huong shook her head as if the logic of the situation should have been clear to me already. "He's a cyclo driver. He doesn't have any money." She pointed to the woman in the pea green suit, who was already puttering away. "She's got money. She can pay for it. They just wanted him to apologize. He wasn't polite."

I may have been witnessing the birth of a capitalist society, but that didn't mean that Vietnam was developing into the same kind of capitalist society as the United States. Communism had had its effect on this country, as had the ancient traditions that dated back over a thousand years. For most Vietnamese, poverty wasn't a predicament so much as a state of being. It was permanent and unalterable, like the geography of the land. Although Vietnamese had hope for their improving economy, few people harbored illusions that the poor would ever be anything but poor.

The cyclo driver pulled himself back up on his seat and slowly pedaled off. He hadn't gotten far when the teenager started after him again, but Tung's friend Phai grabbed the teenager's arm and pulled him back toward one of the mechanic shops.

"Let's go back inside," Huong said. She let go of Viet and he sprang away from us like a rubber band, disappearing into the alley behind our house. Huong walked back inside, turning away from the crowd as if the attention she'd paid the event were one more task completed. I took one last look at Phai and the teenager conferring in front of the mechanic's shop and followed her inside.

Huong had forgotten the commotion instantly, but I was still trying to figure it out. In America, people slow down to glimpse the carnage of accidents, hence our term "rubbernecker." Still, I couldn't imagine a fender bender in America causing the commotion I'd witnessed in the last ten minutes. Despite all the fury, nothing had been broken except the social code and the headlight on one Honda Dream. Why had the traffic stopped? Why did everyone congregate to watch? It began to occur to me that Vietnam was a culture not of rubberneckers, but of kibitzers. They watched the occasional fistfight and commuter drama not simply because they were curious, but because they lived in a society that expected everybody to keep an eye on everybody else.

If for no other reason than this sense of community, Vietnam differed radically from the world I knew in America. The effects were obvious. Outsiders might assume that Vietnam is an aggressive society, but violent crime was rare, and I never witnessed anything worse than the occasional fistfight. I had the freedom—which I did not have in the States—to walk down the street at night without the fear of being assaulted. A society free of violent crime is, of course, one of the reasons repressive governments give for denying their citizens basic human rights. My Vietnamese friends didn't have the freedom of speech or freedom of assembly that I took for granted. But I found myself cherishing the safety I felt on the streets, a safety that Huong, never having to worry about getting assaulted by strangers, would not have even considered. Viet could run all over the neighborhood and any woman who saw him would take care of him with as much care as his own mother, whereas Tra had often complained about how isolated she felt in the States. She could fall down and die on the street and no one would notice. In Vietnam, you couldn't read a book or eat your dinner without someone noticing and discussing it. If you went to visit friends and they weren't home, you simply went next door and the neighbors could probably tell you where your friends had gone.

Over the next few months I would come to realize, all too clearly, the negative effects of being watched all the time. But it was still early enough in my stay that I could appreciate the freedoms I didn't have at home, without noticing the ones that were missing.

The motorbike washing and repair business on my street inspired a busy support network of tea stalls. Motorbike workers and their customers gathered for refreshment around low tables covered with various snacks, drinks, and cigarettes. The proprietor sat at the head of the table, within arm's reach of anything or anybody, investing the atmosphere at her tea stall with the particular attributes of her own personality. My house had a tea stall on either side of it, one run by Grandmother Nhi and the other by Grandmother Ly. Grandmother Ly seemed indifferent to the competition. She was either too distracted by the presence of her newborn grandchild or too busy combing out her knee-length white hair to invest much effort in the business.

Grandmother Nhi worked harder, and she had the more loyal following. The motorbike guys spent the quiet time between jobs lounging next to her tea table, playing cards, smoking cigarettes, cracking sunflower seeds between their teeth and tossing the empty shells onto the sidewalk. Maybe they frequented her tea stall because Grandmother Nhi was lovely, with skin the color of uncooked rice, smooth as the soybean milk she kept in a bottle on her tea table. Or maybe they just liked to hear her gossip.

One afternoon I came home and saw Tung and Phai sitting on the benches surrounding Grandmother Nhi's tea table. Tung motioned for me to join them. I had never spoken to Grandmother Nhi before, and now her smile was huge with anticipation: The foreigner was finally close enough to touch. "Duyen! *Ngồi cho vui!*" she said. Sit down for fun! I sat down. Phai was across the table, and Tung sat next to him. The two looked so different from each other that it was hard to imagine they were friends. Phai was small, dark-skinned, and wiry—in a culture that prized men who were, like Tung, tall, light-skinned, and buff. The other men I knew wore busy fabrics and fancy leather shoes as signs of their sophistication and wealth. Phai wore solid blacks and blues and whites, as if he'd never noticed there was such a thing as fashion. Unlike Tung, he was quiet. He listened closely, but seldom spoke. After he'd convinced his mechanic friend not to clobber the cyclo driver, I'd seen him several times in our living room. I'd never talked to him, but I could tell that I amused him. Sometimes, while struggling through some tricky grammatical turn of phrase, I would glance in his direction and see that he was watching me. I'd smile, embarrassed. He'd smile back as if we shared a secret.

Grandmother Nhi handed me a steaming cup of tea. I knew that she was about to speak, and my brain shifted into a mode of nervous preparation. Then, it came: "Duyen, how old are you?" Easy enough. I relaxed, but before I could get the words out of my mouth, Tung answered. He proceeded to launch into a lengthy and astonishingly assured discourse on the details of my life. Within a few seconds, I had lost the thread of the conversation, but I could tell by the way he continually gestured in my direction that the subject matter had not changed.

Tung made some sort of joke that made both Phai and Grandmother Nhi start laughing. Grandmother Nhi's laugh was persistent and breathy, like the hiss of a water heater. Phai's was louder, but only lasted a moment. I stared into my cup of tea, trying to figure out what had suddenly made Tung such an expert on my life. Since the night he'd brought his brother and cousin to my room, he hadn't come upstairs as often. He was like a child, always focused on the newest toy, and my novelty had worn off. Now he was busy networking to fill the other room in his guesthouse and was often so distracted he'd barely notice when I walked by. At last, I thought, my relationship with him was becoming more normal. We still spent blocks of time hunched over the dictionary downstairs, but the time was no longer simply an exercise in language acquisition. We were really trying to say something. Tung had told me about his years in Germany, about his best friend Hans, a taxi driver from Dresden who had given him the Metallica cassette he always cranked up on the stereo. In exchange, Tung had taught Hans how to cook rice Vietnamese style (never gooey, with each grain so distinct you could pick it up with your chopsticks and see an oval as perfect as an egg). Neither one had had to teach the other about beer. That was one thing they had in common.

Grandmother Nhi began to laugh again and from a few key words I guessed that Tung was describing the limits of my vocabulary. Tung's most recent contributions to my knowledge included "air conditioner," "go downstairs," "go upstairs," and "lock the door." I had, most recently, taught him "it's okay with me," and "fuck you." Was Tung telling that to Grandmother Nhi? He was grinning, seeming to get an inordinate amount of pleasure from making me squirm.

Phai wasn't laughing anymore. His eyes rested on me. As Grandmother Nhi's amusement continued, my discomfort must have been obvious because, for the first time, Phai spoke to me. "Duyen, do you understand?" he asked, his eyes suddenly wide with worry. I nodded and shrugged at the same time, an answer that could have meant anything. Then I hurriedly finished my tea and went inside.

4 The Four Stages of Love

$\mathcal{I}$N EARLY APRIL, THE COLD LET UP and the rains began.
Hanoians called it *mưa xuân,* "spring rain," to distinguish it from
the violent storms of summer. I couldn't call it rain at all. "Rain"
seemed too strong a word for this formless, weightless mist that
didn't fall from the gray sky, but condensed out of the air itself.
The chinaberry trees in front of my house bloomed tiny white
flowers, which fell like snow into the puddles on the sidewalk
below. You couldn't tell if all this water was going up or coming
down, and the living room floors glistened as if they'd just been
mopped. My backpack, shoved into the bottom of the wooden
wardrobe, took on the smell of rotten tomatoes. The adhesive
on envelopes developed colonies of blue fungus, moistened
spontaneously, and sealed. Laundry wouldn't dry at all, and the
clothes hanging neatly in my wardrobe became organic and
began to sprout. I tried to protect myself from so much moisture by pulling over my head a blue and gray hooded rain jacket
I'd bought in Hanoi, which had the phrase SHOWER ATTACK
SPORTS printed in big letters across its back. Vietnam's markets
didn't provide much choice in rainwear, and the weather brought

out mobs of commuters decked in the exact same jacket. But it made no difference whether I was riding down the street or lying in my bed. My body was slick with the moisture of a rain I couldn't feel.

Winter may have been cloudy, but spring seemed worse. We didn't see the sun for weeks. Every morning, we woke to a sky that matched the gray on our raincoats and spent our days picking paths across muddy sidewalks or riding our bikes down muddy streets. I gave up trying to keep the cuffs of my pants clean and got used to walking in shoes that squeaked with moisture. The relentlessly dull quality of the light became so familiar, so apparently permanent, that a blue sky seemed as unlikely as everyone on the streets suddenly speaking to one another in English.

I'd been in Hanoi for more than a month and my life had settled into something resembling routine. Three mornings a week, I left the house at seven o'clock, went to a food stand down the street, and ate the typical Hanoi breakfast, a noodle soup called *phở*. After breakfast, I rode my bike to the Institute of Social Sciences, where my teacher, Professor Mai, and I sat from eight to ten o'clock at a table in a dim and dusty classroom going over my lessons in *Intermediate Spoken Vietnamese*. In a month, I'd worked my way up to "Lesson Five: Planning an Evening Out." Now I was memorizing such dialogues as "Brother Tai: Steve, are you free tonight? Brother Steve: I'm busy tonight, but I'm free tomorrow night; do you have something in mind?"

Intermediate Spoken Vietnamese, published in the States in 1980, was outdated and based on southern dialect. Consequently, it seldom sounded like what I heard around me in Hanoi. I was grateful enough simply to have it, but I knew that these lessons were hard on my teacher. Professor Mai was not a Vietnamese language instructor by calling. He was a linguist who had spent much of his career compiling a French-Vietnamese dictionary. His Russian was effortless; his French nearly perfect. Although he spoke almost no English, he had such a keen understanding of language that he never had trouble comprehending anything I wanted to say. As a teacher, he was patient and devoted, determined to help me learn. Still, the idea of Professor Mai teaching me Vietnamese made about as much sense as a professor from Harvard giving one-on-one ESL training to an exchange student. My lessons were not the most efficient use of this man's time. But he did it anyway. At four dollars a lesson, Professor Mai could make more money in three mornings with me than in an entire week of doing research of his own.

The only real pleasure Professor Mai seemed to get out of teaching me came when we were able to delve, however simply, into sociolinguistics. One morning, our conversation drifted onto the subject of how military terms, which came into common usage during the war, had over the years taken on peculiarly nonmilitary meanings. The word *bắn,* which meant "to shoot," had become, in increasingly corrupt Vietnam, a slang word meaning "bribe." If a wealthy businessperson "shot" an official in order to avoid some troublesome regulation, you'd know the official came out a little richer because of it. Similarly, the word *tấn công,* which literally means "attack," was now often used to describe episodes on the romantic battlefront as well. When a boy flirted with a girl, for example, hip Vietnamese would say, "He attacked her."

Hearing about the evolution of words like *bắn* and *tấn công* reminded me of how, on one of the first days I'd been in Hanoi, Tra had taken me to eat at a little food stall near my house. When I said I wanted vegetarian noodle soup, she'd told me to order *phở không người lái.* I blurted out the phrase, and the food stall proprietor looked at me with surprise, but I got the food I wanted. After that, whenever they saw me walking toward their food stall, the people who worked there yelled, "*Phở không người lái!*" and burst out laughing. It had taken me weeks to get Tra to explain to me that *phở không người lái* didn't actually mean "vegetarian noodle soup." During the war against the United States, she'd finally explained, Vietnamese had marveled at the unmanned airplanes Americans used for reconnaissance missions over North Vietnam. *Máy bay không người lái,* they called the aircraft: airplanes without the pilot. Soon, the notion of a thing without its essential ingredient creeped into the Vietnamese vernacular. Poor people who couldn't afford meat in their noodle soup joked about eating "noodles without the pilot." An American ordering *phở không người lái* seemed doubly funny. First, I was a citizen of the country that had developed that unmanned aircraft. Second, what was a rich American doing ordering poor people's food anyway?

"Is that what you mean about the language changing?" I asked Professor Mai.

He was still chuckling over the story, but he looked at me sympathetically. "Yes," he said. "That's it, exactly."

After class, I would ride home, hang out with Huong in the living room, then go eat lunch. Most afternoons, I taught English at the National Center for Scientific Research, a job I had found through Tra's sister.

One afternoon, as I was on my way downstairs to go teach, I ran into Huong. Her face was flushed with excitement. "Good news!" she said. "We've rented the empty rooms." Tung had spent much of the past month on the telephone, calling anyone he knew with contacts at foreign companies or international aid organizations, trying to spread the word that he had rooms for rent to foreigners. The sight of Tung talking on the telephone had become as familiar an image as Huong sitting on the couch or Viet leaping down the stairs. Now, Tung had managed to rent both of his empty rooms in the same day. Huong and I stood on the landing and went through one of our typical exchanges of information.

"Who?" I asked.

"Chinese from Thailand," she said.

"They're from Thailand?"

"But they're Chinese. It's two wife husband."

It was the "two wife husband"—*hai vợ chồng*—that confused me. I'd never heard a word for "couple" before, but I could deduce that *vợ chồng*—the words for "wife" and "husband" in Vietnamese—could easily mean "couple." What I didn't understand was if "two" (*hai*) signified two couples or one couple, particularly since this party was renting two rooms.

"Is it a wife and husband?" I asked.

"Yeah. Two wife husband."

"Is that two people or four people?" I persisted.

"It's two people. Two wife husband." She wasn't impatient, but it was obvious she couldn't see how to say it more simply.

I was finally beginning to understand when the doorbell rang, signaling the arrival of my ride to the institute.

My student, Harry, was waiting for me on the sidewalk. In keeping with Tra's tradition of giving her American students Vietnamese names, I had come up with American names for all of mine. Harry was a sweet-faced man in his early forties. I was happy to see him. The center was located several miles from central Hanoi, and if I were to ride my bike there I'd spend more time getting to class than I would spend teaching it. But getting lifts to class, so far, had been a problem. At first, a member of the Department of Physics, Jerry, had driven me to class in the institute car, but it was clear to me within a few minutes of our first meeting that I wouldn't enjoy these rides. The institute car was a clunky, mud-yellow Russian model, the first car I had ridden in since arriving in Hanoi. After weeks of getting around town on bikes and the backs of friends' motorbikes, being chauffeured through the muddy streets of Hanoi in a car made me feel like I was riding a water buffalo through a chicken coop.

The real problem, however, wasn't the car as much as the driver. Jerry was tall and heavyset, a body type so unusual in Vietnam that, in comparison to everyone else, he looked like a pudgy giant. A few minutes after we had pulled away from my house on my very first day of class, he had turned toward me. "I see that you are looking so very beautiful today," he said, looking out at me through his thick glasses. The space between the front of our car and the rear end of a truck narrowed precipitously.

"Thanks," I finally said as he jerked the steering wheel and whipped around the truck. "Where did you learn English?"

"Oh, you see, I did this. I taught myself. Only two years. I did that. Study at my house is what I did. Alone. No benefit of teacher . . ." He didn't stop speaking for several minutes, but I had already lost the thread of what he was saying. Jerry's efforts at home study had expanded his self-assurance, but his accent was nearly incomprehensible. He spoke English as if he were speaking Vietnamese, staccato-like, forcing out each syllable like a separate word. It reminded me of a child playing with clods of dirt, throwing them ceaselessly and without aim.

He turned to me again. "And you. I ask. Do you have a husband?"

"No," I said. "Your institute is very far away, isn't it?"

"No husband! I ask. Do you like to dance? I ask. Do you like to disco?"

"Not really," I answered. I didn't know Jerry's marital status, but since most of the men I'd met who were over thirty were married, I took a chance. "Tell me about your wife," I said.

"My wife? Yes. Then I will tell you about my wife. You ask." If the shift in conversation made him pause, it was imperceptible to me. I spent the rest of the ride gazing out the window and vaguely tracking the course of a monologue that centered on his wife's business ventures, a new car shipped from Pakistan, and their efforts to build a guesthouse in Hanoi. By the time we reached the center, I had come to know Jerry more intimately than I desired.

After a few weeks of commuting with Jerry, I contemplated quitting the job simply because I couldn't bear the car rides anymore. Then I found out that another student, Harry, lived near my house. Harry was friends with Tra's sister, and his eight-year-old daughter was one of the children I taught at Tra's house every Tuesday night. I'd had a spate of invitations from married men, asking me to do everything with them from eating at expensive restaurants to dancing at the disco to riding out into the countryside on the backs of their Hondas. I was suddenly more popular than I'd ever been in the States, but none of the attention felt flattering. Rather, it seemed that these men were interested in me because I was a single American woman and therefore available for sex, and probably discreet. Fending off these invitations had become a part-time job for me and a big joke between Tung and Huong, who kept teasing me about not liking Vietnamese men. When Harry offered the ride, I thought that this problem, at least, was solved. I could see by the delight Harry took in his daughter that he was a happy family man.

The center was located at the western edge of the city, on a campus that, given a new paint job and a bit of landscaping, might have passed for modern. Inside, however, I was instantly reminded that this was a poor country with few resources available for aesthetic improvements. My classroom was dank, with wooden tables, dirty windows, and a ceiling fan that, once the warm weather started, would prove itself incapable of redistributing the hot and heavy air. Other institute buildings were hardly more high-tech than the one in which I taught. I never once saw a computer, and the most up-to-date offices I visited looked more like dusty wire- and cable-filled hardware stores than laboratories for scientific research.

Despite their dismal facilities, my students were smart. Most were physicists, but the class also included medical doctors, biologists, chemical engineers, and nuclear scientists. I felt intimidated, having fulfilled my college science requirements by taking courses with titles like "Poetry and Nature." I became even more intimidated when I learned that, on average, each of my students had spent seven years studying abroad, earning doctorates from the ivory towers of the Eastern bloc. These people were fluent in such languages as Czech, Hungarian, and Romanian, and most spoke Russian as well. Now, however, they faced two professional dilemmas. First, the local scientific facilities gave them no chance of keeping up with international research; second, the breakup of the Eastern bloc had made fluency in Czech or Romanian as worthless as the currency of a toppled regime. Even Russian would be of no help at a conference in Tokyo, Geneva, or New York. For that, they needed English. Whenever I walked into the classroom, twenty students greeted me like a visiting specialist called in to help solve a particularly puzzling question in quantum physics.

Harry got me to class much quicker than Jerry's lumbering car ever had and, fifteen minutes after saying good-bye to Huong,

I found myself standing once again in front of the enthusiastic scientists. Today, we were working on chapter 8 of the book *Meanings into Words,* a Cambridge text that was so popular in English-avid Hanoi that it would have easily made the best-seller list. For the first half of class, we discussed a reading passage entitled "Dishwashers," the first sentence of which began, "Over the last fifty years housework has been made considerably easier by the invention of an increasing number of labor saving devices and appliances." For my students, who had voracious appetites for both new vocabulary and information on life in the West, this material was enthralling. It didn't take long before we were holding a passionate discussion on such housecleaning topics as vacuuming options and plumbing problems. After the reading, teams of students came up to the front of the room for a role-playing session in which a customer goes into the neighborhood Sears to check out the latest models.

My students were so satisfied with the dishwasher lesson that, after a brief break, I pulled out a humor column I'd photocopied from the *San Francisco Examiner* about the often odd behavior of tourists. I had never considered the possibility, however, that humor might not translate. For twenty minutes, we moved sentence by sentence through the first paragraph as I tried to explain each joke and the students politely responded with chuckles. By the time we began the second paragraph, however, they had given up listening entirely, and instead sat with their heads buried in their photocopies, hopelessly trying to decipher phrases like "cable car turnaround" and "Bermuda shorts." Even more surprising was how bothered they were by their incomprehension. Jerry, saying he had some office business to attend to, got up and left. Tra's sister bit her fingernails frantically. When I asked Harry a question, he shrugged with despair.

After class, Harry and I walked silently toward his motor-bike. Today's class was not the first time that I'd steered my students in the wrong direction.

Harry could see that I was concerned. "It was a good class," he said. "You taught it very well."

I was touched by his effort to cheer me up. "Thanks so much," I said. "You're really sweet."

We walked on for a moment without saying anything and when we reached the motorbike, Harry stopped and looked at me. "I have an idea," he said. "We should go relax now, because you are tired. We can go to my little country house, next to the West Lake. It's very quiet there, and empty. We can take a nap. It's very pleasant."

Was there some sign on my body that said, "Married Men: I'm available"? After a long moment, I said, "No thanks, Harry. I just need to get home."

When, several months later, I began teaching English at the Vietnam Atomic Energy Commission, which was an easy bike ride from my house, Harry became my only student from the center to follow me to the new locale. Because his enthusiasm never waned, I assumed that he was pleased with his progress in English. It was many months before I learned he had another reason that kept him coming to my class.

Now that I could finally communicate a bit with Tung and Huong, they were able to tell me what they thought of me, and it wasn't always good. Tung decided that the glasses I wore were so unflattering that they made me look like an old grandmother—hardly a desirable quality for an unmarried woman approaching thirty. Huong thought I should do something more with my hair. It just hung there. Why wouldn't I let her take me to the beauty shop down the street and supervise my getting a perm? Both of them considered my wardrobe atrocious. Faded jeans and baggy sweaters were not the fashion statement they expected an American woman to make. Didn't I own a belt?

On top of all that, Huong seemed to be growing increasingly convinced that I was good-natured, but incompetent. I wasn't any good at washing my clothes by hand, and when I hung them to dry on the balcony, I didn't pin them properly and they fell off in heaps on the dusty floor. I didn't know how to peel an apple without slicing my hand. I forgot Vietnamese words she had already taught me two or three times. Once, in frustration, I told her she should come over to San Francisco and try operating a digital answering machine to see how I felt in Hanoi.

To celebrate the impending arrival of the new tenants, I decided I'd cook an American dinner for Tung, Huong, and their families. Surely, hamburgers and French fries would be exotic enough to impress Huong and demonstrate that, in my country at least, I knew what I was doing. She was skeptical about the endeavor, but offered to help.

We went to buy supplies early in the morning on the day of the meal. The Hang Da Market was a three-story concrete building, the cavernous bottom floor of which was dominated by food vendors. I'd been here before, and the sight of dozens of food-sellers squatting over their baskets of bananas, mountains of rice, and buckets of live fish didn't put me off. I'd seen the piles of intestines sitting out on the tile-covered butcher blocks. I'd seen the live chickens and the roasted dogs. I was used to the smells of rotting produce and raw meat, and I knew to walk carefully so as not to slip and fall on the wet and often slimy floor. But I'd never bought anything more complicated than a few tomatoes. The prospect of collecting the ingredients for a dinner for a dozen people suddenly overwhelmed me.

Huong stood behind me. "It must be different from your markets at home," she said.

I nodded.

When I still didn't move, she gently nudged. "What do you want first?" she asked.

To my right, the vegetable vendors sat in little neighborly clusters, chatting with one another while they bent over their morning bowls of *phở*. "Tomatoes, lettuce, and potatoes," I decided, and we started there.

We spent about an hour in the market, though Huong could probably have gone through my whole list by herself in fifteen minutes. She was more puzzled than annoyed, though. It was hard for her to understand how someone about to cook a meal could be indecisive about what to buy and how much of it to buy. I was glad to have her with me, though, and not just for the extra arms (and motorbike) to haul the groceries home. Huong knew the appropriate price of every single item in the market and wouldn't let any of the vendors get anything more out of me. The only things I knew better than she did were the prices for ketchup and mustard, which we bought from imported goods dealers at stalls outside.

When we got home, Huong locked the bike and I started pulling bags off the handlebars and out of the front basket. "Duyen!" I heard a voice call from behind me. When I turned around, I saw Phai squatting on the sidewalk in front of his mechanic shop in his worn blue shirt and black trousers splattered with mud. He had a cigarette between his fingers and a big grin on his face. "*Đi đâu về?*" he asked. Where have you been? It was a standard Vietnamese greeting.

Even though I knew that Phai didn't expect a literal answer, I answered by holding up the groceries for him to see. "I'm cooking dinner tonight," I told him.

Phai's eyebrows went up.

"I know how to cook," I insisted. He didn't look convinced. "I do," I said. "You should come."

The expression on Phai's face didn't change, but he gave a slight nod, which I took as acceptance.

Late that afternoon, I went down to the kitchen to cook. Huong, who had volunteered to be my sous chef, was already squatting on the floor peeling potatoes. "What should we do with these?" she asked.

Hamburgers and French fries had seemed the perfect meal to make, before I started making it. Neither dish was complicated, and the two combined were so quintessentially American that even Huong had heard of them. The problem was, I didn't know exactly how to make either one. Although I loved to cook, hamburgers and French fries were not on the repertoire of things I made at home. I looked at the pile of freshly peeled potatoes and said, "We've got to do this," gesturing with my hands to cut the potatoes with a knife.

Without talking much, we sliced potatoes and tomatoes, washed lettuce, and began to make the burgers. Ground beef was not an item on sale at the market, but I'd managed to explain what I needed to one butcher, who, though puzzled over my request, was willing to take a huge slab of perfectly lean filet — the kind of cut that would have cost fourteen dollars a pound in the States — and chop it by hand with a murderous-looking cleaver. Now I dug my hands into a bowl to mix the meat with eggs and chopped onion and garlic.

We moved on to the raw potatoes. "Now we use that," I said, pointing to a bottle of oil on the shelf.

Huong looked at the oil, then back at the potatoes. "Are you sure?" she asked.

I hesitated. I was only making up this recipe as I went along, but I was sure that Huong would know less than I did about making fries. "You're supposed to use that," I asserted, pointing again to the oil.

"I know what dish you're talking about," Huong said. "Don't you call them French potatoes? They'd be better in the oven."

Of course, after years of French colonialism, the Vietnamese had been influenced enough by French cuisine to have discovered *pommes frites*. But what self-respecting American thinks of French fries as French? I considered arguing with Huong, but then I gave in. I really didn't know how to make French fries. In this case, she might be right.

Vietnamese recipes seldom called for baking, and Huong used her oven for storage. We pulled out a wok, two saucepans, a baking pan, an empty water bottle, and an orange plastic frog that Viet had thought he'd lost. Then we spread the potatoes out on the pan, sprinkled them with salt and oil, and turned on the oven.

By seven o'clock that night, everything was ready. Huong and I had pulled together several small tables to make one large dining table in the living room. Vietnamese usually eat with chopsticks out of small, deep bowls, and so Huong didn't have enough plates and forks for all the people coming to dinner. We improvised by putting platters of French fries at strategic points along the table and deciding that people would eat their hamburgers out of bowls.

We finished just as the guests began to arrive. Huong's parents got there first. Her sister, Nga, and Nga's husband Tan came in a few minutes later, followed by Tung's parents, who rode bicycles over from their house a few blocks away. Tung's younger brother appeared on a motorbike and took a seat next to his mother. Viet, who refused to sit down, lurked near a bowl of French fries, which, not surprisingly, had turned out crisp and perfect. Tung pulled his bottle of Johnnie Walker from a cabinet and began pouring it into glasses. The only person who hadn't shown up yet was Phai.

Huong, Nga, and I shuttled platters of burgers and fries in from the kitchen. Huong's mother, a round-faced woman with a loud voice, picked up the bottle of Heinz ketchup, opened it, and smelled it. She set it down, picked up the bottle of mustard, smelled that, and set it down. As I was beginning to learn, Vietnamese rely on their sense of smell much more than Americans do. If someone describes a food, they'll talk about its smell, either complimenting its pleasant fragrance or complaining about its stink. And when Vietnamese want to demonstrate their affection, they don't kiss. Instead, they hold each other close and inhale deeply.

Now Huong's mother was wrinkling her nose at the smell of the ketchup.

"It's delicious," I told her. "Do you know how to eat it?"

Huong's mother never attempted to communicate with me directly. She looked at her daughter Nga and bellowed, "What is it?"

Nga set a platter of burgers down in front of the two grandfathers, then looked up at me. "What is it, Duyen?" she asked.

Before I could answer, Huong's father pointed to the ketchup and said, in French, as if to translate, "*Qu'est-ce que c'est?*"

Everyone looked at me and waited. I leaned over the table and methodically pointed at the plates of burgers, the "buns" we'd fashioned out of long baguettes, and the bowls of fries, using gesture and a few words of Vietnamese to demonstrate the varied uses of mustard and ketchup. Huong's mother eyed me skeptically. Then Tung's mother picked up the ketchup and, using her chopstick to get it moving, gamely poured some into her bowl. She had a character that Vietnamese would call *vui*, which to describe an experience means "fun" and to describe a personality means "cheerful" or "good-natured." Unlike Huong's mother, who wouldn't talk to me at all, Tung's mother acted as if I could understand Vietnamese as well as a native Hanoian. She looked up at me and said something that sounded like, "Blah blah blah Duyen blah blah." Everyone laughed.

She picked up a French fry with her chopstick, dipped it in the ketchup, then took a bite. She chewed, swallowed, and pondered the experience like a gourmet contemplating the taste of a new wine. After a while, she looked up at me and announced, "*Ngon!*"—Delicious!—and passed the bottle of ketchup to her husband. Now everyone wanted to take a taste.

The next time I returned from the kitchen, Phai was standing in the doorway looking in. His hair was damp and combed back off his face. He had on a gold-colored long-sleeved shirt and a pair of white trousers that were as smooth as a sheet of paper. He looked so clean and fresh that, without even thinking about what I was doing, I found myself pushing my dirty hair off my forehead and straightening my shirt. "Hi," I said, forgetting that I was speaking in English.

"Hi," he smiled.

"Phai, sit down! Eat!" said Tung, who was already biting into his second burger. Phai took a seat next to Tung.

Huong, Nga, and I sat down at three empty spots near the kitchen. "Duyen!" Tung yelled from the far end of the table. "Drink Johnnie?"

I didn't like whiskey, but tonight I took a glass.

We Americans eat our meals very quickly. Even Thanksgiving dinner, which might take eight hours to prepare, can be devoured in twenty minutes. Vietnamese, on the other hand, like to savor their food when they have a chance. On festive occasions, I'd seen men take a bite, stop and talk, take another bite, smoke a cigarette, take another bite, then have another glass of whiskey. A meal like that could last for hours. Tonight, people were laughing and joking as if we were celebrating a holiday, but, for some reason, they rushed through my hamburger and French fries dinner with the speed of a meal at McDonald's. Maybe there was something about the food itself that didn't allow for pauses. Within about half an hour, everything on the table had disappeared, except the mustard, which no one liked.

"Ask her how to make that meat," said Huong's mother, nudging Nga.

"Duyen, blah blah blah," said Tung's mother, nodding enthusiastically.

"*Très bon!*" laughed Huong's father.

Tung's father was going through his teeth with a toothpick.

Tung yelled down at me from the other end of the table. "This dinner is *vui,*" he said. It was the best compliment I got all night.

I looked at Huong. "What did you think?" I asked. Hers was the only opinion about which I really cared.

Huong had eaten one hamburger and a small bowl of French fries. On top of that, she'd consumed several tomato slices dipped in ketchup. "The meat is good," she said, agreeing with her mother. "But it's not good on bread. It would be more delicious over rice." Then she got up and began clearing dishes. Nga and I stood up to help her. I wasn't thrilled with Huong's response, but I told myself that I was making progress.

The party ended pretty quickly after that. While Nga and I cleared, Phai, Tung, and Nga's husband sat at the far end of the table, smoking cigarettes and sipping Johnnie. Each time I emerged to retrieve another armful of dishes, someone else had gone home. First, Huong's parents left, then Tung's, then Tung's brother, then Phai disappeared as well.

Not a single person had thanked me for the meal. I had long ago noticed, of course, that Vietnamese don't say "please" and "thank you" nearly as often as Americans do. As I would later learn, it wasn't for lack of social skills. Rather, with as much logic as an American would use to explain how "thank you" eases the flow of social interaction, a Vietnamese would argue that Americans' use of such terms is excessive, overly formal, and even cold. The mark of a true friendship, a Vietnamese would say, comes from the ability to expect everything from each other, and to give and receive without comment.

I didn't know the Vietnamese side to this argument yet, and even if I had, I would have still been disappointed. You only realize how heavily you depend upon the customs of your own culture when you live somewhere that doesn't follow them. I was raised to say "please" for something as slight as the salt and pepper shakers being passed at the table. My parents had taught me that even "Gesundheit!" deserved warm thanks. As I slowly filled my arms with another set of dishes from the table and walked into the kitchen, I felt unappreciated and ignored. "People don't say good-bye very often in Vietnam, do they," I commented to Huong.

Huong looked up at me from the basin of dishes over which she was squatting. She had refused to let me help her wash, and it was only after some arguing that she'd agreed to let me clear the table. "I don't understand," she said.

I let it drop, telling myself that Tung's assessment of "*vui*" should have been compliment enough.

Tuesday was the night I taught English to the children at Tra's house. My class had five students, who ranged in age from seven to ten. Tra's son Minh, whom I called Mickey in class, was the oldest. He competed for dominance in the group with Harry's daughter, Lily, who was bright and very pretty but didn't like to listen. Next was Tra's niece, Halle, who was good-natured and studious, and a cousin, Georgey, who became the class clown. The youngest student was Toby, a sweet-faced child who wouldn't open his mouth at all, and whom I was surprised to find was the grandson of General Vo Nguyen Giap, the military mastermind behind Vietnam's victories over the French and the United States. After those classes, I had a hard time looking at the general's photos without seeing Toby's face.

The classes were not structured at all. We practiced telling time. We played house. We sang "Head and Shoulders" and "If You're Happy and You Know It Clap Your Hands." One night, a few days after my American dinner, I carried to class a packet of Starbursts I'd brought from the States; using the candies as examples, we learned the words for fruits. When class was over, Lily raced up to her father, who was standing outside our classroom. "Daddy!" she squealed. "Appe! Oran! Bana!" Then she leaped into his arms.

Harry beamed at me. "She's learning so much," he said.

It had been weeks since he'd proposed I go with him to his private cottage, but I still had trouble looking Harry in the face. "Kids learn quickly," I answered.

"Oh, no. She likes her teacher."

The other parents arrived to pick up their kids, and within a few minutes, I was left alone with Tra. "Come upstairs for a while," she said. We hadn't seen each other in days.

With its CD player, VCR, and late-model TV, Tra's living room was the most Westernized space I'd seen in Vietnam. Novels lined the bookshelves, dozens of Vietnamese titles alongside translations of the latest Sidney Sheldon and Danielle Steel. On a piano bench sat video copies of *When Harry Met Sally . . .* and

Touch of Evil and two well-worn Ninja Turtle action figures. On the afternoon I'd first arrived in Hanoi, the sight of this room had surprised me. Against the backdrop of my carefully manufactured concept of Vietnam—the peasant culture I had seen out the windows of buses on my first trip to the country—nothing in this room had seemed Vietnamese. Rather, it had seemed generically cosmopolitan, the happy family quarters of elite professionals in any country in the world. Now, I read this room differently. I knew that the teacups, upside down in their saucers on the coffee table, were perfectly arranged according to local custom, as a way of protecting clean dishes from gathering dust. Beside the teapot, the bowl of mandarin oranges served as the requisite offering for guests. Despite all the Western accoutrements, Tra's living room had as much of a particularly Vietnamese quality to it as the firm swing of a peasant's scythe in the fields of the Mekong Delta.

I settled down on the couch. "What do you think of Harry?" I asked.

Tra was standing at a table a few feet away, absorbed by the task of making tea. "I don't know him. Why?"

I told her about his invitation to go with him to the West Lake. Tra looked up at me, then she began to laugh. "Why should I be surprised? He's just a Vietnamese man. It's a good thing you aren't interested in Vietnamese men."

"I'm interested in Vietnamese men," I protested.

"Not really," she said. In some ways, Tra was like Huong. She often felt the need to teach me things about myself. "Why would you want a Vietnamese man when you could have an American man?"

"I like Vietnamese men. I just don't like the married ones."

Tra looked up at me and shook her head. "Well, you should

know better," she said. Her voice was teasing, but her eyes were serious.

We were silent for a while. Tra carried the tea over to the table and sat down next to me on the couch. "I'm just having a bad day with Vietnamese men," she explained.

The issue of whether or not Tra would go back to the States had been a point of contention with her husband since I'd arrived. She had postponed her return twice already, but now she was scheduled to leave in less than a month. "Are you really going back to Michigan?" I asked.

"Of course I'm going back," she said. She scratched at a mud spot on the cuff of my jeans, sending a tiny cloud of dust into the air. "I don't know, maybe not."

I knew how Tra was suffering to get her M.B.A. When I was still in San Francisco, we'd often talked to each other by phone. Once, I'd gotten a call from her at eleven o'clock at night. In Michigan, it was 2:00 A.M. "Dana, I'm dying here," she'd whispered.

"What's wrong?" I'd asked. In my mind, I was already racing to Michigan to get her to a hospital.

"Exams. And I have a twenty-page paper due next week. How can I write twenty pages in English?" she groaned.

I knew how Tra had to ride her bike home from the campus library in the freezing cold of winter and that she survived on $350 a month, $200 of which went to rent. I knew that her roommate, a nurse on morning shift, liked to run the vacuum before leaving for work at dawn. I knew about the local supermarket that only sold tasteless chicken and about Tra's regular trips across the border to Asian groceries in Canada to stock her freezer with poultry she could eat. Tra had always told me these stories as if she were trying to entertain me with her comical adventures in America, but when I came to Vietnam I began to understand how hard her life in the States really was. I didn't know how much she suffered from homesickness until I saw the pleasure she got from eating a simple bowl of Hanoi *phở*. I only understood her longing for her son when I saw the way she watched him play. It seemed like those years away from Vietnam were tearing her in two.

With Tra's English skills, she could probably do extremely well in Vietnam, even without another degree. An ambitious person with a good grasp of English could earn more in Hanoi these days than almost anyone who didn't speak English, Ph.D. or not. Of course, a Ph.D. was no ticket to wealth in the United States either, but I'd met enough Ph.D.s working as tour guides and secretaries for foreign companies in Vietnam to know that in a country that had traditionally placed a supreme value on education, wealth had begun to supplant knowledge as the great status symbol. With her background in economics and mastery of English, Tra could get a prestigious, well-paying job whenever she was ready. "Are you sure you need that M.B.A?" I asked.

Her head jerked up from her cup of tea. "Of course I do," she said. "You know how much I want it."

"But you have to struggle so much over there."

Tra leaned over the coffee table and opened a plastic bag of yellow candies that looked like sugar-coated garbanzo beans. "This is *mứt sen,* candied lotus seeds. They're a Vietnamese specialty. You should try them," she said. She attempted to pour them into a dish but they fell out in one large clump. "They're a little sticky from the humidity."

I pulled one candy apart from the pile and put it in my mouth. It tasted like a sugar-coated garbanzo bean. "Delicious," I said.

Tra nodded, absently chewing her candy. She said, "You know how well educated my family is."

I nodded. Tra's father was in Ho Chi Minh's first cabinet. Her mother was one of the only Vietnamese ever elected to the French society of engineers. Her sister and brother had gotten doctorates in Moscow. Her husband had trained to be an architect in Prague. "What do I have?" Tra asked. "A bachelor's degree from Hanoi."

"It doesn't make any difference," I said, launching into the same argument I'd given her before. Tra wanted to a be a businesswoman, not an academic.

Tra started scratching at the mud spots on my pants again.

"What does Tuyen think you should do?" I asked. She and her husband had been married eleven years, but because each of them had spent so much time abroad, they'd only actually lived together for five of them. As strange as this sounded, Tra and Tuyen's arrangement was quite ordinary among the educated classes of Vietnam. Apparently, however, Tuyen wasn't satisfied with Tra spending so much time away. He hadn't complained about the separation when he went abroad, but now that she was leaving he advocated a much more traditional model of family. He never showed his resentment openly, but I'd seen the way he teased her. Tuyen was a slight, almost scrawny-looking man, but he carried himself with a confidence he must have earned from his intellect and the power he'd accumulated through his high-ranking position as a government architect. At first, he'd struck me as reserved, even shy, but I quickly learned that his wit could be scathing. His English was terrible, but he used it to great effect with his wife, when he called her "Miss Tra" or "my American wife."

In private, it seemed, he was more direct. "Tuyen thinks I'm wrong," said Tra. "He says, How can I leave him alone here? How can he take care of our little boy as well as I can? What kind of family is that?" When she looked up, she seemed close to tears. "The thing is, I don't even disagree with him."

It was nearly eleven when I stood up to go home. Tra walked me downstairs. When we got to the front gate, the family's new dog, Johnny, ran up and started throwing himself at Tra's legs. In the past year, extremely expensive Japanese dogs had become a new symbol of wealth among Vietnam's elite. At the same time, the ranks of the wealthy in Hanoi were swelling with people who'd made their fortunes breeding these animals. In fact, Japanese dog breeding had become something like a pyramid scheme among Hanoians anxious to get rich. By borrowing small amounts of money from a large circle of family and friends, a person could accumulate, say, one hundred dollars to purchase a puppy, expecting to raise the dog, breed it, then sell its puppies a few years later for a lot more money. The problem, however, was that the dogs were delicate, not well suited to the Vietnamese climate, and they often died. Plenty of Hanoians had lost their shirts on Japanese dogs.

"Is Johnny Japanese?" I asked.

"No. Of course not. He's worthless," Tra said. Indeed, Johnny was cute only to those who equate small with cute. He had a frantic personality and the challenge of his life centered on escaping from the courtyard of the house so that he could dash in mad circles up and down the sidewalks and in and out of traffic. Tra regarded Johnny with a disdain reserved for the very lowest orders. Ignoring his given name, she referred to him as "Stupid Dog."

Now Tra used her legs to block the dog's escape, but she was still thinking about our conversation upstairs. "Vietnamese people say there are four stages of love," she said, going on to define them as *bí mật, trăng mật, vỡ mật, mất mật*. Roughly translated, the first stage would mean "secret honey," symbolizing the moment two people fall in love but haven't told anyone yet. The second stage is "honeymoon," when everything is perfect. The third stage, "broken honey," marks the beginning of problems, and the fourth stage, "lost honey," represents the end of the romance.

"What stage are you and Tuyen at?" I asked.

The dog started to bark, and Tra gave him a shove with her knee. She was coy. "I try to stay away from sweets," she laughed.

I pulled a pen and paper out of my bag. The four stages of love didn't sound too poetic in English, but I liked the idea of it. "Repeat that," I told her.

Tra looked at me. "Why do you want to know these silly things?"

"I'm collecting Vietnamese idioms."

The dog got more determined, and Tra squatted down and held him by the skin of his neck. She slowly repeated the four stages of love while I wrote them down, then she added with a wicked grin. "Why don't you learn an American idiom? Here's a joke my landlord in Michigan told me: What are the three stages of sex?"

"What?" I asked. I was less interested in American humor.

"First there's house sex. That's when you have sex all over the house. Then there's bedroom sex. That's when you have sex only in the bedroom. Finally, there's hall sex. That's when you walk by each other in the hall and say, 'Fuck you!'"

Before I even had time to laugh, Tra poked her finger at the piece of paper in my hand. "It's true," she said, "write that one down."

"It's not Vietnamese," I said. "I'm interested in Vietnamese culture."

"Well, I'm interested in American culture," she said. "Maybe I should start writing things down, too."

⌒⌒⌒⌒⌒   One morning, I walked downstairs at 7:00 A.M.
on my way out to breakfast. Because neither Tung nor Huong held
down a regular job, most mornings they slept later than I did.
Today, though, both of them, as well as Viet, were already out of
bed and downstairs in the living room. Huong had hauled the
couch out from the side of the wall and was sweeping mountains
of dust from behind it. Tung, his face still misty from sleep, was
rubbing a wall mirror clean with a rag. Viet leaned against the
kitchen doorway, eyes half-closed, mechanically sliding a dry
toothbrush in and out of his mouth.

"Viet! Use the toothpaste," his mother ordered.

"I'm hungry," he whined.

"Use the toothpaste or you won't eat," she answered.

I stood watching them. "Why are you up so early?" I asked.

Huong stopped sweeping and glanced up at the clock. "The
new renters arrive today," she said.

I couldn't help but feel disappointed. I had forgotten that
today was the day the Thai-Chinese couple would enter our
lives. I liked being the only foreigner living in the house. I sometimes felt more like a member of their family than a tenant.
Once I became one of a crowd, I felt, my special status would
change.

Actually, the house was more crowded already. Tung and
Huong had hired a young woman from the countryside, like
Lua, the servant at Tra's house, to clean and cook. Sa was a distant cousin of Huong's who had grown up in the countryside
west of Hanoi. She was a tall, fresh-faced girl who had never
been to Hanoi before her arrival at our house. Now I could see
her, scrubbing a sheet in the kitchen, quietly singing a folksong
as she worked. Sa seemed thrilled by every aspect of life here. I
hadn't had a chance to speak with her yet, but every time I saw
her she smiled at me happily, as if the American woman who

slept on the third floor was just one more exciting attraction of the big city.

It was almost noon by the time I came home from my Vietnamese lesson that day. Tung was sitting in the living room with two men I'd never seen before. Both were Asian, but they were so well dressed it was obvious they weren't Hanoians. Even Tung, who looked like a fashion plate compared to most Hanoians, came across as *nhà quê*—the Vietnamese term for "country bumpkin"—next to the two strangers in front of him. One of the men, sitting next to Tung on the couch, had an acne-scarred but not unattractive face. He was wearing a bright green Lacoste shirt, a foreign label I'd never seen, even as a knockoff, in Hanoi. The other man, slumped in an armchair, was portly, with thick jowls and hair drawn like pencil lines across his balding head. His fine cotton button-down was bulging at the seams. All three men were holding Dunhills between their fingers. It was not a brand I'd ever seen in our house.

Tung saw me and grinned. His eyes were shining. "Duyen! This is Mr. Huey, our new tenant," he explained in Vietnamese.

The man with the acne scars stood up and shook my hand energetically. "Hello!" he said in English.

"Hello!" I said. "So, you've just arrived?"

The smile on Mr. Huey's face became slightly less enthusiastic, and he turned and glanced at his companion, who merely shrugged.

Tung jumped in. "He doesn't speak English," he explained in Vietnamese. "He doesn't even speak Vietnamese. He's Chinese, from Thailand. Remember? This is his translator, a southerner, Tuan."

The heavy man looked up at me and grunted.

Tung jumped out of his seat and grabbed the thermos to offer tea. Then he abandoned the tea and pulled his hoard of

Johnnie from the cabinet and began to pour it into four glasses. "Mr. Huey's a businessman," he announced. "He's got a lot of plans in Vietnam." The excitement in his eyes reminded me of the look on Viet's face when I gave him a Barrel of Monkeys I'd brought from the States.

Mr. Huey was wearing a pair of Italian-style leather loafers that, I imagined, would quickly disintegrate in the inevitable Hanoi mud. "What kind of business is Mr. Huey in?" I asked in Vietnamese.

"Trade," said the translator, answering for his boss.

Aside from the small-time deals I watched Tung working all day from his "home office" in our living room, "trade" was a realm of life in Vietnam I hadn't observed yet. Something about Mr. Huey struck me as different from the other people I'd met in Hanoi, and I had a sense that it wasn't simply that he was Chinese. Even though our conversation was purely chatter, he was scrutinizing me the whole time. His gaze wasn't sexual at all, but calculating, as if he felt that the American might have something to offer, if only he could figure out what it was.

After a while, he put out a feeler. "You're from America?" he asked, through the translator.

I nodded. "San Francisco."

"Aah," Mr. Huey said, then added, "San Francisco is a beautiful city. I want to go there. Maybe you and I could do business together there someday."

"Duyen!" Tung fairly exploded. "You should do it. Maybe you'll get rich. Then you can come back here and visit us anytime you want."

"Maybe," I said, smiling at Tung. I had no interest in trade, but even if I had, I wasn't certain that I'd want to trade with Mr. Huey.

I heard the creak of the back door that led to the rooms upstairs. A woman appeared on the upper landing and began to walk uncertainly down the steep treads, clinging to the banister. She carried a bundle in one arm and a large canvas sack in the other. When she finally reached the bottom of the stairs, I saw that the sack was an empty shopping bag and the bundle was a tiny wire-haired dog who growled suspiciously, revealing yellowed teeth. Tung leaned over to me and whispered, "That's Mr. Huey's wife."

Mr. Huey's wife had stringy hair and a frightened, mousy face. She was wearing a mishmash of thin, ill-fitting clothes and looked extremely rural, like an older, worn-out version of our new housekeeper, Sa. With a touch of hesitancy in her gestures, she handed the little dog to her husband. Mr. Huey only glanced at her for a moment, but the look was severe. In quick, sharp syllables, he spoke to her and she nodded quickly, then hurried out the door.

Our conversation sputtered on for a few more minutes before fizzling out. Mr. Huey and the interpreter immediately slid into Chinese, no longer even making a pretense of translating for me and Tung.

"So, anything else new?" I asked Tung.

"Isn't he *vui?*" Tung asked. His eyes were focused on his guests. I knew that I should go upstairs and prepare for my afternoon class, but for a long time I couldn't pull myself away. It wasn't the novelty of Mr. Huey that kept me in the chair. It was the sight of Tung, a man who ordinarily couldn't sit still long enough to eat his dinner, suddenly made motionless by the guttural, meaningless phrases of Chinese, as if he believed that by concentrating hard enough, he could begin to understand them.

⌒⌒⌒ Grandmother Nhi, the tea stall lady, was starting to regard me as a regular. When I got home from studying
Vietnamese one morning a week or so after Mr. Huey moved in,
Grandmother Nhi motioned me over to her table, around which
sat three guys I recognized as motorbike washers who worked
next door. "Duyen!" she said. "*Đi đâu về?*"

I locked my bicycle and walked over, forgetting, again,
that "Where have you been?" does not require an answer. "I
went to school, and then to the bookstore, and then I had to
get my bike fixed," I told her, but Grandmother Nhi was not
paying attention.

"It's too wet. You shouldn't be outside," she said. "Sit down.
Drink tea."

I sat down and she handed me a cup of tea. She refilled the
cups of the motorbike washers, then put her hand on my knee
and began to speak to me so earnestly that I didn't have the heart
to tell her I had no idea what she was saying. I caught a few
words—"poor," "old," "so sad"—and nodded sympathetically.
After a few minutes, she squeezed my hand, then looked at the
people gathered around the table and said, "She doesn't understand." I shrugged, smiled, and sipped my tea.

Over the past few weeks, my comprehension of Grandmother Nhi had improved only a little, though my linguistic
range had expanded significantly. Huong, Tung, and Phai had all
learned how to speak to me, and they had become practiced at
understanding my quirky Vietnamese. Any of them could serve
as interpreters between myself and the rest of the world, simpli-
fying complicated ideas and clarifying whatever mess of mixed-
up tones and grammar came out of my mouth. Grandmother
Nhi never got the hang of this. But I could hear her relaying my
own vital statistics to a newcomer in the assembled clientele. I
didn't have much trouble understanding this because these ex-

planations always answered the same questions: Where was I from? How old was I? Was I married yet?

Today, the discussion hit a snag on the third question. The newcomer, a potato-faced woman I recognized as one of the hawkers from a nearby motorbike washeteria, could not believe that I was twenty-nine and still single.

"Why aren't you married yet?" The woman looked at me suspiciously. Grandmother Nhi, her fingers curled around the toothpick dangling from her lips, was waiting for my answer with the undivided attention of someone planning to repeat the story in detail later in the day.

This question had become part of my daily routine. Now, I tried a little joke I'd learned from an American friend of mine who lived in Saigon. "*Không có gì qúy hơn độc lập tự do,*" I said, adopting the famous saying of Ho Chi Minh: "Nothing is more precious than independence and freedom." Grandmother Nhi understood my attempt at humor. She slapped her knee and said, "*Không có gì qúy hơn độc lập tự do!*" to all the motorbike guys, pointing her finger in my direction.

My interrogator, however, persisted. As if she had a legal right to the truth, she asked again, "Why aren't you married yet?"

"I don't want to get married yet," I said. Unfortunately, my Vietnamese pronunciation was off. I still had trouble with the *muốn* and *muộn*. *Muốn* means "want," while *muộn* means "late." The woman interpreted what I was saying as "I'm not late yet."

"You're late already," she informed me.

"I don't want to," I insisted.

"Late already!" Then she leaned closer and put a pasty hand on my arm. "You can marry my son."

"I don't know your son."

"He's very handsome. He's thirty-one."

"Is he married?" I asked, just curious.

"Of course not!" She turned to Grandmother Nhi. "He's very handsome, isn't he?"

Grandmother Nhi had, I could tell, already decided that she would find me a Vietnamese husband. A single woman from a rich Western country, I was the best catch in the neighborhood. "Duyen," she said, cajoling me, "he's very handsome."

I didn't like the way Grandmother Nhi was looking at me. I could tell that she thought of me as *người Mỹ,* the American. I was like the prized fish she sometimes managed to land at her tea table, the one she could tell her friends about and use to attract more business. Now her eyes glimmered with the prospect of my marrying the motorbike hawker's son.

I stood up. Grandmother Nhi's expression suddenly changed. "Duyen, have you eaten yet?" she asked, not letting her desire to be a matchmaker overcome her instincts as a Vietnamese mother.

"No, I'm going inside to eat," I said.

"Go! Go! You'll get sick," she said. She waved me toward the house, sweeping me away like dust, and as usual refusing to let me pay for my tea.

Inside, I found Tung sitting alone on the couch. Two half-liter bottles of beer, one almost empty, sat on the coffee table in front of him. Next to the beer, our telephone lay in a broken heap. Tung was staring down at it as if it were the remains of a favorite pet.

I sat down. "Do you have a problem?" I asked. My Vietnamese was improving, but I still had to take circuitous routes.

Tung poured some beer into a glass for me. "Huong and I are having a fight," he shrugged.

"What happened to the phone?" I asked.

He made a gesture of hurling the telephone against the wall. "Who?"

"Huong. And now she's not speaking to me."

"Not at all?"

"It's only been one day," he said defensively. Sometimes, he explained, he and Huong didn't talk for a week. Once, they didn't say a word to each other for ten days.

We sipped the beer in silence. The loss of the phone would be a problem. Before the arrival of Mr. Huey, the phone didn't ring that much at our house. Now it rang a couple of times an hour. Calls came in from all over Asia, and Mr. Huey was always telephoning places like Taipei and Shanghai. Though he and I had extensions in our own rooms, the phone downstairs served as switchboard for the whole house.

Tung looked up at me and asked, "Do you miss home?"

"Of course," I said.

"I know how you feel," he said.

I'd heard so much about Tung's years in Germany, but he'd never mentioned feeling lonely there. "Were you homesick when you were in Germany?" I asked.

The question pulled him back. "Sure," he said, but he paused for so long that I could see that he was hesitating, trying to decide what more to say. Finally, he looked straight at me. "No. I miss *Germany*. Now I miss Germany."

Tung had always seemed to me like such an operator here, trying to make himself a big fish in the little pond that was Hanoi. Now I saw that three years abroad had made his sense of the world too big for this place. While his wife thrived in this environment, he was suffocating here.

Tung fiddled with the telephone cord. Suddenly, he looked at me. "Huong's upstairs now. Go talk to her."

"I can't talk to her."

"Talk to her!" he pleaded.

I walked upstairs. Tung, Huong, and Viet shared a small loft, an alcove in the landing off the first flight of stairs, which was big enough for a bed and almost nothing else. I tapped on the door. Huong was lying on the bed like an invalid. "Duyen, come in." She moved over to give me some room and I lay down next to her. She picked up my hand. "Did Tung tell you to come up here?"

"Yes," I said. "Why won't you talk to him?"

"I don't want to. I'm so angry. I don't want to live with him anymore."

"Why not?"

Huong stared at the ceiling for a long time, then leaned over and pulled open the drawer on the tiny nightstand beside the bed. Reaching under some of her son's school notebooks, she retrieved a pile of photographs, all of which had been carefully laminated in plastic—*ép plastic,* as the much-admired process is termed in Vietnam. Huong began to shuffle through the pile, which amounted to the Vietnamese equivalent of the family photo album. The photos not only gave a history of Tung and Huong's relationship, but also of Vietnamese photography over the past six years. The first picture was a purely Socialist venture, a black and white photo of Tung and Huong, the quality of which was so bad it reminded me of those "Olde Time Photographers" in American malls, where customers paid to dress in costume and received yellowed pictures of themselves as gunfighters and saloon girls. "This is our wedding," Huong explained. In the photo, she looked like a terrified virgin, and Tung looked like his little brother. Even in their wedding finery, they both looked too young. Huong pulled out another picture, this one in color but so badly faded that I might have been looking at it through the algae-covered glass of a fish tank. "We'd been married a year already," Huong said. The family was standing in front of a dry fountain in a Hanoi park. Huong looked tired, holding baby Viet in her arms. Tung looked shocked, as if he couldn't believe he could produce a child.

The technical quality of the next picture was so vastly improved that the family seemed to have advanced a century in only three years. Huong explained that Tung had left for Germany a year after their wedding, and just a month or so after Viet was born. When the baby was almost two, Huong took him to Germany for a visit.

Neither Tung nor Huong had ever said anything to me about that visit, but here was proof of Huong in Germany, a family photo with a bunch of Germans at a large table covered with Vietnamese food. Everyone was holding up their beer glasses in one hand and their chopsticks in the other, as if the mixing of the two symbolized the union of two friendly cultures. Tung seemed ready to jump out of his seat with enthusiasm. Huong looked tired.

"Did you like Germany?" I asked.

Huong shrugged. "It was okay," she said, with complete indifference. "The rice is terrible there. Nobody speaks Vietnamese." She was already moving on, searching through the pile again. Finally, she pulled out a recent shot, a clear image of the family in a setting I recognized. They were standing in front of their just-completed house in Hanoi. Huong wore a bright blue *áo dài,* the Vietnamese national dress. Tung had on a nice pair of blue jeans, one of his button-down shirts, and sunglasses.

"Tung's not really Vietnamese anymore. He's a Western man now," Huong said with a sigh. "I'm too sick of him."

I wanted to reassure Huong, but my mind was blank. She was right. Her husband's world had changed, and it was hard to see how she fit in.

An American travel writer once told me that the longer she stayed in one place, the harder it became to write about it. "After a week, I can write something great," she said. "After a month, I start to get confused. If I stay for a year, I'm totally lost." Travelers who spend a short time someplace get a sense of it as static, a motionless image they can study like a photograph and feel they know. But the longer I stayed in Vietnam, the more complicated it became. I could see the society changing before my eyes, as fast as the hypermotion of an early movie. After its government launched market-oriented economic reforms in 1986, Vietnam tried to drag itself out of the Stone Age and onto the Information Superhighway all in the course of a few breathless years. Every day of my life there, I witnessed contrasts between the old and the new. On the spindly legged table of her tea stall, Grandmother Nhi now sold fancy imported cigarettes, but to light one you had to stick a piece of shaved wood into the dim flame of a kerosene lamp and use that as a match. Huong still bought live chickens at the market, but now she carried them home strung upside down from the handlebars of her shiny Honda Dream and wrung their necks in her own modern kitchen. I was used to such contrasts and no longer felt a tourist's need to photograph them. But as someone trying to live in this place, I was beginning to sense that a more serious result of all this change was the intense difficulty people were having in coping with it.

The most obvious sign of that difficulty was evident in my friends' marriages. In Hanoi, at least, separations were a big part of the problem. Even my students, most of whom had graduated from foreign universities, were anxious to go away again. The economic benefits of going abroad were so enormous that almost no one could hope to earn as much by staying home. Vietnam was in desperate need of educated professionals, but few acknowledged the emotional price to be paid for them.

Family separation had evolved into an accepted tradition in Vietnam. The nation's folktales are full of soldiers going off to battle, leaving their heartbroken families far behind. During Vietnam's wars in this century it wasn't unusual for soldiers to be away from home for the duration of the conflict, even if that meant twenty years. With Vietnam at peace, the tradition of family separation had not disappeared, just evolved. But as Tra had once explained, families have a much harder time surviving long separations when the cause is not national defense but personal ambition. And in the gap between those very different motivations lay a hint of what was happening in Vietnam today: This nation, whose very survival had always depended on an all-powerful sense of community, was evolving into one in which the individual took precedence.

Instead of my cheering up Huong, she ended up consoling me. Seeing the glum expression on my face, she started laughing. "Don't worry," she said. "This is normal."

I stood up. "You should talk to Tung," I said.

Huong shook her head, then closed her eyes. "I'm not ready yet," she said.

When I got back downstairs, Tung was still sitting in front of the broken telephone. Both bottles of beer were now empty. "What did she say?" he asked.

I shrugged.

He pulled a cigarette out of his shirt pocket and lit it. "I'm so sick of this," he said.

When I got home from teaching that afternoon, Phai was sitting by himself in the living room with the broken telephone spread out on the coffee table in front of him. The big double doors, usually opened wide to the street, were halfway shut. The overhead fluorescent bulbs were turned off, and the only light came from the slice of dim sunlight that managed to pass through the dense clouds and thick canopy of leaves hanging over the street outside.

I sat down on one of the little plastic-upholstered stools. "Tung and Huong are having a fight," I said.

Phai laughed, as if we were sitting through a typhoon and I mentioned that it was raining.

I smiled. "*Phức tạp,*" I said. The word meant "complicated," but it sounded like "fucked-up," which would have worked just as well.

Phai nodded, looking out the door at the rush-hour traffic. His smooth, dark face was full of concern. The afternoon drizzle was starting to turn into heavier rain, and gray Shower Attack Sports raincoats flashed by like ghosts on motorbikes.

"Do you understand what the problem is?" I asked.

Phai looked at me and smiled. "I don't know. I've never been married. I don't know anything about women." Then he turned his eyes away and picked up the telephone. "I should fix this thing," he said.

I still felt slightly confused by Phai. There was a distance between us that neither seemed capable of bridging. It had nothing to do with mistrust. Unlike all the married men who saw me as a prospect for an affair, Phai seemed willing to regard me as more than The American Woman. He had an empathy that I recognized long before the two of us were even able to talk. During those early months in Hanoi, when I felt as though people regarded my efforts to speak Vietnamese as the ridiculous utterings of a mental incompetent, Phai always watched me like a sports fan rooting for his favorite player. Still, we were complete mysteries to each other.

Phai had what my grandmother would have called "common-sense smarts." He had never been to college, but could install an air conditioner without even glancing at the instructions. In Vietnam, which suffered from a chronic lack of spare parts, exacerbated at that time by the U.S. trade embargo, people made do by fashioning workable replacement parts for everything from radiators and refrigerators to typewriters and photocopy machines. Most Vietnamese knew how to coax aged and delicate appliances into working one more month or year, but, even by local standards, Phai had talent. Tung was clever enough to recognize Phai's skills and turn him into the fix-it man for everything that broke in our house. I had watched him open a busted stereo, scatter the parts across the floor, tweak a few wires, then put it back together so that Tung could blast Metallica through the house as clearly as ever. I often came home to find Phai perched on a ladder, readjusting the electrical wiring, or hidden between the toilet and the wall, unclogging a drain. To me, this was magic.

Phai was using a rubber band and Scotch tape to fix the broken phone. He pried the cover open with his fingertips and thumbs.

"Where did you learn to fix things?" I asked.

He glanced up and grinned at me. "You don't have to go to school for this."

The internal circuit board looked like something I'd seen on a commercial for AT&T, an intricate puzzle of tiny wires and connectors meant to convey to TV audiences the technological sophistication of the phone company. Phai dug his fingers into it, opened a gap, and fixed the rubber band around it. Then, holding a torn section of the board in place, he ripped off a piece of tape with his teeth and reconnected it. He snapped the cover back on the phone, fiddled with the wires in the wall, then picked up the receiver and listened. After a moment, he handed it to me so that I could hear the dial tone myself.

"You must have learned about machines somewhere," I insisted.

"I learned some in the army," he finally admitted, pulling a cigarette out of the box in his shirt pocket and lighting it. Phai was my age, which meant that his mandatory military service had taken place long after the last shots of the war against the United States were fired (but not long after the brief 1979 border war with China). His memory of the American War was probably hazy, but, like all my other Hanoi friends, he still avoided talking with me about it. Sometimes, someone would make a joke about the war, but other than that, when I asked for specifics, I generally met with the same response, a vague smile and an emphatic, question-stopping, "That was the past. I like to think about the future." Once, during an English class, I asked my adult students to describe the scariest moment of their lives. One talked about almost drowning while swimming in a river as a kid. Another remembered a traffic accident in Moscow. All of my students would have been considered members of the "Vietnam Generation" had they lived in the States. But if they had any terrifying memories of war, I didn't hear about them. Talking about the war with an American was bad form, like reminding a guest in your home that she owed you money. Still, the longer I spent in Hanoi, the more I felt the need to find out about it.

"What did you do in the army?" I asked, testing to see how much more he'd offer.

"I was up on the border with China," he said. "I didn't want to shoot a gun, so I studied how to repair cars and motorbikes. I hated the military service, but at least I learned a trade."

I heard the rumble of a motorbike outside the door and turned to see Tung pull up on his Dream. He walked into the house, leaving muddy tracks across the slick linoleum floor, then threw himself down on the couch next to Phai. None of us said a word. In a culture that had so little regard for privacy, there was a great respect for silence.

My impulse to come to Vietnam had sprung from my conviction of the two nations' similarities, not their differences. I was learning that I'd been right. Phai learned to fix motorbikes so that he wouldn't have to shoot a gun. Had I been faced with military service, I would have done something like that. Tung didn't have the patience to sit still on a couch for ten minutes, much less prowl through the jungle on an all-night patrol. But it was one thing to try to imagine Tung and Phai in army gear. It was quite another to hear directly from them how they had experienced the war. Sooner or later, I would have to ask.

I was already able to understand one thing very clearly, though. It was not career military men or the sinister VC I remembered from movies, but individuals like Tung and Phai who would have done most of the fighting. Despite all the rhetoric, all the willingness to die for a cause, war wasn't natural to any of them.

A memory slipped through my mind then, from Maxine Hong Kingston's novel *China Men* describing the experience of soldiers in Vietnam: "[When] they were ordered to patrol the jungle they made a lot of noise, clanged equipment, talked loud. The enemy did the same, everybody warning one another off. Once in a while, to keep some hawk officer happy, they fired rounds into the trees."

I didn't know if Kingston's description was authentic or not, but I'd remembered it all these years because it seemed truer to human nature than anything else I'd read about the conflict in Vietnam. I looked at Tung and Phai and thought of my friends back home. I could picture any of them, lonely and petrified, banging their jackknives against their mess kits.

It seemed like we sat there, silently, for hours, but it was probably only five or ten minutes. Tung finally leaned over and ran his finger across the top of the phone. "Did you fix it yet?" he asked Phai.

Phai picked up the phone and held it over his shoulder like a football. "It works," he smirked. "Now you can throw it all you want." I watched Tung, wondering how he'd react to teasing.

Tung looked at Phai and managed a little grin. "I'm so sick of this," he said miserably.

Tra, her sister Hoa, and her sister-in-law Xuan were discussing how many pairs of black pumps Tra would need in Michigan. Tra couldn't seem to convince them that, given her student lifestyle, she might not need any pumps at all. Like me, she spent a lot of time trying to convince people that, though Americans have a lot more money than Vietnamese, we aren't necessarily stylish.

Laid out on the floor of her bedroom were several open suitcases, piles of clothes, a fake-fur jacket bought on a visit to Saigon, three plastic bags of medicinal herbs, a new Vietnamese-English dictionary, several pairs of plastic sandals, five packages of dried noodles, and six small lacquer paintings Tra planned to give to friends in the States.

The bustle in the room obscured the more central fact that Tra was leaving, and the occasional laughter did nothing to mask the strain on every face. Minh wandered sullenly in and out of the room or lay across the bed, playing with his Game Boy. Hoa squatted on the floor, silently folding shirts.

The three-month struggle between Tra and Tuyen had finally come to an end. Tra's plane left for Bangkok at eight the next morning, and everyone knew, without saying so, that she was buying an education at the cost of her marriage. Tra and Tuyen's marriage was reflective of significant changes that were taking place between men and women in Vietnam's middle class. In word, at least, women had been considered equals since as far back as the revolution, when female soldiers marched right alongside the men on the Ho Chi Minh Trail. These days, women occupied positions in most sectors of Vietnamese society, but, like American women, they were also expected to take care of the children and the home. And few Vietnamese men had begun to accept the possibility that they might, at the very least, help out at home. The women of Tra's generation were beginning to rebel.

Tra had never mentioned the word "divorce," and she planned to return to Vietnam as soon as she completed her degree, but it was impossible to ignore the potential implications of her decision to leave. Tra and Tuyen's marriage, like a bone forced too far in the wrong direction, seemed destined to snap.

I hated the thought of being here without Tra. Besides the prospect of missing her, I dreaded saying good-bye. I remembered too clearly saying good-bye to her the first time, a year earlier, in New York. We had been at the end of a whirlwind rush through Manhattan, two days that had included the Statue of Liberty, the Metropolitan Museum, and the United Nations. Our last stop had been the New York Stock Exchange, where she and I had spent an hour on the observation deck above the market floor, about fifty minutes too long for me and many hours too short for Tra. Before Tra caught her bus to Philadelphia, I'd allowed a few minutes for us to sit and drink diet Cokes, trying to think of anything left to say. There was nothing to say but good-bye, and neither of us was ready to say it. Finally, we stood up, hugged three times, and pulled away.

I had walked a few feet up the street before I gave in and turned around for one last glimpse. Tra hadn't moved at all. She laughed when I caught her, gave a little wave, then slowly began to walk in the opposite direction up the street. The two of us kept on like that for the length of the block—walking, turning, laughing, and waving—until Tra became a tiny black spot that disappeared beneath an ocean of gray business suits.

Now I sat there, watching her pack, telling myself I should get up and leave, but not being able to move. Finally, we heard a knock at the bedroom door, and Tra's elderly aunt poked her face into the room. It was nearly ten-thirty at night. I pulled myself out of my chair and said, "Tra, I've got to go."

Tra looked up from her suitcase, crinkled her nose, and nodded. "I'll go downstairs with you," she said.

Tra held my arm as we went down the creaky wooden stairs of the old house, then walked across the courtyard to the front gate. "Check up on my family sometimes, okay?" she said quietly. "Keep teaching the children English. Make sure that Tuyen learns English, too. He's so lazy. Make sure he learns."

We heard a shuffling behind us and turned to see that Minh had followed us down the stairs. He stood watching us, unwilling to let his mother out of his sight. Tra ran to him and tried to hold him. Minh pulled away. At eleven, he was torn between a child's anguish and an adolescent's refusal to express it. He could only stand and look at us, grinning fiercely. Tra tried again, taking one step closer, but this time Minh slipped away completely, turned his face to the vines creeping up the courtyard wall, and made as if to examine them. Tra stood motionless, both eyes on her son, then turned back toward me and picked up my hand.

"Take care of him. Teach him," she said. In the glow of the streetlight, I stared at her face and tried to think of how to reassure her. I would invite Minh out on Sunday outings to Lenin

Park. In our Tuesday evening class, I would let him play Monopoly as much as he liked. None of that could substitute for his mother, though.

I nodded anyway and squeezed Tra's hand. "Don't worry," I told her. "He'll be fine. Everyone will be fine."

Tra smiled, but now the tears were streaming down her face. I pulled open the gate and we walked onto the desolate sidewalk. "Write," she told me.

"I'll write," I said, and I felt a clinching in my throat. Above us, the streetlight buzzed. Quickly, I hugged her, then turned and walked away. Before I reached the corner, I had to stop and look. Tra was still standing there. She laughed and waved.

5 Pilgrims

A FEW WEEKS AFTER TRA LEFT, I pulled my bike up in front of my house and heard Grandmother Nhi calling my name. When I walked over to her tea table, she greeted me with an enormous grin. "You've had a visitor," she told me, breathlessly, as if she couldn't believe her own good fortune. "Another American!"

I was standing on my balcony late that afternoon, scanning the rush-hour traffic. In my hand was a piece of scratch paper, a note from my friend Carolyn from San Francisco. "Sorry I'm late," she'd scribbled. "I got sidetracked in Nepal. I'll meet you here at five."

"Late" was actually an understatement. I'd expected Carolyn two weeks earlier, but when I'd gone out to meet her at the airport, she'd never shown up. Carolyn was a traveler, and though a lot of Americans love to travel, few would want to travel the way she did. She once hid under the dashboard of a truck in order to avoid rebel fire on a remote island of Indonesia. She trekked alone through the Himalayas. She turned a bottle of aspirin and a box of Band-Aids into a rudimentary clinic for desperate villagers in the hills of northern Thailand. I couldn't help but wonder what had "sidetracked" her in Nepal.

Carolyn and I had known each other for years. During the mid-1980s, we had worked together at *Mother Jones* magazine in San Francisco, but we'd only become friends quite recently, because of Vietnam. Both of us had visited Vietnam in 1990, Carolyn only a few months after me. One day, not long after she returned, we'd gotten together in Berkeley. We sat on a bench on Shattuck Avenue, eating sandwiches and discussing our trips. Carolyn was the first person I'd talked to who completely understood the effect that Vietnam had on me. Like me, she had planned to return ever since.

At exactly five, I spotted a bicycle making a shaky left turn before pulling slowly up in front of my house. A frizzy-haired Vietnamese woman was pedaling. My Western-sized friend was balanced precariously over the back wheel. I watched them disembark from the bike, then I yelled down at them. The two women looked up. Carolyn waved with both arms, then pointed at the beaming woman standing beside her. At the tea stall a few feet away, Grandmother Nhi shielded her eyes from the setting sun to watch. Phai, working on a motorbike out on the sidewalk, paused and looked up.

"This is Linh!" Carolyn yelled up to the balcony. Linh and I looked at each other and waved.

Carolyn's reason for coming back to Vietnam had a proper name: Linh. Linh had been a clerk in the hotel where Carolyn stayed in Hanoi and, somehow, despite the gaps of language and culture, each had felt she'd found a soulmate. A few months after Carolyn left, Linh had asked Carolyn to be her second child's godmother. Carolyn had come back to meet her godson.

Of all the photographs of friends and family I'd brought to

Vietnam, Carolyn's was the least successful at conveying the essence of its subject. Photographs could only capture her physical features, the small frame, thick brown hair, and large eyes that made her pretty in a not unusual way. But they failed to convey the spirit that became so obvious when one met her in person. She had an extraordinary ability to develop deep and lasting relationships with the people she met. Through simple facial expressions and pantomime, she could converse for hours with people without sharing a single common word. Perhaps this ability explained her success teaching English to new immigrants from places like Afghanistan, Eritrea, and Vietnam. She had a magnetism, an ability to draw people toward her. Photographs never revealed that.

A moment later, the two of them stood in my doorway. I turned and smiled at Linh. Carolyn had told me about Linh's tiny one-room house, situated down a muddy lane in a workers' neighborhood. I knew about her husband, a low-level bureaucrat who spoke hyperformal English. I knew about her ten-year-old son and her new baby. I even had a vivid knowledge of Linh's experience as a child during the war. Her parents had maintained their jobs in Hanoi, and every Sunday they rode their bicycles twenty kilometers into the countryside to visit their daughters, who had been evacuated from the city. After each brief visit, Linh had to comfort her hysterical younger sister, who could never understand why their parents kept abandoning them.

Linh held out her hand to me. "I am very happy to make your acquaintance, Dana," she said. She was rather tall and curvaceous, with honey-colored skin and eyes that were both sympathetic and curious. We shook hands and I ushered them both into my room.

Linh was gazing at me, smiling. I thought back to the adjectives Carolyn had used to describe her friend—"kooky" had been prominent—and tried to connect them with this politely professional young woman. Hanoi was full of politely professional young women. Why was Carolyn so crazy about this one?

"I tried to find you," I told Linh. Not long after I'd arrived in Hanoi, I'd gone searching for her at the Bodega Restaurant and Guesthouse, where Carolyn had first met her. (Although the name "Bodega" sounded like the word for an Hispanic grocery, *Bò Dê Gà* meant "Beef Goat Chicken," which the establishment supposedly served.) Though I'd easily managed to find the place, I hadn't found Linh working there. She'd quit her job at the government-owned Bodega in order to work as an assistant housekeeper at the newly restored, French-financed Metropole Hotel. It would have been hard to find a much greater contrast than that between the Metropole and the Bodega. The Bodega represented everything good and bad about the Socialist hospitality industry. It had a large but apathetic staff, good rooms with bad plumbing, and a restaurant that didn't carry most of the items on its extensive menu. The Metropole, on the other hand, was the first swanky digs to open in Hanoi since the government introduced *đổi mới,* its economic renovation policy, in 1986. It had a modern swimming pool, a concierge, and a restaurant that served fine French wines. Well-heeled travelers could expect the same quality of service at the Metropole as they would get at international-standard hotels from Amsterdam to Hong Kong.

After only a month, however, Linh was already unhappy. Compared to the laid-back style of the Bodega, the job at the Metropole was as grueling as indentured servitude, except that the wages, at two hundred dollars a month, were excellent. The Metropole expected a lot for what it paid. Staff could be punished for arriving even a minute late. Linh's uniform had to be absolutely spotless. She had to greet every guest with a big smile, even on days when she had a headache. Plus, she told us, "I have problem with Mr. Dodson."

"What's the problem with Mr. Dodson?" asked Carolyn. "Who's Mr. Dodson?"

"Mr. Dodson. My housekeeper. I have problem with slippers," Linh said matter-of-factly. Though Linh's English rushed out of her mouth with a fluency that impressed me, she made so many assumptions about our knowledge that I had no idea what she was trying to say. After much questioning, Carolyn and I began to understand that Linh's problem resulted from a Metropole policy forbidding staff from taking anything out of the hotel. A few days earlier, Linh had found a pair of bedroom slippers in a wastebasket and brought them to her boss, the chief housekeeper Mr. Dodson, to ask if she could take them home. Mr. Dodson was so enraged by this request that he threatened to fire her.

Linh was shocked. In Vietnam people routinely, and quite practically, sifted through other people's discards. Vendors across the city earned their livelihoods selling empty packaging — plastic Nescafé jars, Coca-Cola liter jugs, wine bottles — to customers who would take these items home and fill them with drinking water, dishwashing soap, or homemade rice wine. On days when the garbage trucks were due to come by my house, scavengers would pick through all the neighbors' trash, collecting twine, pieces of plastic, newspapers, and cardboard, all of which they could later sell. Vietnamese were so thrifty that I once met an American doctoral student who was devoting his dissertation to the topic of waste and recycling in Vietnam, in hopes that we could learn from them. Linh was baffled by Mr. Dodson insistence that a discarded pair of slippers, even in good condition, must be discarded. Even Carolyn's attempts at an explanation of Western concerns about thievery failed to convince Linh that Mr. Dodson was anything but evil. "I hate Mr. Dodson," Linh said. Then, suddenly, she sprang up from her chair, walked over to the mirror, and pursed her lips in front of it. "Caro-leen gave me this lipstick. Is it pretty for me?"

It was a deep red that contrasted nicely with her skin. "It's pretty," I told her.

"How do you say in English—It's pretty for me?" Linh asked.

Carolyn and I looked at each other. "It suits you," I finally said. "You would say that that color suits you."

Linh considered the verb for a moment, repeating it as she gazed at her reflection in the mirror. "Suits me. It suits me." Then she added, "Can I say that this dress suits me?"

We nodded.

"And Mr. Dodson? Can I say Mr. Dodson he does not suits me?"

We nodded again.

Linh began to walk around the room, performing a little dance for us. "This color suits me. This dress suits me. Carolyn and Dana suits me. Mr. Dodson does not suits me," she announced.

Linh ended her parade back at the mirror and did a little fashion-model flick of her head. "I hate Mr. Dodson," she pouted, staring at herself. "He does not suits me."

After Linh went home, Carolyn and I went out to get something to eat. The sky had turned purple, and at the electric appliance stalls by the railroad tracks, the lights of the globe-shaped karaoke lamps were twinkling like colored stars. Inside the open door of one house, a woman was urging a little boy to read a lesson from his school primer. A few doors down, a tiny old woman chewed on a toothpick and gazed at us from the deep recesses of an armchair. In front of us, a bread-seller walked along the street balancing a basket full of baguettes on her head. "*Bánh mì nóng, ời! Bánh mì nóng, ời!*"—Hey! Hot bread! Hot bread! It was one of the last things I heard before I fell asleep at night and one of the first things I heard as I woke every morning. The fragrance of the warm loaves drifted over us.

Despite the long day that Carolyn had had—flying in from Bangkok and getting into the city from the airport—I could not even offer to cook her dinner. I had the materials to do so, but not the capability. Huong had given me an electric hot plate and a refrigerator. Most Vietnamese would have considered these appliances luxuries, but for an American who learned to cook on a four-burner Magic Chef, the hot-plate experience felt like camping. I had to figure out a whole new method of preparing food. Most Vietnamese cooked on the kitchen floor. Squatting down over wooden cutting boards, they would chop their vegetables and clean their fish, then prepare everything on little charcoal cookers about the size of a single burner. Even Huong, who had a full-size stove, did most of her preparations squatting in her kitchen, as I had found, to the detriment of my leg muscles, when we made our hamburger dinner. She could sit like that for hours, while I couldn't last more than a few minutes in that position. Within a few weeks of receiving my new cooker, I was limiting my hot plate use to boiling drinking water and heating up packets of instant noodles. Considering that I could get a very satisfying meal for less than fifty cents, I mostly ate out.

We ended up on the tiny, claustrophobic alley called Cam Chi Street. Lined with bare-bones rice and noodle shops, Cam Chi had the chaotic feel of a Cubist painting. Handmade signs hung off balance, occasionally banging the heads of people moving down the narrow, block-long road. Awnings jutted out from the buildings, their swooping fabric cutting patches out of the rice-colored sky. Inside gaping doorways, wooden tables sat at odd angles on green-and-yellow checkerboard linoleum floors, and stacks of wooden stools leaned like rickety pillars against mottled hospital-green walls. Over everything floated steam and smoke, the steam lifting off the enormous vats of boiling broth and the smoke rising from the glowing coals of charcoal cookers.

Cam Chi's stalls were much like food stalls anywhere in Vietnam. One central table covered with food served as each establishment's low-tech advertisement for what it served—whether it was *phở,* rice porridge, rice pancakes, sticky rice, fried noodles, stewed chicken, or fried eel. At the biggest stalls, this table sat in the open space between the street and the dining room, usually the living room of the proprietor's own house, which was turned into a restaurant during the twelve to eighteen hours that the shop was open for business every day. The bigger food stalls could have as many as three or four people working in them at the busiest time: one or two to take orders and cook the food, another to prep the ingredients and bring the customers their meals, one to clear and wash the dishes, and another to park and watch the customers' motorbikes and bicycles. The smaller stalls on Cam Chi set up tables on the sidewalk itself. Some didn't even have private tables. Customers merely sat down on simple wooden benches lining three sides of the proprietor's table. The proprietor, sitting on the fourth side of the table, was a one-person restaurant staff, able to take customers' orders, dish up their food, handle money, and still have time left over to do the dishes.

This was the street where Tra had taught me to order "noodle soup without the pilot," and Carolyn and I had barely made it around the corner when a young man from my favorite noodle shop saw me and yelled, *Phở không người lái!*" He had such a grin of expectation on his face that I couldn't disappoint him. I ordered the usual.

We chose a table in the corner and sat down. Three well-dressed young men sitting nearby shifted their bodies around and spent the rest of their meal watching us.

Carolyn finally had a chance to tell me why she'd arrived so late in Vietnam. Before coming to Vietnam, she'd stopped to visit her "Tibetan parents," an elderly couple she'd met years before in Nepal. After she had spent ten days with them in their remote mountain village, they'd convinced her to stay another week. "Sorry I didn't call you," she said. "The nearest international phone was a day's hike, then a twelve-hour bus ride away."

Our soup arrived. "*Phở không người lái,*" said the grinning waiter, with a wink in my direction. Carolyn looked at me, waiting for me to translate, but I didn't have the energy to explain. Instead, I concentrated on making sure we followed the appropriate rituals for eating noodle soup. I dug my hand into the canister of chopsticks on the table searching for equal-sized chopsticks for each of us. "It's better to have a mismatched husband and wife than a mismatched pair of chopsticks," I explained to Carolyn, repeating an axiom I'd picked up from Tra. I wiped off all four chopsticks with paper napkins. On a plate in the middle of our table was a mound of fresh herbs, crisp white bean sprouts, sliced chilis, and quartered lemons. I squeezed the juice of a couple of pieces of lemon into my broth, plucked the leaves off a stalk of basil, and dropped them in. I took my chopsticks and my wide, flat-bottomed spoon, and stirred the hot soup. The steam settled like a warm dew on my face.

I told Carolyn about Tung and Huong, about Tra, and about the slow progress of my Vietnamese. After nearly two months in Hanoi, I was finally beginning to feel settled, I told her. When it came to negotiating my way through the basic chores of daily life, I had become quite competent. I could even carry on rudimentary conversations with people who didn't speak any English. But in some ways, the chasm between myself and these Vietnamese was still as deep as ever. I was only communicating in outline form, really. I could mention a topic—say, "age," "homeland," "plans for the future"—but I could never actually discuss it.

Finally, someone was here to whom I could actually express myself. "I'm so happy you're here," I told her.

Carolyn smiled, but she seemed dazed, not simply by the experience of moving in the course of two days from the high Himalayas to the noodle stalls of Vietnam, but by the simple fact of being in Hanoi at all. She'd spent two years focused on finding a way back to Vietnam. Now, she seemed overwhelmed by the realization that she'd finally made it.

Carolyn leaned back against the chipped and faded green wall. "I love the way it smells here," she said, closing her eyes and inhaling deeply. She seemed to be trying to drag all of Vietnam into her lungs, and I felt as though I were watching someone tripping. I breathed a sample of the air myself. It wasn't exotic, more like the muddled ingredients of a stew: burning coal, simmering broth, and the smoke of our neighbors' cigarettes. I had become so accustomed to these smells, to the cries of the street vendors, to the rich taste of cheap soup, that I no longer really noticed such things. Vietnam had already swallowed me whole, and I sat inside it now like a bug in the belly of a dragon.

Carolyn still lived somewhere beyond the thick skin of this place. I wanted reminders of America, reminders that beyond Vietnam a place existed were I could feel at home. I broke in awkwardly. "Carolyn, what's going on in San Francisco?" I asked. "What's happening in the election campaigns? How's Deborah?

Who was nominated for the Academy Awards? Has anybody famous died lately?" I didn't want to miss something important.

We ordered tea, and Carolyn tried for ten or fifteen minutes to satisfy my curiosity. She told me about the presidential election primary season, about her plans for next summer's garden, about the new Vietnamese restaurant near my house. I took in the words as if they were drops of water falling onto my parched tongue. And then, in midsentence, she stopped. She said nothing for a long time, rubbing her eyes with her fingertips. "I'm sorry," she finally said, looking up at me, obviously exhausted. "I can't do this. I'm only in Asia for five weeks. My time here is so precious. I can't think about America now."

Both of us were silent, embarrassed. I stretched my fingers around my cup of tea and blew into it until my face grew hot from the steam and frustration. For a long time, I focused my attention on the little disk of liquid in my cup, and on the image of myself reflected there. That other world was an ocean away. One friend had crossed that ocean, but this didn't mean I'd gone home.

When I came back to the house one afternoon a few days after Carolyn arrived, a brown paper bag was sitting on the living room coffee table. It was a large bag, rumpled and bulky, the kind one would use to carry home a load of groceries in the States. The top of it curled softly to one side, as if it had been rolled tightly closed, then opened, then closed again.

On the couch sat Tung with his brother-in-law, Nga's husband Tan. Mr. Huey's translator, Tuan, sat in the armchair. Phai, smoking a cigarette, perched on a stool near the door. All four of them glanced up at me, then their eyes shifted back to the bag, then back to me.

"What is it?" I asked.

Phai answered. "The money for Mr. Huey's phone bill," he said, explaining that Mr. Huey and Tung, under whose name the phone was registered, would be taking the money to the central telephone office this afternoon. "Take a look," he urged.

I walked over and unrolled the top of the bag. It was stuffed with rubber-band wrapped bundles of 5,000-dong bills, each of which probably contained one hundred individual notes. Five-thousand dong notes, which were worth about 50 cents, were at that time the largest denomination available in Vietnam. They were dark blue and usually crisp, compared to the faded brown 1,000s and the pale red 500s and 200s, which became so worn in circulation that they were as soft and rumpled as Kleenex. In this country, you were lucky to have a little blue in your pocket. Five thousand dong could buy ten loaves of bread, a major bike repair, a pair of shorts and a shirt for a child, several days' worth of rice.

"How much is it altogether?" I asked.

The men looked at the bag, then looked away. It was as if a nude woman were lying on the table and they were trying not to stare at her. "It's worth about five thousand U.S. dollars," Tung told me. Though it had stabilized in recent years, Vietnam's currency had had such a history of fluctuation that, when it came to big sums, businesspeople like Tung often thought in terms of dollars.

"That's about ten thousand five-thousand dong notes," said Phai, who thought in terms of dong.

Even though Vietnam was one of the most expensive places to make international calls in the world, it was hard to believe that one person could rack up $5,000 worth of calls in a month. The figure was astonishing, particularly in a country where the average person only earned about $130 a year. We couldn't talk about $5,000 in terms of Vietnam, and so we ended up discussing what $5,000 could buy in the States. A third of a car, I told them. No, not a house. Almost a year of rent, depending on where you lived. College tuition at a state school. A fourth of a year at Harvard. Three round-trip tickets between San Francisco and Hanoi. Five thousand dollars was a lot of money, even to Americans, but if that was all you earned in a year, you'd be eligible for food stamps.

Tung, Tan, and the translator nodded as I spoke, as if what I was saying confirmed their understanding of economics in the States. But Phai looked amazed. He was barely managing to earn a living. Competition among motorbike mechanics had become fierce. He spent most days sitting in our living room, thumbing through the Vietnamese-English dictionary or smoking cigarettes with Tung. And now I had just transformed myself into a Rockefeller before his eyes.

"What about phone bills?" he asked hesitantly. His effort to understand what life was like in the States was competing with a need to seem unfazed by what he learned.

"I've never heard of a five-thousand-dollar phone bill," I asserted, suddenly compelled to put some distance between myself and the high-rolling Mr. Huey. I pointed out that, while Mr. Huey made international phone calls all day long, I'd only called home twice, for five minutes each, since I arrived in Vietnam. Of course, each of those five minutes cost me twenty dollars, money Phai could subsist on for weeks. But Phai was nodding encouragingly, as if he, too, needed to convince himself that I wasn't rich and he wasn't poor.

The door to the upstairs creaked open and Mr. Huey appeared at the top of the stairs. He hurried down and greeted everyone boisterously, then, spotting the paper bag, he glanced at the translator, asked a question in Chinese, and dumped the cash out on the table. He quickly counted the bundles, not bothering to count out individual bills. Clearly, a bag full of 5,000-dong notes was insignificant to an international trader like himself.

The Vietnamese watched Mr. Huey with a mixture of respect and envy. In all the time that he'd lived in our house, Mr. Huey's big-time living had inspired a number of emotions, especially in Tung, but I'd never seen any hint of resentment. That lack of animosity surprised me, because Mr. Huey was Chinese. Despite the fact that the United States and France had been responsible for most of Vietnam's suffering over the past fifty years, China still managed to elicit the deepest bitterness among Vietnamese. Most Vietnamese had ethnic roots in China, and Chinese traditions had influenced Vietnamese culture in everything from the roots of its language to the rhythms of its poetry, from the way Vietnamese practiced politics to the way they worshiped God. For the past two thousand years, however, relations between China and the region now known as Vietnam had fluctuated between strained and sour. During all that time, the Vietnamese had either been living under Chinese occupation or been consumed by the threat of it.

The fact that Tung and Mr. Huey got along so well was almost as surprising as an old white southerner suddenly setting up business with a black man. The relationship seemed strange, and rather tenuous, but it also represented some easing, at least on an individual basis, of the tension between the two neighbors. I didn't know what to make of it. Maybe Tung was more open to foreigners than other Vietnamese. Or maybe he just needed the money.

Mr. Huey picked up the bag, rolled it closed, and then, with a laugh, tossed it to our landlord. Tung caught it, but the gesture startled him, and he couldn't figure out how to hold it. At first, he gripped the bag uncertainly between his two hands. Then he tried lifting it by the roll on the top. Finally, he shoved the whole thing under his arm and stood up. "Okay, let's go," he said. He looked like an uncertain child desperate to be taken seriously by the grown-ups.

Mr. Huey glanced at the translator and grinned, then said something in Chinese. The two laughed, looked at Tung, and laughed again. Then they walked out the door. Tung squeezed the paper bag tighter under his arm, then followed. Just before he turned away completely, I saw a strange expression cross his face. It was a look one would see on a person racing to catch a train, both focused and panicked, as if a single misstep would seal his fate.

If you set any two Americans down together in Vietnam, they'll inevitably end up discussing history. For Carolyn and me, the war became a ghost that haunted our conversations. We couldn't stop remarking on how strange it was for two Americans to be wandering so comfortably through the streets of Hanoi. With Carolyn around, the war became present in my life again. And if it weren't for her, I would never have followed a one-legged veteran up the side of a mountain, just to ask him some questions.

Carolyn and I had gone with Linh, her husband Son, and their ten-year-old son Giang to the Perfume Pagoda, a Buddhist holy place a few hours outside of Hanoi. The weeks and months following the Lunar New Year celebrations of Tet, which had taken place just before I arrived, served as the main festival season in the north of Vietnam. Thousands of pilgrims were making the trek to the Perfume Pagoda in order to leave offerings to the Buddha and his female incarnation, the Goddess of Mercy.

We left before dawn, drove in a hired car for two hours, then took a two-hour boat trip along narrow canals before finally reaching the base of the Perfume Mountain. From there, we hiked, following a trail that wound its way like a rough staircase up the forest-covered mountain. The path showed signs of years, perhaps centuries, of human passage. Where the trail was dirt, it remained as bare of vegetation as stone. Where it was stone, it had been worn as smooth as paper. Trees surrounded us like lush green walls, and through the leaves I could see a sky so white it seemed that the sun itself had a shade around it. The air was heavy, soaked with moisture, smelling ripe, and the mud that sat in patches on the dirt path and on the great slabs of stone had a deep sheen to it, as if, once wet, it had managed to get wetter.

The trail was as crowded as any sidewalk in Hanoi, but, because of the hundreds of Buddhist pilgrims making the trip to the top, it was much more convivial. Families stopped for snapshots at every shrine and scenic view. Groups of old women sat sipping tea in refreshment stalls crammed between the side of the trail and the edge of the mountain. Teenage boys made daredevil leaps from rock to rock, and young lovers held hands as if their romantic futures depended on their remaining physically attached throughout the trip. Through all of this trudged the laborers, hauling ice, cans of Coke and Heineken, and baskets of apricots—the specialty of the region—from the bottom of the mountain to the refreshment stalls that lined the trail all the way to the top. The scene was some combination of natural wonder, amusement park, and holy shrine, like a Vietnamese version of Yosemite National Park mixed with Vatican City.

Although Son was a Buddhist who had carted a bag full of offerings all the way from Hanoi, Linh let us know that she was "a Catholic person" who had no more reason than we had for climbing to the top of the mountain. Catholics accounted for approximately 10 percent of the population here, and the percentage would have been higher, but the government had already scared away hundreds of thousands of Catholics. Fear of religious persecution led nearly one million North Vietnamese Catholics to flee to the south after the Communist takeover in 1954 (encouraged, perhaps, by a U.S.-sponsored propaganda campaign claiming that "Christ has gone South" and "The Virgin Mary has fled the North"). After the American War ended in 1975, many more Catholics left the country altogether. The repression that followed placed such severe limits on religious practice that by the early 1990s many Catholics, like Linh and her parents, had a hard time even remembering what Catholics were supposed to do.

By the time I arrived in Vietnam, restrictions on religion had eased somewhat, but most of the tension over religion in the country still centered on conflict between those who believed—no matter what god they believed in—and those who didn't. Unlike the religious conflicts taking place in other mixed-religion countries like Northern Ireland or India, people of various religions got along quite well in Vietnam. They didn't even regard mixed marriages, like Linh and Son's, as strange or unacceptable. Perhaps the reason lay in the underlying open-mindedness of Vietnam's majority Buddhist culture. Perhaps the government had succeeded in watering religious practice down to such an extent that there just weren't that many differences between religions anymore. Linh didn't just tolerate Buddhists; she'd married one. And she was as curious as we were to visit the Perfume Pagoda.

Our hike quickly fell into a rhythm, with Son leading the way. He was the only man, and the only Buddhist, in our group, but it was hard to imagine a situation in which he would not have taken the lead. Son was a low-level official in the Foreign Ministry, a translator and diplomat-in-training, and, although he had the fresh and untried face of a teenager, his manner and diction, even in English, were purely bureaucratic. "It is most necessary that we walk at a brisk pace," he had announced to our group before we started up the hill. "We must conclude our program well before dusk." Although he, like most of my friends, was too young to have fought in the war, he was the only person I'd met whom I had no trouble imagining standing at attention or barking out orders.

I followed closely behind Son. His English may have been officious, but he was the perfect hiking partner for me because he was willing to answer all the grammatical questions I'd been ruminating over for weeks. Behind us, often not even within sight, were Carolyn, Linh, and Giang. Linh was the slow one. She wasn't in good condition because her full-time job and duties as a mother and homemaker wore her down. She'd also chosen inappropriate footwear for the trip. She had on a pair of dainty sandals, which kept causing her to stumble as she tried to walk up the uneven trail. For a while, in an effort to distract Linh, Carolyn sang a Vietnamese folksong she'd learned. Every few minutes I caught the notes of the song floating up the trail. Carolyn's strong voice mixed with Linh's shriller one, which was way off key.

Son was listening, too. "I did not marry Linh for her singing voice," he told me, and I could tell by the tone of his voice that he thought he was making a very funny joke.

I didn't do much but chuckle. Even in my sensible Tretorn sneakers, I had to walk carefully, my eyes locked to the ground to keep from slipping. When I heard "*A Di Đà Phật!*" floating down from the path above us, I didn't even look up. *A Di Đà Phật* is the greeting exchanged by Buddhists in their holy places, and we'd been hearing it, and repeating it, for hours. Then my eyes locked on a pair of feet stopped on the ground in front of me. They were tough feet, bony and wrinkled, splayed out over the tops of a thin pair of red rubber flip-flops and covered with mud as thick as grease. I raised my eyes and saw an old woman watching me. Behind her, six or seven other women came to a halt as well. They all wore the same Vietnamese grandmother outfit of thin black trousers, brightly colored long-sleeved shirts, knit vests, and velvet scarves tied like turbans around their heads. "*A Di Đà Phật!*" said the first old woman, holding out her hand to me. For a moment, I thought she wanted money, that she was appealing to the generosity a Westerner might feel in this holy place. But the woman's smile had nothing of entreaty in it. Rather, she was simply offering me a touch of the hand, from one ancient soul who had already made it to the top of the holy mountain to a younger one just beginning to climb it. I smiled and took her hand in mine. "*A Di Đà Phật!*" I said, and the old woman's smile opened into the widest grin.

Maybe she thought she had met a fellow believer. Maybe she thought that despite our different colored skin, different hair, and different language, she and I followed the same path toward God. If so, she was mistaken. I was good at faking. I could hold hands with an old woman on a holy mountain in Vietnam and pretend that four incomprehensible syllables actually carried meaning for me. It wasn't simply that I didn't understand Vietnamese spirituality, or even that I was a Jew and thus felt out of place at a Buddhist shrine. The fact was that spirituality itself was foreign to me.

The old woman couldn't know this. She gave my hand a gentle squeeze, moved on to Carolyn, then shook Linh's hand, and Giang's, and Son's. She turned and continued her walk down the mountain. One by one, each of the old women shook our hands, calling out one more "*A Di Đà Phật!*" before disappearing on down the mountain.

The sound of that chant was steadier than my breathing, more enthusiastic than the cries of the drink vendors, more rhythmic than the *tap tap tap* of a thousand pairs of pilgrim feet. Although I didn't understand it, I loved the sound of it. I loved the way the words flew out of my mouth like little birds. I loved the way it sounded holy, the way it made me feel that it might, in fact, be holy.

I was raised a Reform Jew, worshiping in a grand and impersonal synagogue a God who was no more tangible than the air I breathed. "God's like love," my mother once explained, offering me a vague, well-intentioned definition that hardly helped me find a spiritual path through the long and (I had to admit it) boring hours of Rosh Hashanah or Yom Kippur. Judaism's abstraction stems from its early history, when the Ten Commandments rejected object worship. As a kid, I had a hard time relating to a deity that I couldn't see. I had to ask myself the obvious question: Why did my God exist and not the others? After that, Judaism became even less compelling to me. I was still curious about spirituality, though. Now, in Vietnam, I was drawn to what was taking place in temples and pagodas. In this venture, I wasn't so different from many Vietnamese people, really. I was discovering their religion. And they were rediscovering it, too.

As the morning passed the rhythm of the walk began to lull me. *A Di Đà Phật!* Step. Step. Round a corner. Up a rock. *A Di Đà Phật!* Stop for breath. Step. Step. *A Di Đà Phật!*

Going up the path in front of us was a one-legged man hiking with the aid of a pair of crutches. Middle-aged and dressed in formal military attire, he was moving steadily, only stopping occasionally to hand out alms to the beggars who appeared regularly at the side of the path. Although the trail was steep and treacherous, he didn't even look winded by the exertion it required. Asking Son to come with me, I hurried forward to catch up to him.

"*A Di Đà Phật!*" I said.

The veteran looked up and blinked at the sight of a foreigner pronouncing the Buddhist greeting. Up close, I now saw the strain the hike was taking on him. Sweat was beading the lines of his face.

"*A Di Đà Phật!*" he responded after a moment. Then he turned and continued walking.

We joined him. At first, he and Son discussed the weather, the crowds of pilgrims, the distances we'd all traveled to get here. Like us, he'd arrived this morning from Hanoi. His wife and daughters, he explained, were resting back at a refreshment stall, drinking tea.

Because I felt shy with my Vietnamese, I asked Son to translate my question. "Uncle," Son asked, "where were you injured?"

The veteran didn't pause in his walking, and his answer was casual, as if we'd just asked him his profession, or where he was born. "I was fighting during the American War," he said. "Down in the Central Highlands. I had my leg shot off near Pleiku."

After walking for a while in silence, the old man glanced over his shoulder toward me.

"Where do you come from, miss?" he asked.

"San Francisco," I said.

The old man looked at Son. "Where's that?"

"*Mỹ,*" Son said, giving the Vietnamese word for America.

The old man stopped in his tracks, looked at me, and smiled broadly. "How interesting," he exclaimed. "I want to go there."

"Why?" I asked.

The vet chuckled. "For business," he explained. "Everyone's rich and business is good there. Do you think it would be difficult for me to go?"

I didn't know what to say. It was as if I'd braced myself to watch a movie in which the hero dies of cancer and found myself at a comedy instead. "Well," I finally answered, "the airplane ticket would be quite expensive."

Everyone within earshot became involved in the discussion that followed, voicing strong opinions about the current state of the U.S. economy and whether or not it was worth the effort to travel there. By the time we reached a fork in the path, I was starting to think that you can't make up with someone who doesn't believe he's still at war with you.

The old man was taking the path that led straight ahead to the top of the mountain. We were making a detour to a small shrine that sat on the hillside about halfway up. Everyone stopped and faced one another. The veteran smiled, revealing two large gold-capped teeth at the edges of his mouth. My mind went blank, unable to focus on anything except that I was standing before a Vietnamese man who had been permanently disfigured because of the war my country fought there. Suddenly I had to say it. Even if he didn't want to hear it, I had to apologize. Slowly, I raised my hands in the gesture of supplication I'd seen Vietnamese make before altars to the Buddha. "*Xin lỗi, bác*," I said. Uncle, I'm sorry.

The smile disappeared from the old man's face and he looked away, scanning the line of trees that marched like soldiers down the mountain. "*Không sao*," he shrugged. "*Không sao*." It doesn't matter, he said, and he waved his hand as though we were talking about a mistake I'd made years ago that he'd long since forgotten. Then, without looking at me again, he turned and continued up the trail.

I watched the veteran until he disappeared.

By the middle of the afternoon, we'd arrived at the top of the mountain. One hundred twenty stone steps led down into the great cavern of *chùa trong,* the Inner Pagoda. The cave was thick with people, their bright clothes against the gray stone of the cave like color footage superimposed on a backdrop of black and white. Scores of tea tables and ornament booths spread out in rows across the hard stone floors. Crowds of people swarmed the booths, while in corners and on empty tables, on the sides of the stairways and on the bare surfaces of rocks, the pilgrims prepared their offering platters as if each orange, each apple, and each red plastic pendant was soon to be touched by the Buddha himself.

Near the bottom of the stairs, the one-legged man stood waving at us.

I'd told Carolyn my story. Now she grabbed Son's arm. "I need you to translate something for me, too," she said.

Carolyn walked over to the old man and said, "*A Di Đà Phật!*" The old man grinned. Then Carolyn turned to Son and said, "Tell him not all Americans supported what our government did in Vietnam."

The veteran lost his smile as Son translated Carolyn's comments. He looked her in the eye and said, "I'm a poor man. I have five children to feed. That's why I came here today. I'm praying for good fortune." Then he said something else, mumbling it so quietly that I missed it.

"What did he say?" I asked Son.

Son looked at me. "He said, 'Give me fifty thousand dong.'"

Now we were all embarrassed.

The veteran laughed, as if to break the tension, but it sounded too hearty, unreal. "Just joking!" he said. "That was just a joke." We all laughed politely, but the embarrassment grew worse. He bowed to us and turned away. Within a few seconds, he had disappeared into the crowd.

The unease he left behind him lingered. "Was he joking, really?" I had to know.

Son considered the question for a moment, shifting from an interpreter of language into an interpreter of meaning. "I suppose he was half joking, half serious. If you'd offered him the money, he would have taken it."

Carolyn looked devastated. "Should we have given him the money?" she asked me. "It was only five dollars."

"Maybe," I said. I had no idea.

"But I can't give money to everyone in Vietnam," said Carolyn. "And that guy had gold caps on his teeth."

"But what about his leg?" I asked. The two of us stood there debating every word and innuendo, trying to mine the motivations of the one-legged veteran. Crowds of pilgrims filed past, stopping, even, to stare at us. We ignored them. Beside us, Linh and Giang stood waiting quietly, but Son soon lost patience with the Americans' angst. He had a schedule to follow. Finally, he interrupted us. "Don't feel too bad about that man," he said. "I'm sure he killed some American soldiers, too."

In the pagoda, the air was thick with the smoke of incense, and I wiggled away from all of them, disappearing into the foggy darkness, into the maze of alcoves and crannies and altars filled with Buddhas. In front of every altar, people stood in prayer, their hands raised, their eyes closed, their faces tense with concentration. Exhausted, I sat down on the edge of a raised brick platform where several old women were squatting, carefully arranging their offering trays. They made me forget everything, except that I wanted to believe with a faith like they had. Here I was, a Jew, standing before a pagan altar. For the first time in my life, though, I felt that here in this dark and smoky cave, I might actually make some meaningful contact with God. I looked around at the carefully constructed pyramids of fruit, at the urns full of burning incense, at the big, fat, dreamy-eyed Buddhas. And in that moment, it all became holy to me. It wasn't a holiness that sprang directly from God, but one that emanated toward God, moving outward from the intense devotion of all these people praying. Maybe, I thought, God *is* love, or, more specifically, within each individual.

I sat there for a long time, letting the sensations of the past few hours wash over me—the liquid gray sunrise, the smoke of incense, gooey mud, the glint of gold-capped teeth. I put my hands over my face and rubbed my eyes, then I stood up, walked over to an altar, pulled some sticks of incense out of my backpack, lit them, and raised my hands in the gesture of prayer. *"A Di Đà Phật!"* I said softly.

I hadn't moved when I felt a hand take mine. I looked up at Linh and she smiled at me. "I'm a Jesus Christ person, not a Buddha person," she said, "but I like it here." We stood there for a long time, watching the smoke of all the incense float like a great cloud of prayer out of the mouth of the cave and up toward the sky.

It was Son's voice that finally pulled us back. "Dana, I need to discuss something with you," he said. Beside me, Linh rubbed her eyes, as if she had just woken from a nap. "I can see that you and Carolyn display a keen historical interest in matters of the war. Am I correct?"

I nodded.

He looked at me for a long moment, as if trying to decide whether to continue or not. Finally, he said, "Does the name John McCain sound familiar?"

"Of course," I said. We all knew how Senator John McCain had been shot down over Hanoi in 1967 and had spent years as a POW at the famous "Hanoi Hilton."

"You may not know that when John McCain's plane was shot down, he parachuted into the Truc Bach Lake in Hanoi. He almost drowned." Son looked at me severely, as if Americans would never have heard this side of the story.

I waited for him to continue.

"A Hanoi man rushed to the side of the lake and pulled him out. That man saved his life. Did you know about that?"

I shook my head.

"That man is an old man now," Son said. "He'll probably die soon. It's important that America knows his side of the story. Would you like to meet him?"

"Of course," I said.

6 War Stories

WHEN I WOKE UP ON THE MORNING of our appointment with the man who'd pulled John McCain out of Truc Bach Lake, I felt as though I'd gotten one of those lotus-seed candies stuck in the bottom of my throat. Three days earlier, we'd driven back from the Perfume Pagoda in the pouring rain. The weather hadn't let up since, and I'd been out every day in it, slogging through the mud. The whole city was waterlogged and gloomy. Now I felt the same way. Carolyn had developed a head cold that had somehow migrated down to the muscles of her neck. She'd become so stiff that she couldn't turn her head independently from the rest of her body.

But neither one of us wanted to miss this meeting. We managed to make it to Linh and Son's house just a few minutes past our scheduled appointment time, at eight. Linh greeted us at the door with her baby in her arms. Giang sat on the floor watching a Chinese martial arts serial on television. All I could see was the back of his head, silhouetted by the light from the TV screen.

Linh and Son's house was, in actual fact, a single room with

a concrete floor. It was less than half the size of my room over on
Dream Street. The kitchen was in a shed in a weedy garden out
back. Water came from a cold-water faucet in another shed by
the front gate. The family urinated into the drain beneath this
water spigot. Whenever they had to do anything more than pee,
they squatted over a metal bucket, the contents of which they
later dumped when the night-soil collector passed on the road.
The only sign of wealth was the small Sony television. The only
sign of decoration, aside from a few knickknacks and pieces of
pottery, were several amateurish oil paintings. One was a nearly
pornographic portrait of a buxom, Aryan Virgin Mary with a
lecherous-faced baby Jesus suckling her breast. In a second, another well-endowed and scantily clad maiden lay in a green
meadow with a wine cask at her side and deer and tiny chip-
munks dancing around her. The artistic style was reminiscent of
paint-by-number, but the subject matter must have relied, at
least in part, on the artist's imagination.

Linh had a sour look on her face that I suspected had something to do with Son. The day before, she and the baby and Carolyn had spent the morning in my room. Squatting over my
electric cooker making rice porridge for the baby, she'd made up
a song to describe her feelings. "I hate my husband, I hate my
husband, I hate my husband," she sang gently, as if these were the
lyrics to a lullaby. According to Linh, Son was selfish and she
couldn't stand it any longer. Every day she had to ride her bicycle to work at the Metropole, which took forty-five minutes
each way. Son had a motorbike, but he would never let her drive
it, and he told her he didn't have the time to give her a ride.

Now, instead of hello, Linh said, "Son makes me so pooped
off."

Carolyn rolled her eyes. She walked slowly over to the bed,

the only place to sit in the room, and, with a wince, lowered herself into a sitting position.

Linh put the baby down on a mat on the floor, then she
looked up at us, her eyes suddenly glowing, and whispered, "But
I'll tell you something. Last night, Son make me very happy in
my coont."

Carolyn gasped. "Don't say that word. Where did you learn
that?"

Linh looked confused. "I learned it from my friend at my
Metropole. Why I can't say 'coont?'"

"It's 'cunt,' not 'coont,'" Carolyn said. "It's a terrible word."

Linh's lips started to tremble, as if she were being unfairly
denied a new privilege. "But I like the slang word, Caro-leen.
Why?"

Carolyn began to explain the difference between slang and
obscenity, but Linh wasn't listening. "Why?" she wailed. "Why?"
The baby started to cry.

Carolyn grabbed Linh's hand. "Get hold of yourself," she said.

Son walked into the room from the back porch, and Linh
picked up the baby and walked out.

"Good morning, Carolyn. Good morning, Dana. You are
late," Son said. His face was flat, expressionless.

"Son, I don't feel well," said Carolyn, trying to control the ir-
ritation in her voice.

"Oh," he said. "Our friends are waiting for us at the hour of
our appointment. We must hurry with great dispatch."

Carolyn looked at me but said nothing. We got up and followed him out the door. He turned down a narrow lane lined
with rows of ugly concrete houses. Son walked quickly, a few
paces ahead of us, ducking under eaves to keep out of the rain.
Beside me, Carolyn, who hadn't bothered to put on her poncho,
held it above her head. She looked upset. Personally, I was de-

pressed over the whole subject of marriage in Vietnam. I never heard about anything but problems. Linh's admission that she was happy in her "coont" was the best thing any of the wives I knew had said about their husbands.

Our destination turned out to be only a few minutes' walk down the lane. Son's friend, a prematurely balding man named Bac, was standing in the rain waiting for us. "Hello!" he said, taking my hand in both of his and shaking it passionately. He turned and did the same to Carolyn.

We followed Bac into a large, simply furnished room that had a mud-speckled motorbike in one corner, a wooden bed in the middle, and a blackboard hanging from a center wall, on which had been written, in English, HE WALKS TO THE SHOP. HE WALKS FROM THE SHOP. HE WALKS AROUND THE SHOP. Bac was an English teacher, and it quickly became apparent that having two Americans in his home was a very big deal. Not only were we the first Americans he had ever entertained, but we were the first ones he had ever met. He unrolled a straw mat on the concrete floor and invited us to sit down. Son and I sat. Carolyn perched on the only chair in the room, a large wooden armchair that sat against the blue mildew-stained wall.

Bac was anxious to tell us his story, which he did as soon as we were sitting down. "When I discovered English—your native language!—I fell in love," he explained. Then he jumped up, pulled four glasses and a bottle of mulberry wine out of a cabinet, and poured some for each of us. Lifting his glass, he proposed a toast. "To both of you, my wonderful new American friends, whom I have the honor to welcome into my home." I raised my cup for the toast, then took a sip. It tasted like melted Slurpee, but it felt good on my throat.

The morning passed slowly. Neither Bac nor Son mentioned Senator John McCain. Occasionally, Carolyn and I looked at

each other in confusion, but neither of us had the heart to inter-
rupt the pleasure that Bac was getting from hosting us. The conversation meandered in different directions, with Bac and Son
doing most of the talking. We heard about their days as students
in the Soviet Union, how they always wanted to learn English
more than Russian, and how, when they formed a band with a
group of friends, they agreed to sing every song in English. I
knew they weren't just flattering us. I had heard Vietnamese
make enough disparaging remarks about the Russians to realize
that, despite Vietnam's history of animosity with the United
States, and despite the fact that the Soviet Union had been a solid
friend, Vietnamese felt a much greater attraction for English and
American culture.

With the mention of the band, Bac got up and pulled a guitar from underneath the bed. He handed a notebook full of sheet
music to Son, who paged through for a moment, then announced, "We will play Abba for you. They are the most important international pop stars, so you will like it very much." He
looked at me. "You like Abba, don't you?"

"Abba!" was all I could say in reply.

I can't say that Abba sung by Vietnamese amateur musicians
was really that much worse than Abba sung by Abba. Son and
Bac began their serenade with an upbeat version of "S.O.S.,"
slowed it down with "Knowing Me, Knowing You," then slid
right into "Dancing Queen." They sang with merciless enthusiasm, their eyes half-closed. Bac handled the notes with spiritual
appreciation, as if he believed himself a conduit for an angel's
hymns. Son was less devotional, but his voice carried the conviction of a member of the Communist Youth Brigade chanting
slogans of revolution. Neither of them could actually carry a
tune. The thin black minute hand of the chicken-faced clock on
the wall had made significant progress before Bac finally slid the

guitar back beneath the bed. "I am in Vietnam," he told us, "but, you see, my spirit is American."

Carolyn and I offered him weak smiles.

Bac sighed, then added simply, "This is the happiest day of my life."

It was nearly eleven when we heard the front door open. A white-haired man appeared in the doorway, clutching a cap in his hands. He was wearing a thick brown turtleneck sweater and a dark green army coat. "This the man who saved the pilot," Son explained, ushering him into the room. "We will talk to him now."

Looking at me, then Carolyn, the man made quick but solemn bows of greeting. He was an old man, but I couldn't tell if he was closer to sixty or ninety. Deep wrinkles traced diagonal lines from either side of the bridge of his nose to the edge of his chin. But his body was supple, and he moved with grace.

Son and Bac made space on the mat, but the stranger refused to sit down. He slid his feet out of his shoes and squatted in his socks. Son lit a cigarette and handed it to him. The old man took a long drag, then began to speak.

He explained that in 1967 he was working as a cadre for the government. Although most of Hanoi had been evacuated because of the bombing of the city, his work was considered necessary and so he had remained in town. Walking home for lunch one day, he suddenly heard an airplane overhead and the sound of artillery fire. He looked up and saw the pilot parachuting toward the ground.

The old man's voice was soft and carried the unmistakable quirk of a working-class Hanoian—a tendency to switch his "l's" for his "n's," which made him pronounce his birthplace as "Haloi, Vietlam" instead of "Hanoi, Vietnam." On top of that, he spoke quickly, mumbled, and used words I couldn't identify at all. I could hardly understand a word he said. Luckily, Son was translating for Carolyn. As I'd learned during our day at the Perfume Mountain, Son was a very conscientious translator. But I could understand enough of what I heard to know that something important got lost in the translation. This old man was not a government official speaking in the exacting style of modern political debate. Over the course of nearly thirty years, his vision of an American pilot falling into a lake had grown into an epic tale, its cadences less similar to the officious arguing of diplomats than to the mesmerizing chants of the Buddhists I'd seen worshiping in the pagoda. But Son approached his mission with a diplomat's agenda and the condescension the educated classes, even in Communist society, reserve for those they consider beneath them. Son didn't even bother to introduce the old man to us by name, referring to him instead as "this man," as if his identity were irrelevant to his story.

"This man ran toward where he'd seen the pilot falling," Son continued. "It took him only a few seconds before he spotted the pilot floating in the Truc Bach Lake. The pilot was struggling in the water. He couldn't get the parachute straps off his back, and the weight was pulling him under. He was gasping for breath. Before this man had time to think of anything else, he grabbed a bamboo pole and held it out to save the pilot. The American took hold of the pole and this man pulled him onto the shore."

Son's translation may have sounded like a just-the-facts-please testimony at a criminal trial, but the old man's presence conveyed much more. Because he couldn't understand a word of English, he didn't recognize the way that Son's translation dehydrated his story. Every time he paused to let Son speak, he looked down at the floor, nodding slightly at the sound of the English words. His concentration was reverent.

Son took another swallow of his mulberry wine. "Within just a few minutes," he said, "people were swarming around the two of them. These people, these Hanoi citizens, were angry. They grabbed things from the pilot, snatched pieces of his clothing as if they wanted souvenirs. This man, however, only took one thing. He took a knife with a red handle. He did not steal a single thing."

The difference between taking a knife with a red handle and stealing a souvenir was lost on me and Carolyn. "Why did he take the knife?" Carolyn asked.

Son translated the question into Vietnamese. The old man looked up at both of us and, as he spoke, fear, dug out of memory, hung on his wrinkled face. "He wanted to protect himself," Son explained. "He was afraid this foreign pilot might try to hurt him."

Son picked up his cup, saw that it was empty of wine, then said something to Bac in Vietnamese before telling me and Carolyn, "You will have some more wine."

Bac poured more wine into my cup and I took a sip. The old man was still squatting motionless, staring at the mat beneath his feet.

"But why did he even bother to save the pilot?" I asked. "That man was the enemy. He ended up in that lake because he was bombing Vietnam."

When Son translated my question, the old man looked at me and chuckled. He and Son exchanged a few words, then Son said, "Of course, he supported Vietnam's fight for victory. But he could see that the young pilot was a human being, too. Watching him out there in the lake, this old man felt that he could not let him drown. He says that he cannot explain to you his reason why."

All of us were silent. Despite the blandness of Son's words, some flash of feeling from that long-ago moment did slip through. The ash on the end of the old man's cigarette, forgotten now, dropped off. After a while, he looked up and spoke again.

"There was one moment," Son translated, "right after this man pulled the pilot out of the water, when he looked into the pilot's eyes and thought about the wife, the children, the elderly parents in America who must have been waiting for this young man to come home. That was the moment he says he stopped seeing the American as his enemy. After that, the crowds swarmed around them, then the police arrived and dragged the pilot away."

The old man, Son translated, harbored a dream. He wanted to meet John McCain one more time before he died.

Carolyn leaned stiffly forward on her chair. "So many years have passed," she said. "Why does he want to meet the senator now?"

After a minute of discussion in Vietnamese, Son replied. "When John McCain returned to Vietnam several years ago, this man read in the newspaper that the senator wanted to thank the person who saved him from drowning in the lake. Because of the senator's interest, this man made efforts to meet him, but our government would not allow it. Now that he's met you two American friends, he hopes that you can help him to make contact."

Bac refilled our glasses with wine. I was starting to feel woozy. It was hard to turn it down, though. The sweet liquid cut the chill blowing through the open window and seeping up through the damp floor. The old man sat quietly, looking back and forth between me and Carolyn. He no doubt also hoped that the senator, one of the most powerful men in the most powerful nation in the world, might surely offer this poor and tired Hanoian a bit more financial security than he now enjoyed.

Carolyn's face was flushed. I could tell that she was already working on a plan. Carolyn and I often differed in our reactions to Vietnam, but now we only had to glance at each other to know we were in perfect agreement. Someone was asking a favor of us that, like a penance, we would actually have to try to accomplish.

Son looked at his watch. "This completes our allotted time," he announced. "Our next engagement begins in ten minutes." He stood up. The old man immediately sprang up beside him.

Carolyn was annoyed. "What engagement?" she asked. "We have to discuss how to arrange a meeting with the senator."

"No problem," said Son, waving her concerns away as if they were as insignificant as a fly. "You will speak to the senator about our friend here and we'll make all the arrangements after that."

Vietnamese regularly made the assumption that Americans had a direct line to power. Sometimes, people would address me by saying, "Tell your president . . ." None of my Vietnamese friends had chats over coffee with their prime minister, but somehow they assumed that a more open government would have more open doors. "It's not that easy," I said.

Son was already walking toward the door. "I suggest that you telephone him," he said. Carolyn and I could do nothing but rush through our good-byes with the old man and Bac, then hurry off after Son.

The rain had finally stopped, but the runoff from roofs and tree branches kept a steady drizzle falling around us. The sky was still overcast, the ground still covered in mud. I picked my way carefully over the broken pieces of pavement that formed the only stable islands on the slippery path. In my mind, I was writing letters to John McCain's office in Washington, planning a meeting here in Hanoi. Where might be a good location for such a meeting? By the shore of the lake?

Son opened the door of his house. Linh and her sons weren't home, but a man was sitting on the bed, reading the *New Hanoi* newspaper. He was sixty-something, wearing a fedora, and had a smart blue-and-white striped ascot tucked neatly into his wool blazer. "Hello! Hello! Hello!" he said in English, jumping up to shake our hands. "I am so happy to meet you two lovely young American women."

"This is my uncle," said Son.

"I'm sorry," Carolyn said. "I need to go home now."

Son looked at Carolyn and smiled knowingly. "You must stay. Believe me. This meeting will be for the mutual benefit of everyone involved."

Carolyn looked at me, but I only shrugged. I was curious. Son, sensing the opportunity, hurriedly cleared the newspaper off the bed, then invited me and Carolyn to sit down. I crawled over to the side against the wall. Son crawled over and sat down, cross-legged, next to me. His uncle leaned against the head-board. Carolyn, treating her neck gingerly, lowered herself gently onto the edge of the bed.

"My uncle painted all the beautiful artwork you see here," said Son, sweeping his arm across the room to encompass the lurid paintings of the Virgin Mary and the maiden in the woods.

The artist looked at me expectantly.

"They're very beautiful," I said.

"So, what's this about?" Carolyn asked, shifting her body to look at Son's uncle.

The uncle reached into an inside pocket of his jacket and pulled out a photograph. "I've made a painting at home of this photograph. I know it will have great meaning for you and every other American."

Carolyn examined the photo and then handed it to me. The black and white image had begun to yellow but remained clear. Eight Western men in military gear stood posed for a portrait. I looked up at Son's uncle. "Who are they?" I asked.

He smiled broadly. "These men are Americans. That's right.

Americans. Like yourself. But, unlike you, they are not happy visitors to Vietnam. They are Poes and Meeas."

Carolyn looked at me, confused. "POWs and MIAs," I told her. I'd heard the Vietnamese pronunciation before.

The uncle looked deeply into my eyes, then he did the same to Carolyn. "I have their remains," he said. Then he paused to let this information sink in.

I looked down at the picture. The smiling men stood in front of a row of palm trees. The ground beneath them was flat and could have been an airport tarmac, a parking lot, or even the boardwalk at the beach. My eyes focused on each face, each cocky smile, each pair of eyes squinting in the sun. I thought of Captain Raymond Stacks, my MIA. Even though I'd prayed for his return, deep down I'd wondered if he'd ever really existed.

But a photograph—particularly one that came with its own set of bones—well, that was more substantial proof. Captain Raymond Stacks could have been the light-haired little guy, shoulders lifted, straining to be taller. Or the burly mustached one, brows bunched like worry above his eyes.

Son's uncle was watching me and waiting. I looked at him. "Where'd you get the bones?" I asked.

He grinned, revealing two rows of cracked and yellowed teeth. "I have a friend in central Vietnam," he said, explaining that this friend had found the bones and brought them up to Hanoi, then asked Son's uncle to contact the organizations representing the American POW and MIA families in order to return the remains. He stressed the word "remains" as if he thought the euphemism would prove his sincerity.

I handed Carolyn the photograph and she examined it for a while. "Do you know who these people are?" she asked. She appeared to be fascinated.

The uncle leaned back against the headboard of the bed and

examined his fingernails. "We have a list of names, from U.S. military dog tags," he said. "We believe that several of these men come from the region of Wisconsin in America. Or maybe from a place called Milwaukee. We are certain that the families will be so happy to have the remains of their soldiers returned. You know, we Vietnamese are like Americans. We, also, insist on burying our dead. Did you know that?"

"I know that," I said.

The uncle raised his eyes to the heavens dramatically and laid his hands against his cheeks with dismay. "We Vietnamese are *haunted!* Do you know that? *Haunted.*"

His performance was making me ill, even though I knew he was right. Vietnamese *were* haunted. They had a much worse MIA problem than we had. Through an agreement with Vietnam, the United States had recently begun an active search for American MIAs, and the U.S. teams had been able to settle all but a few dozen cases, either by discovering and identifying the remains or by gathering enough evidence to verify each death. The Vietnamese, on the other hand, had barely begun to search for answers to the fates of some three hundred thousand of their own soldiers and civilians who remained unaccounted for, even twenty years after the end of the war. Still struggling to feed their living, they didn't have the resources to search for the dead. This inability remained a wrenching problem. According to the religious beliefs of the majority of Vietnamese, it's necessary to bury the dead, then worship them at family altars. A body that goes unburied cannot be worshiped, and the soul is left to wander. Vietnam, to the Vietnamese, was haunted by the ghosts of so many wandering souls.

"We've got to bury these poor men, don't we?" asked the uncle, throwing the responsibility for doing so on Carolyn's shoulders. Turning to her, he said, "Son tells me that you are leav-

ing our country in just a few days. You must help these American
families by returning the remains of their sons to them."

Carolyn looked at him. "What do you want me to do?" she
asked.

"We need you to help us set up a relationship with the
American families."

I was afraid Carolyn was about to commit to something she'd
later regret. "The United States has an office in Hanoi to settle
these problems," I said. "Why don't you take the bones there?"

Son's uncle looked at me. "Of course I know about that office, Miss Dana," he said. "But you must understand our situation. Our government will punish us for contacting them."

"But your government has been cooperating with them," I
argued.

The uncle sighed and smiled sadly, as if there were aspects
to his government's behavior that I, a foreigner, would never
understand.

"Why don't you let me take the bones to them?" I asked.

The uncle's smile disappeared. "No," he said.

"That's really the way to do it," I insisted.

The uncle muttered something to Son in Vietnamese, and
then the truth came out. "My friend went to a lot of trouble to
procure these remains," he said. "He carried them all the way
here from central Vietnam. He spent his own money to do this
service for the American families. We know that the American
families will want to thank him." He was looking earnestly at
Carolyn now. "We know that they will want to thank you, also.
The compensation can be quite large. Sometimes several hundred dollars for each set of remains."

His ignorance of U.S. domestic politics was staggering. The
people he imagined giving him money—the organizations representing POW and MIA families—would see this bone-selling

scheme as proof that the Vietnamese were trying to extract as much money as possible out of the search for the dead. In this case, at least, they wouldn't be wrong.

Carolyn sat looking down at the picture for a long time, her eyes completely focused on the faces staring out at her. Finally, she lifted her eyes and calmly handed the photograph back to the uncle. "I don't want money for bones," she said.

The uncle rushed to reply. "Yes, of course not. But my friend went to a lot of trouble. Don't you think he deserves something?"

Carolyn's eyes settled on me. "I have to go home," she said.

Neither the uncle nor Son tried to argue after that. The uncle shook his head like a disapproving parent, trying to make us think that we were making a gigantic mistake. Son, to my surprise, didn't even look disappointed. He got off the bed, helped Carolyn gather her things, then walked us out to the street and hailed a cyclo. Then he shook our hands, thanked us for coming, and stood waving while our cyclo rolled away.

Carolyn did not wave back. For the entire ride home, she fumed. Son's bone-selling scheme had been the last straw. She didn't like Son's officious manner or the way he treated Linh. He'd also speculated, incorrectly, that Carolyn liked Linh because Carolyn was a lesbian. And Carolyn had gotten tired of how often her visits with Son and Linh involved expenditures of money—Carolyn's money. If she went with Linh to the market, Linh expected her to pay for everything. Son and Linh were always suggesting restaurants they'd like Carolyn to take them to for dinner. Linh was as guilty of mooching off Carolyn as Son was, but Carolyn cared so much for Linh that she put up with it.

"Just wait," she said. "The next time Son says to me, 'Now you will drink tea,' I'm going to tell him. 'No, Son, I will not drink tea,' just to make him mad."

I tried explaining to Carolyn that Son's lack of social graces had as much to do with the Vietnamese language as with his own personality, that Vietnamese just didn't say "please" that much. But Carolyn wasn't mollified a bit. She was so angry that she threatened to stop speaking to Son altogether. She never got that chance. Two mornings later, something happened that made Carolyn's relationship with Son completely irrelevant.

The doorbell jarred me out of a deep sleep. I knew it was Linh because her ring had a signature insistence to it. I forced my eyes open and glanced at the clock. It was 6:10 A.M. The buzzer sounded like a motorbike barreling through my bedroom. I pulled some sweatpants on under my T-shirt and hurried out onto the balcony.

Linh began yelling up from the sidewalk as soon as the top of my head appeared over the railing. "I'm going to my mother's," she declared. "I'm not going to live with Son anymore."

"What are you talking about?" I asked. As soon as I pronounced the first word, a sharp pain cut across my throat.

Linh continued. "I want a divorce."

This sort of news wasn't easy to digest so early in the morning. "Do you want to come upstairs?" I finally asked, leaning over the railing and almost whispering to protect my throat.

"No! I have my little son with me," Linh said, pointing to the edge of the road. For the first time, I noticed the cyclo parked there. Piles of suitcases and blankets covered the seat, with the baby squeezed in between. The cyclo driver was leaning over Linh's belongings, trying to humor the fussy baby.

"What about Giang?" I asked, thinking how calm the ten-year-old had looked the other day, watching ninjas slice each other open on TV.

"Giang is at Son's mother's house. He must stay there to go to school." Linh already had every angle figured out.

"Tell Caro-leen my terrible story!" Linh said. She turned around and, with more bounce in her step than I'd seen in a while, she hurried back to the cyclo, lifted the baby, then sat down. The cyclo driver climbed back on his seat and started pedaling away. Just before they slid out of yelling range, Linh turned around. "I am single woman now!" she called triumphantly. She raised her hand into the air and gave the thumbs-up sign that Carolyn had taught her.

When I left for my Vietnamese lesson a half hour later, Carolyn was still asleep. I quickly scrawled out a note telling her about Linh, then I rushed off to get breakfast and go over my new vocabulary words before my lesson at eight.

By the time I got home late that morning, the sky was beginning to darken, and I could see the storm clouds rolling in over the city. Grandmother Nhi was packing up her tea stall to avoid the shower.

Tung and Phai were sitting in the living room watching the day's installment of the Chinese ninjas. Huong wasn't around. Her interest in imported TV drifted closer to the cowboy drama from Brazil, the Chinese soap opera *Beijing People Living in New York,* and the Mexican poor-girl-makes-a-million miniseries *Maria* and its sequel, *The Rich Also Cry.* Tung, like his son, was crazy for the ninjas. He hardly noticed when I walked in, threw myself onto the couch, and let my keys and backpack slide to the floor.

"Is Carolyn still here?" I asked Phai.

He shook his head.

"Do you know where she went?"

"She went out," Phai shrugged. Carolyn spoke no Vietnamese and Phai spoke no English.

I put my hands on my throat and tried to massage it. After two hours dedicated to perfecting the pronunciation of a Vietnamese folktale, the pain in my throat had begun to creep north toward my ears.

Phai watched me. "Are you sick?" he asked.

I shook my head and stood up. "My throat just hurts a little. I need to drink some hot water." The words came out shredded into pieces.

Phai jumped out of his seat and got to the kitchen first. By the time I reached the door, he had pulled a tall glass down from the shelf and filled it with hot water from the thermos. He handed it to me. "If you're sick, you shouldn't talk," he said.

"I'm not sick."

Phai grinned. He rested one shoulder against the refrigerator and looked at me. I leaned against the doorway, gazing down at the floor. Neither one of us made a move to return to the living room.

"Mr. Long just came by," Phai said.

Mr. Long was a neighbor who lived somewhere in the back alleys behind our house. Tall, muscular and very *vui,* he seemed about sixty, but was actually eighty-five. Sometimes when I left for my lessons early in the morning, I'd spot Mr. Long from the landing. He'd be standing in the concrete courtyard between the houses, eyes closed, arms raised in the air, doing calisthenics. Mr. Long lived alone. His entire family had been killed in 1972, during one of the U.S. bombing raids on Hanoi. Sometimes, in the afternoons, he'd come by the house. He and Tung and I would sit listening to Metallica.

"I still don't understand why he likes me," I said to Phai.

Phai grinned and shook his head. "You think he shouldn't be friendly to Americans because he lost his family during the war."

I considered the idea for a moment. "You're right," I said. "That is what I think."

"You just don't understand Vietnamese people," said Phai. "We think of the war like a volcano."

"What do you mean?" I asked.

Phai explained. "There's nothing you can do to stop it. You just do what you can to save yourself. The American air raid was like a volcano, and the people in Mr. Long's family couldn't save themselves." He added, "It's their destiny."

As I'd discovered over the past few months, the idea of destiny was very important among Vietnamese. In one way or another, it could account for almost anything that happened in life. "If I had a better destiny, I would have found renters who could pay one hundred dollars more a month," Tung would gripe. Linh, calculating her finances, would moan, "Because of my bad destiny I don't have my own motorbike." Sometimes, I tried to convince myself that appealing to destiny, or số phận, was more of a figure of speech than a worldview, like a Vietnamese equivalent of "God willing" or "God forbid." My friends were sophisticated urbanites. Most of them followed a modern lifestyle that hardly seemed driven by worry over whims of fate. In a sense, they reminded me of my Jewish ancestors, who had abandoned their prayer shawls and kosher diets. My Hanoi friends' attempts to Westernize themselves made it seem that they, too, had given up the old-fashioned superstitions.

But they hadn't. Once, when I urged a friend to drive more carefully on her motorbike, she had assured me that because her fate was to die by water, she didn't need to worry while she was out on the road.

"Then why not drive three hundred kilometers an hour?" I'd asked. "Why show any caution at all?"

"Because you never know," my friend had explained. "I'm going to die by water, but I could still die on a motorbike. I could be hit by a truck hauling water. Or I could have an accident when I cross a bridge."

Still, I thought Phai's explanation oversimplified the complexity of the war.

"What about responsibility?" I asked.

"Responsibility is something different."

"Why?"

Phai tipped his head back and stared up at the ceiling. After a moment, he said, "Okay. If I lock my bike and it gets stolen, that's my destiny."

"And if you forget to lock it?"

"Then losing it is my responsibility."

I still didn't get the connection to the war. "What does that have to do with Mr. Long?" I asked.

"Mr. Long did what he could to protect himself, but his family died anyway. That's destiny."

Phai was looking at me as if, now that he'd explained his logic in detail, it should make perfect sense. But when I'd spoken of responsibility, I hadn't been thinking of Mr. Long. I'd been thinking of the Americans, the ones who'd dropped the bomb on his family. According to Phai's volcano model, primary responsibility lay in people's duty to protect themselves: with the person who locked the bike, not the person who stole it. In my admittedly Western view, the blame for what had happened in Vietnam fell on many shoulders: French colonialists too greedy to give up a prime piece of real estate; Americans too eager to define a civil war in terms of superpower politics; Vietnamese leaders too intent on consolidating their power. Every one of those groups had been willing to destroy Vietnam in order to save it. But the people themselves—it was hard for me to assign them blame or to see how destiny had dictated their losses. Through generations of Buddhism or generations of war—or both—the Vietnamese had developed an acute ability not only to endure the worst, but also to accept the worst as fate and move on. I had to admit that it was a good defense.

"Hey, Phai," Tung yelled into the kitchen. "Do you have a cigarette?" Phai looked at me and smiled, then walked back into the living room.

Outside, the rain had begun to fall in thick sheets, and the trees were whipping in the wind. Dream Street was deserted, but the thunder sounded like dozens of invisible army trucks rattling down the road. The air had grown chilly. I sat down on the couch and knotted my scarf more tightly around my neck, clamping my fingers around the warm sides of my glass. Phai sat down next to me, pulled a pack of 555s out of his shirt pocket, and offered one to Tung. A Vietnamese documentary was demonstrating the modern production line of a provincial pencil factory. Tung lit his cigarette, then leaned back in his chair. Despite his ardent desire to participate in the affairs of Mr. Huey, on most days he was still pretty idle. Sometimes, he rushed off to rent a car when Mr. Huey had to make a trip out of town, or he arranged an interpreter when Mr. Tuan was away in Saigon, but for the most part Tung's days weren't any busier than before. I couldn't see how Mr. Huey had that much to offer anyway. Despite his promises of big deals "about to happen" and the phone calls at all hours from Hong Kong and Taipei, I never saw any sign of actual commerce. Every move in this business revolved around elaborate plans for the future. Tung still insisted that everything would come together soon, even if I couldn't see it.

Today, as usual, Mr. Huey was sitting upstairs, talking on the telephone, and Tung was sitting downstairs doing nothing. "Who came by so early this morning?" he asked, for want of entertainment.

I told Tung that Linh had left her husband. Tung's eyebrows went up in surprise. "What's wrong?" he asked. His own recent marital tiff had somehow been resolved, though I never heard the details. One night they weren't speaking to each other. The next night, they'd appeared at my bedroom door together, all dressed up and giggling, and told me they were on their way "*đi chơi*," to go out together, in this case for a night on the town. Everyone Tung and Huong knew had problems in marriage. Tung wasn't surprised that Linh was unhappy; he was surprised that she'd actually left.

I described Son's refusal to let Linh ride the motorbike, the way he bossed her around, and how tired she was from working all the time and trying to take care of the house and the kids, too. Tung interrupted. "*Bình thường*," he said. That's normal. "What else is new?"

Actually, I wanted to change the subject anyway. I'd been waiting for a chance to talk to Tung and Phai about the man I'd met who said he'd pulled John McCain from the lake. Since that meeting, I'd thought of questions I wished I'd asked at the time. Like why would he have been walking home for lunch during the middle of a bomb attack on the city? And, if he had been a hero, and so humanitarian, why was his government reluctant to take advantage of such a great PR opportunity as a reunion between these two men?

"I met a man who saved an American pilot from drowning during the war," I said.

"The one who fell in the lake?" Tung asked. I nodded. A stone statue stood by the edge of Truc Bach Lake, memorializing the fall of the pilot.

I recounted the story as the old man had told it. "Do you think the story's true?" I asked.

Tung considered the question, then shrugged his shoulders. "Imagine that you were a civilian during the war," he said. "Let's say you worked in a factory. Suddenly the American warplanes flew over the city and dropped bombs on you. What did you do to deserve that? Whole families died that way."

He continued. "People who didn't know a thing about politics were suddenly buried under the rubble of their houses. Imagine that, after surviving a bombing, you saw an American pilot parachuting toward you."

He paused and lit himself a cigarette. "I'm not saying the old man's lying," he said. "How would I know? But if he's telling the truth, he's an unusual man. Maybe he's a great one. Most Vietnamese hated those pilots. Sitting in those bomb shelters makes you crazy. I remember being nauseated. I couldn't breathe. I thought I'd die. And I was just a kid. What did I know? An adult would feel rage. The police had to race to get to those pilots every time one of them landed in the city. If civilians got there first, they'd try to kill those guys." He looked over at Phai. "Is what I'm saying true?"

Phai nodded, looking down at the floor.

Tung took a long drag and looked out at the rain. "I never saw a pilot myself, but I might have done the same thing." He glanced at me, curious to see how I'd react, but I wasn't upset. What he said made more sense to me than Phai's ideas about destiny and locking your bike.

Lightning sent a flash across the sky. The living room, already fluorescent bright, got brighter. And then the thunder crashed. The bombing campaigns were two campaigns, really, taking place in two separate, parallel universes, the universe of the earth and the universe of the sky. Down on the ground, loudspeakers blared out the danger, sirens screamed, citizens jumped into bomb shelters and covered their heads. Up in the air, million-dollar machines clicked into gear. Above and below, people took deep breaths, maybe their last, and mumbled prayers. And then two separate universes would briefly collide, with a flash of a bomb, the explosion of a plane, or maybe a parachute slowly descending, a human being pulled by gravity from one universe down into the other.

The rain outside gradually slowed to a stop, delivering the eerie silence that follows a storm. Tung went upstairs to check on some papers he was going to deliver for Mr. Huey. Outside, the trucks and motorbikes reappeared. Grandmother Nhi hurried past the front door to reopen her tea stall. Phai's cigarette had burned out. He lit another one. I collected my keys off the floor.

"Duyen," Phai spoke softly.

I looked at him.

"We didn't all hate the pilots," he said. "When I was a kid, I lived near the prison where they kept the Americans. Sometimes, they were brought outside and taken for a jog around the building. We children liked to stand there and wave to them. Sometimes, we gave them cigarettes. It was exciting. They were so big. We'd never seen Americans before. We'd never seen skin so white." He added, "Once, when the pilots were jogging by, one of them reached over and patted me on the head."

I took a sip of water, cringing as it slid down my troubled throat. I wanted to believe that story, too. But I'd never heard of prisoners going out for jogs on the Hanoi streets.

By evening, I couldn't speak at all. I was sitting up in bed with the covers pulled to my shoulders and a large scarf wrapped around my neck.

"It's the wind," Huong said. She sat down on the edge of the bed and peered into my mouth. "It's very bad these days. It's *dangerous*."

Huong's and my arguments about health always pitted my "germ theory" against her "wind theory." She found it incomprehensible that I could ignore the strength and intensity of the spring breezes, while I made her laugh when I tried to explain that a sick person could spread disease by sharing chopsticks or a glass of water. "You can't get sick like that," she'd say, shaking her head. We were like two cooks with competing family recipes for chicken soup. We'd both learned a formula handed down by our ancestors, but neither of us could explain why it worked.

Still, when Huong checked my symptoms and diagnosed a "wind cold," as opposed to a "cold cold," I almost believed her. After all, every time I walked outside, the wind sliced at my throat like a knife across a piece of steak.

But as Huong started counting little pink pills into her palm, I objected. Vietnamese pharmacies sold everything, even the strongest antibiotics, over the counter. Many of these medications had passed their expiration dates. Others were fakes. I waved Huong away.

"You don't want the pills?" Huong asked, her eyes narrowing to slits.

I shook my head.

"But these are from France!"

She said the word as if to offer evidence that the medication must be excellent. I didn't even know what it was, though. I was positive that Huong didn't either. Miserably I pointed to the bottle of honey she'd brought upstairs. That I could take.

We heard a knock on the door and Phai, his face lined with worry, came quietly into the room. "I brought you something," he said. He sat down on the armchair across from my bed and handed me a fist-sized plastic bag of something that looked like sawdust.

"It's *ô mai*," he told me. "When I told my mother you were sick, she made you some to soothe your throat."

I only knew one thing about Phai's mother, that she was a big fan of Jane Fonda, the movie star Americans still called Hanoi Jane. Phai's mother had gotten her hands on a Jane Fonda workout routine and she now followed it every day.

Phai leaned forward. "It's made with shredded ginger and salted plums," he said. "Just take a pinch and put it in your mouth. Suck on it for a while. Don't swallow it."

I unwrapped the rubber band from around the neck of the bag, pulled out a pinch, then set it like a wad of tobacco between my teeth and gums. A sour taste spread through my mouth, but it had a hint of sweetness in it, too.

Huong and Phai were both watching to see how I would react. "Do you like it?" Phai asked.

I nodded. My mouth was filling with saliva. I glanced across the coffee table, which was littered with books, an old *Atlantic Monthly,* the wrappers from a couple of Hershey bars, and the pages of a letter from my sister. I was looking for a place to spit.

"Now try to swallow," Phai said.

I grimaced. Asking me to swallow was like asking me to stab my throat with a pair of scissors.

"Just try," he said gently.

I took a deep breath, then did it. The pain that cut into my neck was so severe it made me gasp, but at the same time the sweet tang of the *ô mai* slid into my throat muscles like water into parched earth. Something softened and grew numb.

I smiled and looked at Huong and Phai. Expressions of relief crossed their faces. Huong stood up. "I have to cook dinner," she said.

Phai lingered. "Do you need anything? Do you want some tea?" he asked, his face full of concern. I shook my head. Phai followed Huong down the stairs. I leaned over and pulled another pinch of the *ô mai* out of the bag, then lay back down against my pillows, sucking on it. I wished Phai hadn't left so quickly. Even though I couldn't say a word to him, I'd wanted him to stay.

I must have dozed, because then Carolyn was sitting on the bed beside me.

"How are you?" she asked, brushing the hair out of my face.

I sat up, leaned over, and picked up a pen and paper off the coffee table. "Linh?" I scrawled.

Carolyn shrugged. "No change," she said. "I saw her a little while ago."

I turned the paper over and jotted, "Do you think it's possible that the Vietnamese would have taken U.S. prisoners out to jog around Hanoi during the war?"

Carolyn read what I'd written and laughed. "Does this relate to Linh?" she asked.

I shook my head.

Carolyn considered the question for a moment. "You know," she finally said, "it sounds strange, but I guess it's possible. What were they going to do, run away? This whole city was a prison. The whole country. They didn't need any walls."

I nodded. The prisoners would not have had anywhere to go. They might have jogged.

I put a bit more *ô mai* in my mouth and leaned back against my pillows.

"I've been thinking about the old man," Carolyn said. "When I get back to San Francisco, I'm going to call Senator McCain's office in Washington. I want to find out if, the next time he's in Hanoi, he'd be willing to meet with him."

"Get some rest," she said, then went downstairs. For a long time, I lay there unable to sleep, watching the sky outside grow dark with dusk.

⌒⌒⌒   It didn't take us long to get our answer from Senator John McCain. A few weeks after Carolyn returned to the States, I received a letter from her saying that she had telephoned Washington and relayed the old man's story to one of the senator's aides. The official was not surprised to hear the tale, nor did he deny it. Rather, he told Carolyn that Senator McCain wasn't interested in meeting anyone connected with his capture in Vietnam. As the aide explained it, "That was one of the worst days in the senator's life," and he didn't want to relive it.

Months later, I learned a bit more on the subject. My friend Norma Cline, an American writer who lived in Hanoi, showed me a response to a letter she'd written to John McCain, also about a Vietnamese who claimed to have saved him from drowning. "Dear Norma," he wrote,

> Thank you for your letter regarding Nguyen Ngoc Huan and the circumstances surrounding my capture by the North Vietnamese.
>
> Over the years, numerous people have contacted me to inform me that they participated in pulling me from the Western Lake. I appreciate your interest and, of course, I am grateful to anyone who may have been motivated by humanitarian concerns to help pull me from the lake.
>
> In any event the war is behind us and it serves no purpose to revisit the circumstances surrounding my

capture. I'm sure you will agree, what's important now is to improve relations between the two countries, and to focus our efforts on building a future that is worthy of the many people who paid the ultimate sacrifice for freedom and democracy.

Again, thank you for your letter. With regards.

Sincerely,

John McCain

United States Senator

I didn't know how to tell the old man the bad news, so I put off contacting him. Son never brought it up either.

7 Liberation Days

*O*NE MORNING, ABOUT A MONTH after Carolyn's departure, I woke up and the world had changed. As soon as I stepped outside, Dream Street flashed before me in a burst of color. The commuters whizzed past on their Hondas and Chalys, their bright clothes trailing pink, orange, purple, and green across the blue-black asphalt of the road. Children, scattered in chattering pairs and trios along the sidewalks, appeared in their elementary school uniforms like moving blocks of white and navy blue. Even the drab concrete sidewalk sparkled, as if dusted by diamonds. Up until now, had I been director of *Hanoi: The Movie,* I would have cast the film in a muted black and white. Something miraculous had happened, though. Today, the city shined in Technicolor.

I walked across the street to where the sticky-rice vendor squatted on the sidewalk behind two shallow baskets full of steaming rice. Every morning for two or three hours, she set up a food stand in this exact same spot and served sticky rice. She arrived on foot, everything she needed dangling from the long wooden balancing pole she carried across her shoulders. She set three or four tiny wooden stools down on the sidewalk, pulled the burlap cover off her rice, and opened for business. This morning, the motorbike washers perched on the little stools, carefully scanning the morning papers. The office workers loomed above, tottering on their high heels, and the children stood shyly to the side, exact change wadded between their fingers.

The sticky-rice lady looked up at me. She was a sturdy woman with skin as mottled as a bar of Vietnamese soap. "You want yours as usual?" she hesitantly asked. Even though I frequented her stand, the sight of a Westerner always unnerved her.

I nodded. Her sticky rice came two ways, either with green bean cake shaved on top or with large grains of butter-colored corn mixed into it. I liked a combination of the two, topped by a handful of crisp fried onions. Hold the dried pork. Hold the extra splash of oil. Wrapped to go in a banana leaf.

I had my bundle of rice in my hands and was pausing at the curb, waiting for a truck to pass, when something, perhaps the glint of light on steel, caused me to glance up. Then I realized that it wasn't Hanoi's colors that had changed; it was the light. For the first time in months, the sky spread above me in a solid blanket of blue. Looking up, I saw the sun, an acquaintance I remembered only vaguely from California, rising above the railroad tracks down the street. After the relentless mud of spring, the city was clean, crisp, and dry. Hanoi had become a different city overnight, one I'd have to get to know.

Summer had arrived.

Linh was a single woman now. At least that's what she called herself. She'd always dressed nicely, and her appearance didn't change in any obvious way. But these days she had a kind of raffishness about her I hadn't seen before. She went around spouting the slogan of Ho Chi Minh—"Nothing is more precious than independence and freedom"—which she'd learned to use, in this context at least, from me. And she wanted to do the kinds of free, independent things that single women did, like go to the movies. One Saturday afternoon, she left me a note that said, "Dana, today is my holiday, your holiday, too. Tonight we'll take dinner outside for short time and go to cinema at Ngoc Khanh cinema hall. It will take us forty-five minutes by byke. The very interesting film will begin at 8 P.M. Hope to see you soon."

When Linh arrived on her bicycle, she was in no hurry to leave again. "Today our holiday," she said. "No one waiting for us. Tonight, we go slow, not quick, quick, quick." We spent ten or so minutes lying on my bed, resting our eyes, then Linh popped back up again, went to the mirror and put on lipstick, and announced that it was time to go.

We rode to a small *cơm bình dân,* a "regular rice shop," not far from my house, where we stood in front of a table covered with prepared food and picked out what we wanted. Linh insisted that we "eat like the pigs," so we ordered plates of fried tofu simmered with scallions and tomatoes, four pieces of grilled fish, stewed bamboo shoots, a ham omelet, two deep-fried hard-boiled eggs, sautéed water spinach, a bowl of vegetable broth, and two large bowls of steamed rice. The entire meal didn't cost three dollars.

At Linh's request, we ate slow, slow, slow, then we sat for a while over tea. Linh had decided that the only way to salvage her marriage would be if Son would agree to find them a house somewhere closer to the center of the city. If they lived in a more convenient location, she wouldn't have to ride so far to her job every day and she wouldn't be so exhausted when she got home. She'd have more time to spend with her family. All their problems would be solved. Linh had been dreaming about this idea for years. But recently, it had seemed a true possibility, and then that hope had been dashed. After ten years of service in the Foreign Ministry, Son received a bonus, which was intended for the purchase of a home. But instead, Son came home with a small Sony color TV.

"That must have been an expensive TV," I said.

Linh shook her head. "You don't understand," she told me. "I was wrong about the money. The ministry, they tell you they give you this money to buy a house, but when the money comes, it's not enough. Vietnamese dong worth so little now that the same money used to buy a house now only good for a small TV—not even a big one. So my dream become like glass, broken."

"Is that really why you're so fed up with Son?" I asked.

Linh shook her head. "When I married my husband," she said, "I loved him with all my heart. He loved me with all his heart. But then, after some years, he was not faithful anymore. That's why I become fed up on Son."

Linh's raffishness, I was coming to realize, was mostly superficial, and, with the discussion of her marriage, she fell into a funk. I looked at my watch and saw that it was nearly seven-thirty. I pulled her up, paid the bill, and we rode out to the cinema. Somehow, the memory that we were two single girls going off to the movies cheered her up enough to serenade me with songs along the way. The theater was a fairly new brick building, simply built, with a crowd of mostly teenagers waiting to get in. Linh had a friend who worked in the ticket office, which meant that we got in for free. Screaming, "We are VIP!" in English, Linh pulled me past the paying customers and led me into the cinema.

We took seats in the back row. As the rest of the audience began to file in, each person made sure to take a long look at me, the foreigner. I was the most interesting thing in the house, apparently. And somehow there was a pervasive sense of dreariness about the whole enterprise, as if no one was there by choice, but because there was nothing else to do in Hanoi.

But Linh was already staring up toward the screen in anticipation. "The film is an American film," she told me. "I know that you will enjoy it very much." She pulled from her purse two bags of sunflower seeds and handed one to me. As the lights went down, the entire theater became alive with the steady crackling of seeds. On the screen, the credits began to roll. The film was called *The Tower of the Screaming Virgins,* based, supposedly, on a novel by Alexandre Dumas.

The movie was in English, simultaneously dubbed into Vietnamese by a woman speaking into a microphone from the projection booth behind us. Between the pauses in the Vietnamese translation and over the cracking seeds, I could just make out some English, spoken in American accents. Although the film was set in eighteenth-century France, the haircuts, the particular thrust of the cleavage, and the grainy color made me suspect that it had probably been made in the 1950s. How it ended up in Vietnam I couldn't begin to guess. The characters didn't speak to one another so much as exclaim, crying and moaning and saying things like, "The walls have ears!" It was hard to pay attention, not just because it was silly, but because soon after it started, Linh began to fidget. She stretched this way and that, moving her body, taking deep breaths. A character by the name of Blanche Dubois began to cry. Linh lifted her knees up to her chest and buried her face in them. "Are you okay?" I asked.

Linh nodded. Her shoulders were heaving. Then, suddenly, she jumped up, squeezed past me, and ran out of the theater.

I raced after her through the darkness. I discovered her at the side of the building, leaning with her head against the wall, gasping for breath.

"Are you okay?" I asked.

"It's no problem," she said, between great gulps of air.

"But what is it?" I was trying to figure out if she needed a doctor.

She couldn't answer immediately, but she put her hand on my arm to keep me near her. It was several minutes before she could speak. "No problem," she finally said. "I have this once time before, when I'm sixteen." Her hands were trembling and she was clearly shaken.

"Do you have asthma?" I asked. Linh shook her head to let me know she didn't know what "asthma" was. Slowly, her breathing became more regular. It didn't seem to be asthma. It was more like a panic attack, but I didn't know how to say that in Vietnamese. For most Vietnamese, the only ways to cope with depression or anxiety were to make a trip to the pagoda, talk to a fortune-teller, go home to mother, or ignore it.

After a while, Linh said that she felt well enough to get on our bicycles and ride slowly back home. We unlocked our bikes and started the long ride, but we'd only made it a few hundred feet when she had to stop again. We pulled over near the shore of a small lake and sat down.

We leaned against a tree and looked up at the night sky. The clouds hung low and I couldn't see a single star. For a long time we said nothing. Linh's breathing slowed until I couldn't hear it anymore and then, a few minutes later, she began to speak. Two years earlier, when she was still working at the Bodega Hotel, she told me, she'd met a man who came from Bulgaria. Every night for a week, he came to the Bodega for dinner. "He was so nice to me," she said. He told her stories about his homeland. He lived near the ocean, in a house with a slanted roof, not a flat roof like hers in Hanoi. He could lie in bed and hear the ocean waves running up against the shore. He told her that she should come visit.

Linh was quiet for a moment. "I knew him for only one week," she said, "but that man asked me about my hobbies. Do you know, Son has never asked me about my hobbies in ten years. This man, one week!"

A mangy dog came and nosed around in a pile of trash, then tried to get into Linh's purse. She shooed the dog away, then we got back on our bikes. Linh held the handlebar of my bike so that we could ride next to each other through the streets. She never saw the Bulgarian after he left Hanoi, and she'd never spoken of him to anyone. But now she had to ask, "Is it possible to love someone you only know for just one week?" I thought about the question for a long time, but I didn't know the answer.

Vietnam celebrated two major holidays at the end of April, the April thirtieth anniversary of the Liberation of Saigon, followed by the May first celebration of International Workers' Day. To have a two-day holiday was a very big deal for Vietnamese, who only had Sundays off every week.

On the evening of April 30, I sat in my room writing a long-overdue letter to my mother. I'd put on a cassette that Tra had recorded off an easy-listening radio station in Detroit. The tape wasn't much, just a bunch of Barry Manilow, Neil Sedaka, and Carpenters interspersed with advertisements for Maytag washing machines and Kentucky Fried Chicken. But I relished it. I could listen to those saccharine tunes, even to the Maytag man, over and over without growing sick of any of it.

Tonight, though, even Karen Carpenter at full volume couldn't drown out the sound of Vietnam. Down on Dream Street, it sounded like all of Hanoi was charging by. In the intermittent lulls between the honks of horns and the roar of motors, I could hear the screams of the children playing flip-flop toss on the sidewalk in front of the house. I went out onto the balcony and looked out. Just below, Viet and his friends were standing in the blue dusk, hurling their shoes across the sidewalk, then huddling over them trying to decide whose flip-flop had come closest to the mark. A bike pulled out of the traffic and parked in front of them. Phai grinned at Viet and his friends, then he saw me peering down from my balcony above.

"Duyen!" he called. "What are you doing?"

I shrugged. "Writing a letter."

Phai shook his head, then locked his bike and disappeared into the house downstairs. I watched the children for a few more minutes, then went back into my room.

After about an hour, I heard a knock on the door. When I opened it, Phai was standing on the landing holding two glasses of lemonade. The sight of him surprised me. I felt like I'd forgotten what he looked like, how beautiful he was.

"Today's a holiday," he said, grinning. "You've got to enjoy it."

Vất vả is a word that doesn't translate well into English. The dictionary defines it as "hard" or "strenuous," as in "hard work," but this definition ignores the broader scope of the concept. Among Vietnamese, the word often connotes absolute and unending exhaustion. In this onomatopoetic language, even the sound of *vất vả*—pronounced "vut vo," with tones that trudge up, then down, then halfway back up again—comes out of the mouth like laborious breathing. Although my urban friends had plenty of time to hang out in front of the TV watching the latest Chinese soap operas, most Vietnamese were poor and lived harder lives. From sunup until sundown, each day was a chain of duties. Life itself was *vất vả*. When the rare holidays finally rolled around, the populace flooded the streets to enjoy them.

It was eight o'clock, and Phai and I were driving Tung's Honda Dream up Hang Bong Street, joining the stream of vehicles flowing toward Hoan Kiem Lake for a night of cruising. Within a few blocks, the stream had turned into a giant, churning rush of motorbikes racing down the narrow canyon of the road and emptying into the avenues that led around the lake. The momentum alone pulled us along, leading us through humid air scented by engine exhaust, squid grilling over charcoal cookers, and sugar-sweet perfumes. Whole families squeezed onto single motorbikes—Dad in front, Mom in back, and two or three balloon-gripping children sandwiched in between. Other motorbikes carried young men with slicked-back hair and wildly patterned polyester shirts, who forced their big machines to pass all the rest. Guys with dates steered with one hand and rested the other proprietarily on the woman's stocking-covered knee. The women sat sidesaddle in their short, straight skirts, one leg daintily crossed above the other, as if the back of a motorbike were as stable as a barstool. I sat in the standard, one-leg-to-a-side position behind Phai, trying to figure out what to do with my hands. I should have clasped my arms around his waist, but I couldn't do it. The gesture seemed too intimate, and so I hung on to the bike's steel frame, telling myself that we were moving too slowly for any crash to be fatal.

Inside the arc of all the traffic, white lights sparkled on the trees surrounding the banks of the lake, and the black water reflected these lights as if they were so many stars. Out on a little island in the middle of the lake, a twinkling electric Vietnamese flag seemed to flutter, mimicking the effects of a breeze. These displays of lights weren't all that unusual. Hanoi made any excuse to light itself up, whether to celebrate a Communist party anniversary, to welcome visiting dignitaries, or to commemorate the birth of Ho Chi Minh.

Phai pulled up to a vendor selling balloons twisted into the shapes of elephants, dogs, and rabbits. We picked out a pink rabbit, Phai revved the engine, and we sped back up Hang Bong Street. Within a few minutes, we were in Ba Dinh Square, the great civic plaza in front of the Ho Chi Minh mausoleum. The lawn that faced the resting place of Uncle Ho was dotted with families enjoying the holiday.

Phai slowed down, then came to a stop next to the sidewalk. I pulled myself off the backseat to let him park the bike. Several policemen were standing smoking cigarettes, and they motioned to Phai to come closer. They were curious about the foreign woman he'd carried here on the back of his bike. I wandered away, staring across at the black marble mausoleum, which faced the square like a gigantic gravestone on a cemetery lawn. The words Chủ Tịch Hồ Chí Minh, "President Ho Chi Minh," had been chiseled into the somber stone.

I heard someone say my name and turned around to see the policemen leering at me. Phai pulled a pack of 555 cigarettes out of his shirt pocket and handed it to one of the cops, then he quickly walked over to where I was standing. "Come on," he said.

We hurried across the street and onto the great lawn. "What was that all about?" I asked.

"Nothing," Phai said. He walked more quickly than I did and I had to hurry to keep up. We turned down a cement walkway that led across the lawn. A young couple walked by us holding hands, pausing in their conversation to look at me. On either side of the square, towering panels of electric lights made the grass glow like a football field lit up for a night game.

"Why did you give them your cigarettes?" I asked. I knew he'd offered cigarettes to keep them from bothering us.

Phai glanced at me, then looked away. "I was just being friendly," he said.

We walked along silently. Perhaps Phai wanted to keep me from seeing how the police managed, in the subtlest of ways, to promote a sense of fear among the people here. I think he imagined me innocent, unable to understand that this place might be quite complicated. Maybe that was why I suddenly blurted, stupidly, "You know, cigarettes are really bad for your health." I needed to show him that I knew a thing or two about the world.

"I know," Phai said.

"You should quit smoking," I told him.

"Okay," he said.

"When will you quit?" I pushed.

"I just quit," he said. He pulled his remaining cigarettes out of his pocket and offered them to a young man who was just then walking past us. "Here you go, friend," he said. The man, a young soldier, accepted the cigarettes with surprise, then continued on his way.

After a while, Phai asked. "Have you visited Uncle Ho yet?"

I nodded. I'd been to the mausoleum, seen Ho's body, lying like a wax doll in a silent, guarded room. "Phai," I said, "what do you think of Ho Chi Minh?"

Even among northerners, Ho was not always respected with the quasi-religious fervor the government demanded. My neighbor, Mrs. Thu, was a retired French literature professor. One afternoon when I visited her, I wore a shirt with a sketch of Ho Chi Minh's face on it that I'd just bought. Just as foreign tourists might wear "Big Apple" T-shirts that New Yorkers wouldn't be caught dead in, Vietnamese couldn't understand the fashion impulse behind wearing a shirt with the visage of Ho Chi Minh. Still, I wasn't prepared for the vitriol with which Mrs. Thu responded to my outfit. She'd hissed, "Why are you wearing that shirt?"

"I just bought it," I said.

"I hate it," she announced. "Drink your tea."

I lifted my cup and took a sip, unsure of what to say next. Was a T-shirt too lowly a frame for the exalted form of Ho Chi Minh? Had I been culturally insensitive to buy it?

"Are you crazy?" Mrs. Thu scolded.

"But I bought it in front of the post office!" I cried, hoping that the government connection would bolster my decision.

Mrs. Thu waved her hand scornfully. "I don't care," she said, then added, "That terrible man."

"What?" I said. Now I was totally baffled. I'd met plenty of people who detested Ho Chi Minh, but all of them had fought against him in the war. Mrs. Thu was a northerner, even a member of the ruling class. "You hate Ho Chi Minh?" I asked.

She leaned forward and looked me squarely in the face. "That man. He ruined this country. Look at the poverty here. Our people don't have enough to eat. What kind of rubbish is communism? Tell me that! I never trusted him from the start, let me tell you. Disaster. They should have known it would come to this. Drink your tea."

Before I had a chance to take another swallow, Mrs. Thu was off again. "And let me tell you," she said. "If you plan to go into business, don't you ever visit that mausoleum."

"Why not?"

"It's bad luck. Vietnamese businesspeople never set foot in that place. Drink your tea."

Since then, I'd been less positive about people's opinions of Ho Chi Minh. But Phai only said, "Uncle Ho was a great man. He made Vietnam a free country." Of course, while Mrs. Thu remembered Ho as the controversial leader who had led Vietnam down the path to communism, Phai was seven when the old man died. His Ho Chi Minh was a character in history, a portrait in elementary school textbooks, a name in a song. George Washington, really.

I felt a cool breeze blow in from the West Lake and across the square. The dust in the floodlights glowed like fireflies, and my balloon jumped on its stick. Phai was so quiet that I finally asked, "Is everything okay with you?"

Phai looked up, startled and embarrassed, as if I'd scolded him for failing in his duty to keep me entertained. He nodded firmly. "Everything's great," he said.

We made a slow loop of the square. Then Phai stopped. "Did I ever tell you about my friend in Moscow?" he asked.

I shook my head.

In front of a us, a tiny girl raced by on an intersecting path, making a monkey balloon bob in the air in front of her. Phai said, "We went to school together. She wasn't my girlfriend. But she was easy to talk to. Two years ago, her father got her a position as a guest worker in Moscow, so she went. We've been writing since then. I got a letter from her yesterday."

"Is something wrong?" I asked.

"No. I just . . ." He stuffed his hands in his pockets. "I don't know. I don't understand these things. She's coming home pretty soon."

I had to guess at the rest of it. "Do you think you'll marry her?" I asked.

Phai shrugged. His face was sullen. "Probably. Our parents like one another. I think that's what we'll do."

In my mind, I tried to make a shift. "Do you love her?" I asked.

Phai laughed. "I don't know. What do I know of love? I guess it's my destiny to marry her, so that's what we'll do."

I paused. "Don't you think you should love her?" I said. Phai said nothing.

We walked back to the motorbike. The city had grown quiet now, with only a few dateless guys cruising the deserted streets. We drove up Dien Bien Phu Street, which led past the dark, half-timbered embassies of the former Eastern bloc. In the guard-houses, solitary soldiers rested their elbows on the windowsills, their heads slowly turning as we passed.

"How do you say 'I quit' in English?" Phai asked.

I told him.

"I quit," he said, trying out the sounds on his tongue. It sounded like "I kit."

A balloon-seller pedaled by us, a single blue monkey whipping back and forth against his wooden vendor's frame. I closed my eyes and saw the image of Uncle Ho, lying dead and fragile under glass. I leaned into Phai's back and set my hands upon his waist. For the first time, I felt his body beneath the soft, thin fabric of his shirt.

8 · A Typhoon and a Full Moon

*I*N JULY, THE TYPHOON HIT. For weeks leading up to it, the air was hot and as sticky as syrup. Even the slightest rain made steam rise off the pavement, as if the entire city were a kettle of simmering soup. Almost worse than the weather was the mood. Although Hanoi was a city plagued by bad climate almost year round, summer brought hopelessness, as if no one could decide if life was worth living.

A few weeks into the summer, Huong's sister, Nga, had opened a dress shop in the downstairs living room of our house. Nothing changed in the makeup of the living room itself. The couch was still there, and we still spent great chunks of time on it. The TV still flickered in the background, and Tung still played his Metallica at full volume. The only difference was that now dresses also filled the room. There must have been a hundred of them, plaids and polka dots, long-sleeved ones with lace-covered collars, a rusty wool with a matching cowgirl vest, and the same thing in pink. The dresses hung from long wooden poles attached to the living room walls and dangled from the front doors of the house, making it look like the entrance to a harem. Each dress cost about thirty dollars, in a country where most people earned that much money over the course of a month. But, in a sign of the wealth in Hanoi, Nga was selling a lot of dresses.

Two of Nga's biggest customers were a pair of Chinese women who'd been introduced to Tung by Mr. Huey and who were now staying in Mr. Huey's second room, the one on the fourth floor. They were big-boned, sturdy women I could imagine as urban factory workers in China. It was hard to figure out what had brought them to Vietnam. They didn't act like tourists, but they didn't have any apparent work to do here either. They never left the house until the middle of the afternoon, and they always came home with shopping bags full of new clothes—blue jeans mostly, but also denim shirts and jackets, frilly dresses, and straw hats with big, bright flowers on them. They were determined to wear every single thing they'd purchased, even the jackets, despite the heat. But they moved stiffly in their outfits, pulling at the seams and checking their zippers, as if they weren't quite sure how to wear them. Huong and I would sit on the couch and watch them try on Nga's dresses. We smiled at them, doing our best to be friendly, but we never spoke at all. Neither of us knew a word of Chinese.

I was in the living room, with Huong, when I first heard that the typhoon was approaching. She called it a *bão,* with a tone that swooped up, then down, then up again, as if mimicking the weather. The newspapers and TV were full of predictions, but I had so much trouble comprehending the language that I had to rely on the news as it trickled down, second- and thirdhand. On the afternoon that Typhoon Chuck was supposed to arrive, Huong hauled the big stone planters down from my balcony railing. Downstairs, Nga and her husband pulled all the dresses off the front doors and hung them inside, far from the entrance to the house. Outside, Grandmother Nhi disassembled her tea stand, and the motorcycle mechanics put away their tools, boarded up their storefronts, and hurried home. Everyone seemed quite worried. But Hanoians were always upset about the weather, and I couldn't tell whether this storm was really that much worse than any other passing crisis.

I hadn't seen Phai in two days. In fact, I hadn't seen much of him at all lately. He no longer fixed motorbikes next door, so he didn't have reason to spend all day in the living room. He hadn't been fired, or even laid off, exactly, but over the past few months he'd worked less and less, until the job just didn't exist anymore.

I felt sure that he'd come by tonight. The two of us never made plans. But he followed an unspoken pattern of stopping by, a pattern I'd come to predict and depend upon. Surely, I thought, he would appear tonight. But we'd never had a *bão* before. At four in the afternoon, I stood out on my balcony, surveying the sky. A thin, gray haze stretched out over the military housing complex across the street.

At six, the sound of howling wind made me look up from the book I'd finally started reading. I turned the latch of the door that led out to the balcony and found I had to force it open. Up and down the street, tree branches waved like arms at calisthenics. A wall of dark gray clouds had rolled across the city and, down below, fat raindrops had already begun to crash against concrete. On a typical Wednesday evening, it would have been rush hour on Dream Street, but tonight the road was empty. I leaned out and let the rain splash against my face. The air smelled like sweat. Even in those first few minutes of the typhoon, the heat refused to break.

I spent the rest of the evening reading and watching the storm. I wasn't afraid; from where I stood, the trees were swaying back and forth, but none of them had toppled. I was fascinated by the drama of it. As the wind picked up, the house began to rattle and shake. A water stain appeared on the ceiling and began to expand down my bedroom wall. I couldn't keep myself from stepping onto the balcony, where the fat drops of rain had turned into broken lines, then ropes, then dense sheets of water. Even in my childhood in Memphis, where the storms rolled across the Mississippi Delta in the summer, I'd never seen such wind as this. The shiny metal Christmas tree ornaments on Huong's potted plants whipped in the air like Ping Pong balls.

Across the street, a few lights twinkled in the windows, but I couldn't see much of anything. The storm, the darkness, and the distance kept me from spotting a single person. I couldn't re-member another moment since I'd arrived in Vietnam when I felt such an absence of human life. Even when I lay in bed at night, motorbikes would regularly roll by and break the silence. Now, all of us were trapped inside. What was everybody else doing? Drinking rice wine? Playing cards? Standing at their win-dows looking out toward me? So many times, I'd felt desperate for privacy. Now all alone, I felt stranded. I contemplated brav-ing the elements and running downstairs to sit out the storm with Tung and Huong and Viet, but I knew they'd yell at me for venturing down the slippery stairs.

The enormous muscled trees hunched like old men protect-ing themselves from a beating. I looked out toward the Old Quarter, toward the Red River, no doubt swollen now, and the neighborhood where Phai lived.

The next morning, metal hooks were all that remained of Huong's Christmas tree ornaments. The sun made gold mirrors out of the puddles on the sidewalk, and small branches lay scattered up and down the road. The bright green awning of the beer bar across the street now hung from the lower branches of a nearby tree. The city looked sloppy, but also clean and fresh. Actually, from my position on the balcony, the damage didn't look too bad.

When I walked downstairs, though, Tung told me of the devastation. Somewhere between three hundred and a thousand trees had fallen in the city, some crashing into houses, many others blocking streets and crippling traffic. Hanoi was paralyzed. Tung had tried to take Viet on a ride to survey the damage, but they hadn't made it past the railroad tracks a block away. The huge trunk of a tree was blocking an entire intersection. According to Tung, these were all trees that the French had planted. Beautiful and generous with shade, they had shallow root systems that made them topple easily in violent storms.

"At least our Asian trees are flexible," he said.

I sat down next to him on the couch and he poured me some tea. "Were you scared?" he asked, grinning like an older brother daring his little sister to tell the truth.

I shook my head. I hadn't been brave, I told him, just ignorant.

"People died," Tung said. "Over on Thi Sach Street a guy died. He was a security guard at that outdoor market. He stayed in a little hut during the night and a French tree fell on him. Crushed the whole hut."

Footsteps made us both look up. It was Mr. Huey's translator, Tuan, who didn't bother to greet us.

"Are they off to Saigon?" Tung asked.

Tuan grunted an assent.

"You'd better leave early. It'll take you hours to get to the airport."

The translator surveyed his image in the big mirror Nga used for her customers. He leaned forward and picked something from between his teeth. "We'll leave at ten," he said.

"They'll be back the day after tomorrow?" Tung asked.

Tuan grunted again. He adjusted his belt, fiddled with his collar, and raised his eyebrows, apparently satisfied with what he saw. Then he sat down in an armchair, pulled a cigarette out of his breast pocket, and lit it. Tung pulled out a 555 of his own and lit it.

"He's getting rich," I mumbled to Tung in English, which the translator couldn't understand.

Tung looked up, startled, as if he hadn't remembered that I was there. When my meaning registered on his face, he shrugged. "I guess so," he said in Vietnamese.

Someone yelled down from the top of the stairs in Chinese. The translator jumped out of his seat and went up. Tung watched but didn't move. The translator reappeared, a large suitcase in each hand. Mr. and Mrs. Huey followed him down the stairs, each of them carrying several smaller parcels. The yellow-toothed dog peeked out of a canvas shopping bag.

Mr. Huey stopped, put down his parcels, and grinned at me and Tung. He pulled a package of Dunhills out of his pocket and offered cigarettes to both of us.

I shook my head. Tung doused his 555 in his teacup and took a Dunhill. Tuan returned from putting the bags in the car and translated a brief exchange between Tung and Mr. Huey. "You're off to Saigon?" Tung asked, his voice full of respect.

Mr. Huey nodded and took a drag on his cigarette. His eyes closed slightly as he sucked, then he looked out the door toward the car, exhaling slowly. He was as relaxed as ever, cheerful and distracted, as if his mind were wrapped around some big deal he planned to make that afternoon.

"Anything you need me to take care of while you're gone?" Tung asked.

Mr. Huey looked at the ceiling, considered the suggestion for a while, then he shook his head. "Everything's taken care of," he said. "We'll have a lot to do when we get back here." Then he picked up his bag, put out his barely smoked Dunhill, and shook Tung's hand, then mine. "See you soon," he said.

Tung and I waved good-bye. "I'll keep a list of phone messages for you," Tung yelled after him, but Mr. Huey and the translator were already getting into the car.

Tung poured me another cup of tea, and we watched an old Chinese martial arts film, dubbed into Vietnamese, on the television. The traffic on the street began to pick up, and the morning after the typhoon began to resemble a normal day. After a while, the sound of footsteps made me turn and look toward the door. Phai stepped inside. "Still alive?" he asked.

The next night, a full moon hung in the sky, and hundreds of dressed-up young supplicants packed the Quan Su Pagoda like revelers at a disco. Phai squatted on the ground, using a Bic to light a large bunch of incense. He handed half the burning joss sticks to me, and we began our circuit of the pagoda, leaving prayers and incense at each of the dozens of altars that filled the shrine.

We'd been praying at the pagoda together nearly every full and new moon night since my visit to the Perfume Pagoda several months earlier. I still couldn't explain what had come over me on the mountain that day, but the feeling hadn't disappeared. Every two weeks now, I joined the crowds of Hanoians paying tribute to the waxing and waning of the moon. All I had to do was stand in front of an altar with incense in my hand and the feeling—What was it? Fervor? Spirituality? God?—washed back over me. Now, the experience of going to the pagoda felt central to my life. Mine might have been the only white face amid a thousand praying Asians. Teenage boys and wrinkled old women might have stared at me. I hardly noticed anymore.

Of course, I was watering down the religion itself, but I rea-
soned that most of these people were watering it down as well.
It had been forty years—a few generations—since Vietnamese
had had complete freedom to practice their beliefs. It was impossible to quantify the loss or define what it meant if a family no
longer knew how to pay homage to its dead, or if no one in a village was alive anymore to teach the movements of a sacred
dance. Tra had complained that people didn't even recognize the
difference between pagodas and temples anymore. At a pagoda,
one prays to the Buddha, she'd told me, and at a temple, to local
and national spirits. The difference was essential for many reasons, she explained, not least of which had to do with what you
prayed for in each place. "You go to the pagoda if you're worried
about love or health or happiness," she'd explained. "And if
you've got money problems, you need to appeal to the ancestors." She'd seen people in the pagodas asking the Buddha to give
them good fortune.

"Is that rude?" I'd wanted to know.

"No, it's not rude. But what's the point?" she'd asked. "The
Buddha knows nothing about money. Go to the Buddha to ask
for favors in love."

Tonight, it looked as though most of Hanoi needed favors in
love. With all the young people walking through the corridors
holding hands, the Quan Su Pagoda might have been the most
romantic destination in the city. At the very center of the main
sanctuary, Phai and I stood waiting our turn to pray. The smoke
of the incense was so thick that it burned like onions, and my
eyes began to water. Phai looked at me. We were the same
height, and in this dense crowd our faces were so close together
that I could almost feel his breath.

We made our way through dozens of people and squeezed
through a side door that led outside. An altar was hidden in a

niche in the wall, and we waited our turn among the people massed there, eyes closed, whispering their prayers. When space cleared, Phai and I stepped forward and stood next to each other, facing a serene Quan Am, a female Buddha. I glanced at Phai. His eyes were shut already, and his hands were raised in supplication. I watched as his lips moved through their silent prayers. After a few seconds, his body swayed slightly and his shoulder touched mine. I forced my eyes closed then, lifted the sticks of incense grasped between my fingers, and had a hard time focusing on the Buddha.

The night was hot. Hanoi had enjoyed one day of air so fresh that it felt like nature's sweet reward for making us suffer through a typhoon. The respite hadn't lasted, though. Today, the second morning after the storm, had dawned so hot and humid that the sky above us felt like the top on a steaming rice cooker. Even now, at well past eight in the evening, with a moon like a scoop of ice cream in the sky, the heat refused to break, and the air was so moist that even people sitting motionless had to wipe the sweat off their faces with handkerchiefs.

"Let's go get a lemonade," Phai said. I nodded. Ice-cold drinks made life bearable. Even the recent outbreak of water-borne cholera in central Vietnam hadn't stopped people from filling their glasses with cubes of ice. I drank at least three lemonades a day.

Back in the street the air seemed almost refreshing. "Let's walk up to the lake," I suggested.

Hanoi's municipal authorities had yet to make a dent in the job of clearing the massive trees off the city's streets. Nonetheless, the amount of debris had already begun to shrink. What Americans might have seen as enormous obstacles, the Vietnamese looked upon as free firewood. For two days now, men and women had been straddling trunks and branches with hand saws.

Falling trees had pulled down so many power lines that the city had shut off electricity. Our way through the streets was lit by the moon, flashlights, and candles. Without electric fans or air conditioners the entire population had moved outdoors in search of a breeze, hauling tables, chairs, and even folding metal beds along with them.

Phai walked through it all without emotion, as if the sight of people eating their dinner in the middle of the sidewalk was the most natural thing in the world. Our path was so circuitous that we walked in single file. Phai led the way, weaving carefully around children tossing balls, old men playing chess, and even older men already curled up in bed and snoring. Every so often, he'd pause and look back at me, his face full of concern, checking to see if I'd made it through some particularly narrow space between the side of a building and the trunk of a fallen tree. In addition to the scavengers hacking away at the branches, children were using the trunks as giant jungle gyms. Because the road itself was often blocked, people with motorbikes and bicycles were up on the sidewalk, too, trying to maneuver their vehicles past.

After half a mile or so, we reached Hoan Kiem Lake. Hanoi is a city of lakes, brought about over the centuries by the Red River's myriad floods, expansions, and diversions. The lakes invested the crowded neighborhoods with light and air and a sense of space that made quite livable what would otherwise be a fairly claustrophobic urban environment. I'd never seen a lake in Hanoi that wasn't necklaced by benches and circled by people out enjoying the view. People fished in them, swam in them, and waded out into them to harvest wild *rau muống,* a waterborne vegetable that could add a few extra vitamins to a bowl of rice.

Hoan Kiem Lake wasn't Hanoi's biggest, or its deepest. It wasn't even the cleanest. But it represented the spiritual heart of the city. It was possible to stroll its circumference in less than thirty minutes, but the role that it played in Hanoians' sense of their city—both historically and in the present day—was enormous. The lake drew people toward it as a body draws breath. I had seen the crowds at the lake on Liberation Day, thousands of revelers on their bicycles and motorbikes, moving slowly, packed tight, endlessly circling the lake. During the wedding season, I'd seen professional photographers snap shots of brides and grooms on the green lawns beside the water. Traditionally, at midnight on the first night of the Tet New Year celebration, the most significant moment in Vietnam's year, the smoke cloud of a million exploding firecrackers covered the lake like a blanket on a newborn. Hanoians didn't even call Hoan Kiem Lake by its proper name, but used a shorthand term of endearment, *bờ hồ,* "the shore of the lake." No one had to ask, which shore? which lake? *Bờ hồ* wasn't merely the heart of the city, but its lungs, and mind, and soul as well.

Bờ hồ was quiet tonight, its wide sidewalks nearly empty. A few young couples walked hand in hand, or sat on benches looking out over the water. I hadn't thought of Hoan Kiem Lake as a particularly romantic spot, but now I felt embarrassed for having proposed it as a destination.

Phai fit in well here, even if I, the American, didn't. His outward appearance had changed dramatically over the past few months. Abandoning the T-shirts and work pants, he now wore neatly pressed shirts and belted, baggy trousers. It was a look that was very much in vogue among Hanoi's smart set. Personally, I didn't like the flashy new outfits, but I did understand the significance of Phai's new look. He had decided to aim for something more ambitious than fixing motorbikes for the rest of his life. He was, wishfully or not, willing himself out of manual labor and into the middle class.

Now that we had plenty of space in which to walk, it was hard to tell that Phai and I were even together. There was still so much distance between us that another person, or two, might have fit between. He walked silently, his eyes on the ground, and I was beginning to worry that I'd done something to offend him. Then I heard him say, very quietly, "Duyen."

I said, "Yes?"

"Do you remember when I told you about my friend in Moscow?" he asked.

"The one you're going to marry?" I asked.

He shrugged, kicking a small branch out of our path. "I said maybe."

The Moscow pen pal had made me jealous, but I had also felt relieved. I still didn't know what I wanted from Phai, but I was sure I wouldn't marry him, and I didn't want to hurt him, either. I didn't mind the pen pal, so long as she stayed in Moscow.

We passed a fallen tree, its root system exposed to the air, its branches deep in water. "Is she coming home?" I asked. As soon as I asked that question, the jealousy returned. How would I feel if Phai suddenly showed up at Tung and Huong's with a girlfriend from Moscow?

Phai shook his head. For a long time, he didn't speak. The hot air in my lungs suddenly felt heavy and useless. When I exhaled, the breath came out like a gasp, and its force surprised me. The sound made Phai look over. "You're driving me crazy," I told him in English.

"What?" He looked confused.

"Totally bananas," I said, articulating every syllable with the precision I used when speaking to my students.

"Is that English?" he asked.

I nodded, but I couldn't look at him.

"I don't speak English." His tone was polite.

"I know that already," I said in Vietnamese.

Phai said, "I wanted to tell you. I got a letter from her a few days ago. She's getting married."

I stopped and looked at him. "What do you mean?" I asked.

Phai paused, shrugged, then started walking again. "She's getting married to a guy she met in Moscow. That's all I know."

For two years, Phai had considered the pen pal his destiny. And now, in a single letter, she'd effectively ceased to exist. Now what?

"Are you upset?" I asked.

Phai ran his fingers through his hair, and his laugh sounded less distraught than confused. "I don't know," he said. "It's just that we've been writing these letters for such a long time, but I hardly even knew her."

Neither of us said anything for a while. I think we were both trying to come to terms with his sudden freedom. What if I did something I'd later regret? Still, I felt like an obstacle had been removed, and I was surprised by how light and happy I felt.

"Let's go get a lemonade," I said.

We headed beyond the end of the lake, then turned down Hang Gai Street. The sidewalks were empty and we walked closer together. Something had changed between us in the past few minutes, but neither of us said a word.

The power was still out on Hang Bong Street, and the only light poured down from the glowing moon. It was nearly ten o'clock. Parents sat whispering to each other, holding their sleeping children in their arms. An old woman squatted at the edge of the road, brushing her teeth with one hand and holding a cup of water, for rinsing, in the other. Phai's rubber sandals softly slapped the pavement.

The café was eight or ten tables scattered along a wide swath of empty sidewalk. We pulled two low wicker chairs together and ordered drinks. Phai picked up my hand, not acknowledging the gesture. He suddenly became chatty, as if nothing more concerned him than the prospects for the cleanup after the typhoon. I couldn't focus at all. The more I tried, the more I found myself mesmerized by the way his thick black hair nestled like the tail of a cat around his ear. Phai's eyes swept the road, scanned the trees, settled back on the road again, looking in every direction but at me.

"Phai," I said, interrupting some observation about how long it might take a single crew of road workers to clear each fallen tree.

His face turned to mine, and I leaned close and kissed him on the lips. He pulled away, looking at me in shock. Then he dropped my hand and covered his face.

"I'm so sorry! I'm so sorry!" I gasped, watching him rub his hands across his temples. I felt mortified, as if I'd made a terrible mistake.

"No. It's okay," Phai finally said. He looked up at me again. "I told you. I don't know about these things." He took my face in his hands and pulled me toward him.

When I woke up the next morning, I lay beneath the covers, watching the sunlight shine through my pink sheets. I needed to think back over everything that had happened the night before. I didn't see a way to back out now. At home, an exchange of a few kisses could be forgotten, or retracted, without causing too much damage. Even here in Vietnam, a man might have moved past a brief physical encounter with a foreign woman, viewing the experience as one more adventure among a string of them. Not all Vietnamese men seemed as vulnerable as Phai did. A couple of my American women friends had had brief affairs here, and their reports were dismal. The "events," as they called them, had lasted an average of five minutes, and the men had offered their partners about as much affection as might be bestowed upon a tree or a chair or some other inanimate object. I'd planted my affections on Phai, a man who, at twenty-nine, had not only never had a girlfriend, he'd never even kissed a girl. Maybe he hadn't been entirely truthful about his history. I doubted it, though. Even in Vietnam, which was more traditional than the United States, sexual ignorance was not the sort of thing a man would lie about. He'd be more likely to lie about exploits he'd never actually had. But that wasn't the reason I believed that Phai was telling me the truth. I'd always trusted Phai. Now that I'd kissed him, though, I had another reason for believing him. His kisses were lovely, sweet, and uncertain, as if he was tentatively exploring something absolutely new. It would be extremely difficult for a kiss like that to lie.

If either of us were to become callous about this affair, I realized, it would probably be me. Despite my sudden fear that he would break my heart, I would more likely be the one to hurt him.

Such possibilities, however, bore no relation to my present condition. I felt a debilitating need to see him. My hand slid across my cheeks and over my lips. These lips touched his lips, I thought. So many times already. First in the café, and then when we reached the front door of my house, again and again. I had no idea how long we had lingered there. Mosquitoes bit constellations around my legs. Rats zigzagged down the sidewalks, quite close by. When I finally pulled myself away from Phai, it was not out of fatigue, but from a different motive. For the first time since I'd known him, I could look into his eyes without needing an excuse to do so.

A sliding metal gate had sent a screech into the night, and our two heads had jerked around at the same time. We both suddenly worried that a neighbor might see us. Worse, Tung and Huong could catch us. I doubted they would turn us in to the authorities, but they'd be angry. My visa to stay in Vietnam did not include the possibility of having a Vietnamese boyfriend, and my doing so could cause problems for them. Phai could be arrested for having intimate contact with a foreigner. And I could be kicked out.

We pulled ourselves apart, and I opened the gate in front of my house. Upstairs where Tung and Huong slept was dark and quiet. Phai gave me a reassuring smile, pulled his bicycle out of the living room, then carried it down the steps. Without a word, we waved good-bye.

When I finally ventured downstairs the next morning, the front doors were shut. Nga's dresses still hung where they had been placed for the night, even though it was well past the time that her shop usually opened. Although it was dim and silent, the room was full of people. Tung's parents, Huong's parents, and assorted siblings were drinking tea and smoking cigarettes. Tung was in one of the armchairs, staring at the wall. Huong sat between her mother and Nga on the couch, holding their hands.

My first thought was that Huong and Tung had seen me kissing Phai. I stood for a moment on the stairs, bracing myself for rebuke, but no one said a word. Huong's brother Phuong sucked on a cigarette and stared at the floor. Only Nga seemed to notice me, but she said nothing. I hurried down the stairs and out the door.

By the time I came home late that afternoon, Huong was in the kitchen cooking dinner. Someone had switched on a light. Tung was holding an open bottle of *rượu,* homemade rice wine, and pouring shots. Without saying a word, I went up to my room. I knew now that their problem didn't have a thing to do with me. No matter how indiscreet I might have been, a few kisses between a local and a foreigner would not throw an entire extended family into turmoil. Had someone died?

The phone rang at about seven, and three buzzes on the bell in my room indicated that the call was for me.

"How's everything going?" asked my sister, Lynne.

Her voice had traveled all the way from California, and now it sounded so close that I almost cried when I heard it. I paused before answering. I'd long ago written home about Phai, but the attraction I'd developed for a Vietnamese motorcycle mechanic did not translate well. Once, after receiving a particularly fervent declaration of my feelings for Phai, my friend Grace had telephoned. "So," she'd begun, making her amusement quite obvious in the tone of her voice, "did you two do the monkey yet?"

"Grace!" I'd shrieked across the ocean. Slang that sounded funny and racy in America came across as obscene and cold here in Vietnam. Within the context of quick and easy American sexuality, our slow and careful courtship seemed quaint, even prudish, though it seemed to generate more heat than any one-night stand. The prospect of actually doing the monkey, as Grace would have it, had seemed not only overwhelming, but also surprisingly irrelevant.

Now, with my sister, I tried again. "Last night," I began, "I kissed him."

"Who?" asked Lynne.

"The mechanic."

Someone in the house picked up the phone and began speaking loudly. I recognized the voice of Mr. Huey's translator, Tuan. I hadn't seen him or Mr. and Mrs. Huey since the couple's departure for Saigon two days before, and Tuan's voice signaled an end to the peace I'd enjoyed during their absence. Once again, they would tie up the phone day and night.

I waited for him to realize that I was on the phone. When he continued to speak, I said in Vietnamese, "I'm on the phone. Hang up." After a long pause, the line clicked.

"Are you still there?" I asked in English.

"Yeah," Lynne said. "How did it happen? What happened? How do you feel?"

I paused. "We went to the pagoda," I said, and then the translator picked up the phone again.

"Get off the phone," I said, my tone getting sterner now.

He rambled on for a few seconds, then hung up.

"We went to the pagoda," I repeated. "I really like him."

The voice came on again. "Get off the phone," I yelled. He kept talking, for longer this time, neither responding to my complaint nor yielding to it. "Get off the phone!"

When he finally hung up, Lynne said, "If he picks up again, I'm just going to hang up. I'll call another day."

"Will you call me soon?" I asked. I felt like I was pleading.

The translator picked up again. Beneath his sharp, guttural syllables, I could just make out the voice of my sister. "I'll call again. I love you. Bye!"

I hung up the phone and sat staring at it for a few seconds, trying to control myself. Then I raced down the stairs. Tung was standing by the phone, his eyes locked on the translator, who was speaking to someone in Chinese. The rest of the family was watching the two of them like an audience at the climax of a film.

"Why is he so rude?" I asked. "I was talking to America."

Tung didn't even look at me.

"He can't just ruin my call like that," I said, raising my voice so that they would pay attention to me. "He doesn't even live here," I added.

Without taking his eyes off the translator, Tung muttered, "Duyen, be quiet." Huong, her face a sheet of anxiety, gestured for me to stop.

I pushed my voice even louder. "Was he quiet?"

Tung turned and looked at me. His face was so full of fury that it scared me. "Go upstairs," he ordered, and he indicated the way with a clenched fist.

I turned and walked back up the stairs. For a long time, I sat on my bed, doing nothing. I was angry, but worse was the feeling that I'd misunderstood something essential about my place in this house. Over the past few months, I'd come to think of it as my home and Tung and Huong as my family. What Tung had said to me, the look on his face, the way he'd held his fist, told me that I wasn't family at all. I was an outsider, a pest, just someone who gave him money. It was time, I thought, to find a new place to live.

⌁ Early the next morning, I prepared myself to go downstairs and tell Tung and Huong that I was moving. But Huong got to me first. I heard her rattle the door at a little after eight, and when I let her into the room, she looked so pale that, instead of keeping a cool distance, I immediately took her hand. She smiled, but looked as if she could cry at any moment. "Please forgive Tung," she said. "Something terrible has happened." She walked into the room and sat down on my bed.

When Huong cleaned the tenants' rooms, she picked a time when we were out. Once or twice a week, I would come home to find clean sheets on my bed, a mop-slick floor, and my toilet seat dripping from a generous dousing of soapy water. On Thursday afternoon, a few hours after the Hueys left for Saigon, Huong had picked up her wash bucket and an armful of clean sheets and towels, then trudged up the stairs. She started at the top, in the room where the two Chinese women were staying. Then she cleaned my room. Then, finally, she moved downstairs to the Hueys'.

By the time Huong reached the Hueys' door, the sun was low in the sky. After a morning made fresh by the storm, the heat had returned. By five in the afternoon, the sweat was rolling down her face. She pulled the keys from her pocket, unlocked the door, and, before doing anything else, turned on the air conditioner, which sat in the wall just above the door. For a few sweet seconds, she stood there with her eyes closed, letting the cool, artificial air blow down into her face. Then she opened her eyes, switched on the light, and turned around. Except for the furniture and the pot the Hueys had used to boil their rice, the room was empty.

"Tung," she'd cried, running to the stairs. "Tung!" She was screaming now.

9 Private Rooms

*T*UNG AND HUONG HAD SPENT that Thursday night trying
to stay calm. Sitting on the bed in their loft, he insisted that an
empty room did not mean the Hueys had left Hanoi for good.
Huong, never an optimist anyway, was already hopeless.

By Friday night, Tung began to admit that Mr. and Mrs.
Huey probably weren't coming back. On Saturday afternoon,
when they had, in fact, failed to return as promised, Tung drove
over to the home of the translator, Tuan, who told Tung that
when he dropped the Hueys off at the airport, Mr. Huey had
not made an appointment to meet him again. Although Tuan
had never been civil to Tung, he was sympathetic to this new
predicament. When it came down to it, the ties between two
Vietnamese, even if they were a northerner and a southerner,
were stronger than either of them felt toward a Chinese. Tuan
came back to our house and telephoned Mr. Huey's business
contacts in Saigon. Late that night, not long after Tung ordered
me to go to my room, they finally located a Chinese trader in
Cholon who said that Mr. Huey had flown to Bangkok that
morning.

The tenants had gotten away with more than the $2,000 they still owed in rent. Mr. Huey had brought total disaster on Tung and Huong in a way that any of us should have suspected.

Mr. Huey hadn't paid for a single phone call since the day, more than a month earlier, when I'd seen him and Tung take a bag full of 5,000-dong notes to the central telephone office. Since that time, he'd made calls to Thailand, Hong Kong, Taiwan, and South Korea. Sometimes several times a day. When the June phone bill had arrived on Friday, the day after Mr. Huey left for Saigon, it added up, once again, to $5,000. Tung's name was on the bill.

A middle-class American would have to owe something like $50,000 for this calamity to have the same effect; $5,000 was all the money Tung had managed to save in three years of hard labor in Germany, and he'd spent much of that building his house. The debt would eat up his entire savings.

A gloom settled over the house. Tung spent half of every day rushing around town searching for a solution to the crisis. The rest of his time he sat motionless on the couch, his face as blank as that of a man determined to let himself drown.

Huong and her family went into permanent conference. She spent mornings whispering with Nga. Later, she'd stand for an hour on the front steps, discussing matters with one or another of her older brothers. In the evenings, she and her mother stared at the television set, rarely bothering to turn up the sound.

"Mr. Huey was so polite," Huong said to me one evening when I'd joined them.

"He sure dressed well," I said.

On the television, three dancing swans were singing songs for children. Huong turned and faced me. "There was something

in his eyes, though. I could see it. He had eyes like the Mafia."
She leaned her head against the couch and gazed at the dancing
swans. "I told Tung, but he wouldn't listen. He trusts too easily,"
she sighed.

I'd noticed Mr. Huey's Mafia eyes, too, but I hadn't said a
word. I felt as if a friend had just committed suicide and I could
have prevented it. Mr. Huey had always seemed just a little bit
slippery to me, but I'd never expressed my suspicions. How
could I, a foreigner with no business experience, judge the hon-
esty of wheeler-dealers in Vietnam? I wished there was something I could do to help, but the only thing Huong asked was that
I promise not to tell anyone what had happened. That included
Phai, which made the promise more difficult to keep.

After months spent working my way toward a single kiss, I
was now obsessed with the question of when Phai and I would finally be able to sleep together. Like many Americans, I regarded
sleeping together—not merely sex, but *sleeping together*—as a
necessary step in the development of an intimate relationship.
But I lived in a country that forbade me to have such a relationship with a Vietnamese. I wasn't even supposed to kiss Phai,
much less invite him over to spend the night.

We hadn't told anybody what had happened between us, but
people might have guessed. We were suddenly showing up all
over the place together. One night, I took Phai with me to the
third-year death anniversary of Linh's father-in-law, a big family
dinner celebrated in the dead man's honor. Linh's life as a single
woman hadn't lasted more than a month, and now she was back
to her old life with Son, happier, perhaps, but still complaining.
If she had to go to her father-in-law's death anniversary, then, she
insisted, I had to go too. I dragged Phai along with me. Linh's
family was gracious toward him, politely including him in their
conversations, but they were obviously quite puzzled by my

choice. Although Vietnamese had lived through forty years of socialism, ancient Confucian attitudes toward education and class
were still central to the way they assessed one another. In the
same way that I might guess the background of another American within a few seconds of meeting him, Linh's family took one
look at Phai and knew that he wasn't educated.

During those weeks, I lived what seemed to be a 1950s version of life. In the evenings, Phai and I would ride out to the
shore of the West Lake, where dozens of couples stood kissing in
the moonlight and necking beneath the trees. I'd never been to
a lover's lane, even when I was in high school, and it was fun, for
a while, to sneak around. But that only lasted a couple of weeks.
I was nearly thirty years old. I didn't want to act like a teenager
anymore; I wanted Phai to spend the night.

Phai was perplexed for completely different reasons. He
came from a culture in which spending the night at your girlfriend's house was not an option. Not only did he personally have
no experience with such activities, but he'd never heard of any
other Vietnamese having such experiences, either. In Hanoi, unmarried couples rarely slept together. Certainly, they had sex,
but seldom in the bedroom. Whose bedroom would it be? Most
unmarried Vietnamese lived with their parents, and the entire
family slept together in a single room.

Such circumstances, understandably, gave bedrooms a low
ranking as sexy places in Vietnam. The couples who had sex in
their bedrooms were married, and even they would have to have
it quickly and on the sly. Linh and Son had efficient relations at
three or four in the morning while their young sons lay fast
asleep beside them. Married couples with older children, I'd
heard, didn't have much sex at all.

Unmarried couples in Hanoi didn't have the luxuries of soft
mattresses and privacy, but they could be nearly as sexually ac-

tive as their counterparts in the States. They just had to be more creative about the location. Some couples frequented the "hugging" cafés, where proprietors used poor lighting, thin partitions, and leafy plants to provide privacy between tables. Many cafés rented their customers tiny cubicles equipped with narrow pallets and even doors that shut. Less affluent couples made do, weather permitting, in the great outdoors. The particularly dexterous, I'd heard, could complete the act of intercourse while balanced together on a motorbike. And then there were Hanoi's many tree-filled parks, and the banks of its lakes, which provided ample—if rather too public—space. An American photographer friend of mine once visited Hanoi's Lenin Park at dusk, hoping to discover a peaceful setting in which to take pictures. Instead, she found herself the only solitary person in a park full of embracing, and copulating, couples.

And unlike most other couples in Hanoi, one of us was foreign. As an American, I was used to privacy. But, also as an American, I was even less likely than a Vietnamese person to find it in such venues. If Phai and I rented a cubicle in a hugging café, the proprietors would be telling friends about it for years. If we found a cozy-looking tree in Lenin Park, we'd have a mob of seven-year-olds surrounding us in minutes.

Something else bothered me more than the possibility of prying eyes, however. Sneaking around felt demeaning.

Luckily, I did have my own room and a habit of inviting my Vietnamese friends to visit me in it. As long as Phai only visited during the day, no one in the house or neighborhood would suspect a change in our relations. Besides, Tung and Huong were so preoccupied with their own problems that they hardly noticed anyone else. For a time, we enjoyed a privacy unimagined by other couples in Vietnam.

Whole afternoons passed with the two of us locked inside

that room. Once, we lay side by side on our backs while I dragged my Vietnamese through ridiculous contortions to explain menstruation, the biology of intercourse, and the creation of a baby. I'd long known that Phai was sexually inexperienced, but I was shocked, and somewhat unnerved, to discover that he knew almost nothing about the facts of life.

"There's blood every month. This thing goes in here," I told him, indicating the appropriate locations on our bodies. "A baby grows right here." My hands floated everywhere, pointing, gesturing, demonstrating. The two of us stared at my hands as if they were characters in a foreign film. After a while, he pulled one out of the air and kissed it.

Phai was learning in another way as well. By now, the two of us had spent a good bit of time in bed together. He now knew, quite well, what he was doing.

Once, when I opened my eyes, he was watching me, smiling. That afternoon, I split in two. Half of me lay in bed with Phai. The other half stood a few feet away, incredulous. What was I doing to myself? To him? Where did I expect this thing to go? Would I marry him? The me in bed wouldn't respond. She had never thought someone like Phai could happen. She could hear the questions, but she couldn't answer them.

Not surprisingly, those afternoons of privacy didn't last long. Eventually, Huong discovered the truth. And she might never have suspected had Phai and I not given it away.

No one paid attention to what time Phai arrived and, as long as he went home in the afternoon, they didn't notice him leaving, either. If he left at six, the family, already leaning over the coffee table eating dinner, would simply invite him to join them. A seven o'clock departure might attract a curious look, but only if Phai left my house alone. If I went with him, they'd assume he'd dropped by to pick me up for dinner. If Phai left at eight, and alone, we were cutting it close.

Early one evening, we fell asleep. By the time I woke and looked at the clock, it was 10:30. I lay back down on the pillow and stared at the ceiling, panicked. Tung and Huong would be brushing their teeth already, getting ready for bed. When I first arrived in Vietnam, I'd laughed at the restrictions imposed on people's lives by the government. Once, a friend had asked me what kind of government permission he'd need in order to stay overnight at my house in San Francisco. I'd answered him seriously, but I'd had a hard time keeping a straight face as I did so. Though I was willing to abide by such laws while living here, I'd done so with a sense of their absurdity.

Now that I'd lived in this country for almost half a year, my perspective had changed. Rights that I'd always taken for granted as an American now struck me as privileges, luxuries even.

Phai wasn't nearly as upset as I was that it was too late for him to leave my house. "It doesn't matter," he told me, more interested in running his fingers across my forehead.

"You won't say that when I get kicked out of the country," I told him.

Phai laughed. I couldn't help but think how much better he functioned in this place than I did. He not only accepted the repressive laws, but he had a very well developed ability to subvert them. His twenty-nine years of experience had made him a much better sneak than I was.

Phai promised to leave without waking anyone up the next morning. I couldn't imagine how he would do so, because the stairs, which ran outside the house on the top three floors, slipped inside the house and passed right by Tung and Huong's sleeping quarters on the way down to living room, and front door. The architecture of the house offered no other route to the street. When I tried to question Phai, however, he changed the subject. My mind hadn't made the leap yet, but his had. For the first time, he was going to spend the night.

He nudged me awake at a little after six the next morning. He already had his clothes on, and his hair was wet from the shower. When I got up and opened the door for him, he gave me a quick kiss, then leaped up to the iron railing that separated the outdoor staircase from the three-story drop to the ground below. "Watch out," I whispered.

Phai grinned, balancing so easily that I remembered how I'd once been stunned by his agility and grace. "I'll come over to-morrow," he said. Then he stepped along the top of the railing, leaped across a two-foot gap to my neighbor's roof, then disappeared around a corner of the building. I ran back into my room, then out to the balcony at the front of the house, which over-looked the street. After about five minutes, Phai emerged from an alley.

After that, we didn't see any reason why Phai couldn't spend the night quite regularly. And so, on three occasions over the next week, he utilized our newly discovered escape route across the neighbors' roofs and down the trellises that clung to their balconies.

After the fourth morning, Huong knocked on my door. Grandmother Nhi's son, she told me, had come over that morning with a worried look on his face. "Your friend Phai," he'd begun. "Do you know that he's been creeping around here early in the morning? The next time we see him, we're going to call the police."

Huong had immediately thought of me. After convincing Grandmother Nhi's son to let her investigate, she'd rushed upstairs.

"Why didn't you tell me?" she asked.

I shrugged my shoulders, a recalcitrant teenager confronted by Mom.

"Why don't you trust me?" she wanted to know.

I stared at the floor, shocked at my own inability to discuss the matter like a grown-up.

"We could get into a lot of trouble because of this," Huong said. "Tung and I have too many problems already."

I nodded.

"You can trust me," Huong said. "I take care of you already."

I looked up at her, confused. "What do you mean?" I asked.

Huong paused for a moment. Once every few weeks, she explained, secret police would come by the house to question her about my activities in Vietnam. Who are her friends? Where does she go? What does she do? Huong always professed ignorance. She was only my landlord, she'd claim, how could she know such details about my private life? Without ever actually lying, she managed to keep from them the one fact that would have made them push her harder. She never told them that she and I were friends.

The news didn't surprise me, particularly in light of something I'd learned from my student John only a week or two before. Late one evening, when John was driving me home on the back of his motorbike, we got into a conversation about Harry and how he'd once taken me out to Ha Long Bay. "I still don't understand how he managed to take a foreigner outside of Hanoi without government permission," I said.

The motorbike puttered to a stop in front of my house, and John paused before heading home. Two dogs were poking through a pile of trash my neighbors had put outside for the street sweepers to pick up. "Harry's very powerful," John said.

"What do you mean?" I asked. "As a scientist?"

John laughed uncomfortably, then looked down at the ignition on his motorbike and toyed with the keys. "You can have many careers in Vietnam," he said. "Look at me." Although John worked every day as a physicist, he made his money on the weekends, as a guide for French and Italian tourists. With Harry it was the same thing, John explained. He was a scientist. And he was also a high-ranking member of the secret police.

It took a moment for the idea to register that Harry—small, lascivious Harry—was also a cop. "How can he be both?" I'd asked.

John explained that many institutes in Vietnam had employees who were also members of the secret police. It was a perfect way to keep tabs on what was going on in the country.

I must have looked upset. John had laughed. "Don't worry about it," he said. "Harry is your friend. It's no problem."

I'd nodded, not knowing what else to say. Harry's interest in me had suddenly seemed more complicated. He wasn't just a student looking for a date.

Huong wasn't critical of her government, but she was critical of me. "How can I help you if I don't even know myself what you're doing?" she asked me now. "You act like you want to make the police suspicious—having Phai climb across the neighbors' roofs. Tung and I can help you."

Huong's words were harsh, but her eyes were smiling. After all these weeks of secrecy, I felt enormously relieved to discover that Tung and Huong not only wouldn't condemn my relationship with Phai, but that they would actually encourage it. It turned out that they'd been wondering when the two of us would finally get together.

"I thought maybe you would look down on me for sleeping with him without being married," I said.

Huong shook her head. "You're not like Vietnamese women. You're an American. You always sleep with your boyfriends."

I started to object, but stopped myself.

"You're lucky," Huong continued. "Maybe if I'd slept with Tung, I never would have married him." She laughed loudly then, thoroughly enjoying it.

Huong and I came up with a more practical—and physically safer—plan than the one Phai and I had figured out. Phai could spend the night, but he couldn't leave the house before nine in the morning, an hour that was late enough to guarantee that none of the neighbors would notice.

Huong stood up and walked to the door. Just before she closed it behind her, she looked at me again, her face more serious now. "Duyen," she said, "Tung and I care about Phai. He doesn't know anything about these things. You'll hurt him if you don't really love him."

I was asleep, and Phai's words nudged me like gentle fingers. "*Yêu quá,*" he said. Two words that, translated, meant "so much love." Pronouns weren't necessary in Vietnamese. All that mattered was the noun itself, and it came out of his mouth as easily as a sigh. But my mind was clouded with sleep and, at first, the words didn't register. I lay on my stomach and when I opened my eyes, I could only see the lower half of his body sitting on the bed beside me. As usual, he'd woken well ahead of me. A towel covered his waist, and drops of water glistened on his bare legs. He pulled down the sheet and draped a hot wet towel across my back. I closed my eyes again and fell back to sleep.

It wasn't until later that morning that I remembered what Phai had said. He'd said it quietly, not knowing if I was asleep or not, as if he only wanted to try the words on his tongue. Perhaps he wanted to give me an out. That might have explained my own

behavior, had I been the one to whisper words of love to someone sleeping, but Phai's mind didn't work like mine. Whether he
was fixing a broken faucet for Tung or spending his last few thousand dong to buy an ice cream for Viet, Phai's generosity flowed
freely. Love would be a gift from him, like a warm towel draped
across my back. He'd whispered it because he felt it. And, for
that moment, at least, he needed nothing back.

From my previous romantic relationships, I'd come to believe that love was a complicated experience that filled you with
passion one day, aversion the next, and, on the third day, tor-
tured you with some mind-numbing mixture of the two—so
many emotions piled on top of one another that love itself ended
up a tiny pearl buried beneath a heap of trash. With Phai, it
never seemed to include the trash. He loved so completely, and
without hesitation.

Still, I wanted to avoid the subject. If I could have controlled
our relationship, I might have decided that we'd only say such
things while the other person was absent or sleeping. Words
seemed to complicate things. Loving Phai was easy, but our future together wasn't.

I wasn't the only American to fall in love with
a Vietnamese. During the time that I lived in Hanoi, I came to
know a number of Americans, most of them my age, most of
them scholars or staff members of international aid organizations. Our small circle of expatriates relied on one another for
everything from emotional support to loans of money to carrying letters and packages for one another when we returned to
the States. Other groups of foreigners were trying to create
tiny Western enclaves for themselves in Hanoi, and the city did
have its cocktail parties at the Australian embassy and a pizza

parlor or two. But for more than financial reasons, my friends were not among this set. Jack spent his free time translating an ancient Chinese text into Vietnamese. Olivia learned to play an obscure type of bamboo flute. Norma raced off to every village festival that took place within a hundred miles of the city. We didn't focus our intellectual or personal passions on one another, but on Vietnam. Not surprisingly, few of us became involved with each other romantically and almost all of us fell for Vietnamese.

Most of the men in that circle have since married Vietnamese women. Only a couple of the women have married Vietnamese men. Somehow, the cultural gap between our nations has been easier to span for one gender combination than the other, and the traditional interest of Western men in Asian women doesn't fully account for it. My male American friends did not travel the countryside in search of fresh-faced farm girls to cook, clean, and raise babies for them in Kansas. Jack married Nga, who became such an asset to Save the Children in Vietnam that the organization sent her on a year-long study course in Australia. Steve married Lan, who raced so quickly up the corporate ladder at Cathay Pacific in Hanoi that, when the couple decided to move to the United States, the airline offered to transfer her to its prestigious Los Angeles office. David married Thuy, who, while completing a fully funded graduate program at Harvard, had to rush back to Vietnam to translate for groups of visiting VIPs who refused to hire anyone else.

The American women I knew didn't end up with partners like these, probably because of two factors: our nationality and our gender. Two specific attributes—being American and being male—were the qualities most likely to enhance one's power in one of these cross-cultural relationships. If a member of a couple was both American and male, there wasn't much of a problem.

Jack, Steve, and David could marry phenomenally successful Vietnamese women and not feel threatened by the success of their mates. All three of them could both believe in equality for women and, at the same time, appreciate having a wife who felt she had a duty to cook dinner. Such relationships didn't disrupt the established dynamics of power.

When American women took up with Vietnamese men, however, power got split down the middle, and not always with positive results. Though Vietnamese men may have appreciated our independence, most of them were raised to expect dinner on the table when they came home at night. If I cooked, I'd expect the guy to do the dishes. In more subtle ways as well, such as my desire to have male friends or his need for a wife willing to be subservient to his mother, my nationality would invariably clash with his gender. We American women gravitated toward Vietnamese partners less likely to make oppressive demands on us: eccentric artists, easygoing workers, curious but unambitious intellectuals who sat around all day drinking rice wine and talking about books.

It was hard to imagine, though, bringing a guy like that back to the States. Nga, Lan, or Thuy could make it in any country in the world, but Phai couldn't. As long as we remained in his own country, where he functioned well, power remained fairly balanced between us. Once we got to the States, however, the scales would tip dangerously in my direction. After a blissful honeymoon spent standing atop skyscrapers, riding escalators, and sampling Big Macs, we'd settle into normal life. Phai would look for a job fixing motorbikes and, because he didn't speak English, no one would hire him. Unable to work, he'd stay home alone, squatting in front of the television, trying to make out the meaning of every episode of *Days of Our Lives.* At some point, my mother would fly out to meet her new son-in-law, and her brows would bunch with worry because she couldn't even speak to him.

No, I couldn't imagine that kind of future with Phai.

～～～   Phai lived with his parents and younger sister and brother in a neighborhood at the edge of the Red River. He had described for me the large room where the family slept, his father's garden, and the shed where his mother was raising a pig. But these descriptions weren't enough for me. I kept asking him so many questions that, finally, one afternoon, he invited me for a visit.

On our way out the door of my house, I heard the sound of running water in the kitchen. For reasons I could never understand, Huong regularly left water running in the sink. I regularly turned it off. Now, however, when I walked into the kitchen, I nearly tripped over Huong herself. She was squatting on the floor, ardently scrubbing a black cloud of mildew that hovered like a thunderstorm above the tiles. Her posture suggested that she was involved in some form of meditation.

Phai leaned through the door behind me. "Where's Tung?" he asked. Neither of us had seen Tung for days. The two Chinese women living on the fourth floor had left a few days earlier, and I assumed that Tung had been busy searching for someone to rent his two now-empty rooms.

Huong's hand moved in slow circles across the floor. She mumbled something about a business trip to Saigon, but didn't look up. Her head was bent so that I couldn't see her face at all, and, like a robot, she continued scrubbing. She had never been an ardent housecleaner, but now she was acting like nothing in the world interested her so much as the sparkle on her kitchen floor. I knew that she was lying. Tung didn't have any business. Had he gone off in search of Mr. Huey? The idea seemed ridiculous, expensive, even dangerous. If it was true, then of course Huong would be upset. If it wasn't true, where was he? I couldn't ask Huong anything. I was still keeping my promise to her, that I wouldn't tell the truth about Mr. Huey's departure to anyone, including Phai.

"Can we borrow the Dream for a while?" Phai asked.

Huong nodded, still not looking up. Phai took my hand and pulled me away from Huong.

Phai's neighborhood, Nghia Dung, not only sat right next to the Red River, but was actually situated somewhat below it, protected from the water by the strength of Hanoi's ancient dikes. In recent years, Hanoi's building boom had begun to transform areas like Nghia Dung, converting land traditionally devoted to small houses and flower cultivation into real estate for private mansions and luxury hotels. Much of the construction had taken place without government approval, or with the help of corrupt officials willing to look the other way. Development had grown to such proportions that scientists and engineers now warned of a potentially disastrous strain on the dikes. Although Phai's neighborhood had yet to see much physical change, the threat was obvious: on one side, developers sat anxious to get their hands on this valuable swath of land; on the other, the river strained against the beleaguered dikes, a trapped monster, biding its time.

Phai's house lay between two lanes in a small line of long, narrow concrete houses that paralleled the dike. As soon as we arrived on the motorbike, the requisite group of curious children immediately crowded around to look at the foreigner. Phai parked the motorbike, then grabbed one little boy by the shoulders and drew him closer. "This I cousin," he said in English.

Phai had been studying my language on his own for several months already, mostly by the extraordinarily inefficient method of paging through the Vietnamese-English dictionary, reading the words. He rarely tried out his new skills on me, however. Communication between us was difficult enough, and so we relied on Vietnamese, our strongest common tongue. But I smiled at him encouragingly and looked at the boy, whose face was buried in Phai's leg. "*Chào cháu.*" Hello, Nephew, I said.

The little boy's face burrowed deeper. Phai laughed, then forcibly turned him around and nudged him until he said hello. All the other kids screamed with laughter. They found it unbelievable that they could communicate with a foreigner.

An elderly face peeked out from a doorway and looked at us. It was a soft, gentle-looking face, but it disappeared quickly. Phai turned and walked into the house, motioning for me to follow. The old woman hurried down the hallway in front of us. Just inside the doorway, the opening to a small, dark pen revealed black mud, hay, and a large pink pig.

I leaned across the railing of the pen and looked at the pig. "He's kind of sweet," Phai said. "I'll be sad when my mother sells him."

"Was that your mother?" I asked, feeling remiss at not saying hello to her.

Phai nodded and gave my hand a squeeze. Then he led me farther down the corridor. We weren't inside or outside, exactly. The narrow hallway opened into a roofless, plant-filled space. Traditionally, Vietnamese homes had two courtyards. The "dry" courtyard was usually full of plants and trees, a space in which a family might sit on pleasant evenings to enjoy the fresh air. The "wet" courtyard, fitted either with running water or a storage tank, served as a domestic work area, where the women rinsed vegetables, washed dishes, and scrubbed clothes. My house on Dream Street, being more of a Western-style home, had no courtyard at all. Phai's house used one space for both purposes. In one corner, a water spigot stuck out from the wall above a drain. A plastic bowl of green beans and another of lettuce sat on the concrete floor, next to a pile of wet clothes.

I followed Phai into a spacious room that looked out over the courtyard. The room had a concrete floor and plaster walls painted in the pale turquoise common in Vietnamese homes. Decorating one wall was a monthly calendar with a picture of an Asian man kicking a soccer ball. The other walls were bare. We sat down at a table in a corner. In the other three corners were positioned broad wooden platform beds, their thin bedding rolled into cylinders and placed against the wall. Phai's mother and younger sister slept in one bed, his father and younger brother slept in another. Phai had a third bed to himself, which was separated a bit from the others, at the far end of the room. On Phai's bed sat a wooden guitar and the only piece of technology I'd seen since we left Tung and Huong's Dream out in the lane: a portable radio that might have been manufactured in the 1970s.

"I'm planning to build a private room for myself," Phai said, pointing out the window and explaining that he would wall in a small section of the courtyard and put a bed in it.

Phai's mother reappeared with a thermos of hot water. Phai had told me she did a Jane Fonda–inspired aerobics routine every day, but it was hard to imagine. She was a tiny, fragile-looking woman and wore the loose-fitting black trousers and thin cotton blouse favored by most matrons in Northern Vietnam. I was struck, all over again, by the strangeness of my situation here.

Phai's mother would remember all of the war, the air raids, the bombs dropping on the city, her fear of Americans. How would she feel, right now, to have an American in her living room? How would she feel—did she know?—about an American sleeping with her son? If she felt any concern, she didn't show it, but then again, she didn't show any other emotion either. She moved about the room without even looking at me.

"Mother, this is my American friend, Duyen—Dana," Phai told her. "She lives at Tung's house."

I started to say hello, but Phai had barely completed his introduction before his mother, in a sudden burst of nods and smiles, disappeared again out the door. That was the last I saw of her.

I didn't have time to react. A moment later, we heard a shout from the other side of the courtyard and a white-haired man in a T-shirt, shorts, and sneakers appeared in the doorway. He was small, thin, and probably close to sixty, but his body moved like that of a very young man. In his face, I saw Phai's eyes.

"*Bonjour! Bonjour!*" he said, rushing over and taking my hand in both of his. "*Je suis Papa Phai.*"

"I father," Phai tried to translate the French into English. His father threw himself into a chair.

In Hanoi, traditionally, people who perform the same craft or trade settle in the same neighborhood. Phai's neighborhood was a community of bronze workers, many of whom still practiced their craft, either by making Buddhas and other ornaments for religious shrines or by making smaller objects to sell to the growing tourist market. I'd once gone with Phai to a pagoda where we'd seen a bronze bell bigger than a small room that had been made by his grandfather. Many of Phai's relatives still practiced the ancestral trade. Phai's father, however, had given it up in favor of a career in sports fitness. He taught swimming to members of the army.

I tried to say a few words in Vietnamese, but Phai's father insisted on speaking in French and Phai insisted on speaking in English, neither of which I could understand. After a few seconds, this form of discourse came to a halt and we sat in silence. Phai's father leaned back in his chair, grinning at me. Phai poured tea.

"You have a nice house," I finally said in Vietnamese.

"You speak our language!" exclaimed Phai's father in Vietnamese, as if I hadn't just been talking. "You like our house?"

I nodded again. Phai's father looked at his son. "Your American friend likes our house," he said emphatically. "Is it nicer than the houses in America?" he asked.

I considered the question for a moment, then said, "It's nice how you have all this outdoor space. We don't have that in America."

Phai handed his father a cup of tea. The older man said to his son, "She likes our houses here better than in America."

We lapsed again into silence. Then, suddenly, the questions began. Phai's father spoke quickly and, because I couldn't easily understand him, I turned to Phai for help. In the months that we'd known each other, he'd become a competent translator for me, converting complicated Vietnamese into words and phrases I could easily understand. Now, however, he insisted on using his English vocabulary of about twenty words, only three or four of which he could pronounce accurately.

Phai's father shot out a question about my stay in Vietnam. I wasn't sure if he wanted to know how long I had been here or how long I planned to stay.

When I looked over at Phai for help, his eyes grew wide and he pursed his lips in concentration. "Vietnam many days," he finally said, then cocked his head in order to let me know these three words constituted a question. Phai's father acknowledged his son's facility in English by clucking admiringly. Phai, who seemed to believe his English actually made sense, waited patiently for me to respond.

I took a sip of tea, trying to figure out what to do. I knew I would embarrass Phai by insisting he speak to me in Vietnamese. But I was annoyed that he was using me to show off his English. I turned to the older man and said, "I've been here five months."

Phai's father continued to stare at me expectantly, but when I didn't say anything more, he looked over at Phai and mumbled, "She's still learning, isn't she?" Phai nodded like a patient teacher.

Phai's father leaned closer toward me. "You stay in Vietnam a long time," he said, in language so slow and simple that I could understand every word. "When you take a Vietnamese husband, you'll learn to speak just like one of us."

I smiled, unable to answer, unable to look at Phai. I took a sip of tea and glanced out the window into the courtyard, at the space where Phai and his future bride would enjoy the luxury of a private room.

Phai didn't stay over that night, but I still couldn't find a chance to talk to Huong. Her mother had now apparently moved in. Every time I came home, she was sitting in the living room, staring at the TV, or standing out on the front steps, shouting for Viet. It wasn't as if Huong wasn't taking care of herself and her son quite adequately. She hadn't fallen apart. But she seemed distracted. Something was definitely wrong; Huong, who almost never left the house was, these days, hardly ever home.

For a few days, I lurked around, trying to find an opportunity to talk to her, even to see her. Then, late one night, I heard the familiar rattle at my door. "What's wrong?" I asked, as soon as I'd let her in.

Huong smiled grimly. She walked over to one of the armchairs and sat down. As usual, my room was a mess. The remains of several oranges created a little mountain in the middle of the coffee table, and books and papers lay in heaps all around it. One armchair was completely covered with clothes. My bed was a mass of tousled sheets. "I'll come clean up this place in the morning," Huong told me.

"Don't worry about it," I told her. "What's going on?"

Huong looked at me. "Don't tell anyone, even Phai. Okay?"

I nodded impatiently. "I haven't told Phai anything."

Huong sighed and leaned back, letting her head fall against the chair. She stared up at the ceiling and said, very quietly, "Tung's in jail."

10   Dreams, and Waking Up

*H*UONG, HER SISTER NGA, AND I were sitting in the downstairs living room/dress shop, arguing with a tall, skinny Frenchman. He was insisting that $325 a month rent would put an unhealthy strain on the small salary he earned teaching French at the Foreign Language College. Huong and Nga turned to each other and conversed quietly in Vietnamese, then Huong sat for a moment, doing silent arithmetic in her head, before turning back to me. "Tell him I'll give him breakfast every morning, whatever he wants." Then, she added, "And laundry. Tell him I'll throw in laundry for free."

Huong's face was set. Her eyebrows bunched over her eyes in an expression that suggested firm determination. To look at her at that moment, one might have guessed that she was an experienced businesswoman, the type of high-heeled Hanoi lady who zipped from meeting to meeting on a pink Honda. Of course, she wasn't dressed like a businesswoman. She was wearing the same old flat rubber sandals she always wore, and her soft, pajama-like shirt and pants. But Huong had a look on her face that even the Frenchman could recognize as shrewd. She'd picked her price and she wasn't budging.

It was my job to be translator, but, unlike Linh's husband Son, I wasn't a foreign ministry diplomat trained to be objective. I turned to the Frenchman and did my best to make Huong's offer of breakfast and laundry sound inviting. "It's a good price," I told him, not mentioning the fact that I only paid $220 a month myself. "And Huong's an excellent cook."

"Ffffft," said the Frenchman, half closing his eyes and letting his fingers flutter through the air dismissively. He was about my age, with close-cropped dark brown hair and an air of stubbornness that made me curious to see which of them would give in first. "As if I cannot buy my own breakfast on the street every morning for two thousand dong," he said, looking at me and rolling his eyes.

In the few minutes since Huong had dragged me down the stairs to act as her translator, the Frenchman and I had conversed just enough for me to establish that his name was Hugo, he came from Bordeaux, and that, on several occasions, he'd visited the States. Now, after that brief conversation and, more importantly, because of the implicit solidarity of Westerners, Hugo was treating me as his ally. He regarded Huong and Nga skeptically, and he spoke to me as if the two of us were in this thing together.

Huong had seen enough old French movies to know what "Ffffft" meant. She tried another tactic. "Tell him I'm an excellent cook," she urged.

I mumbled, "I did already," then I turned to Hugo. "It's a good deal for you," I told him. "I don't get breakfast, and I have to do my own laundry."

Hugo shrugged and looked around the room uncertainly. I could easily remember the morning Tra and I first trudged up the stairs to that multicolored, overfurnished room I now called home. I'd once wondered if that uneven staircase would lead me to break my neck, and now I raced up and down it ten times a day without a thought. I'd once looked at Tung with the same suspicion with which Hugo now gazed at Huong. In a country where the average citizen made less in a year than he was being asked to pay in one month's rent, the Frenchman probably thought that she was trying to grab every dollar he had. In addition, Hugo, like me, came from a country that had a rocky history with Vietnam. Maybe he was wondering if the high rent demonstrated how much the Vietnamese still hated the French.

Hugo sat back and looked around the room. A recent shipment from Hong Kong made it appear even more like a dress shop and less like a living room than ever. "These two sisters own the place?" he asked.

I shook my head. "It's just Huong and her husband, who's away on a business trip to Saigon." I said. "He lived in Germany for a long time." Hugo's eyes opened wide, and I could see that the European connection impressed him.

"So, is he very Westernized?" Hugo asked.

I nodded. "Very," I told him. I went on to describe Tung as a Vietnamese in blue jeans and loafers, a fan of Metallica, drinker of Heineken. I could see Hugo begin to relax. Tung became comprehensible, which was a very attractive quality to foreigners just starting out in a city as incomprehensible as Hanoi. At the mention of Metallica, Hugo began to laugh, but the memory of Tung standing in front of his stereo, tapping his feet and cranking up the heavy metal, just made me sad. I wasn't just trying to paint a portrait of Tung. I was trying to conjure him.

Huong had told me that on the previous Tuesday afternoon, two policemen had arrived at our house. They weren't the regular guys who came by periodically and sat in our living room drinking tea with Tung and questioning him about the foreigners who rented his rooms. Within a few minutes of their arrival, they had already disposed of the requisite small talk and had begun to interrogate Tung about the Chinese women who'd been staying on the fourth floor. Tung said that he didn't know much about the women, only that they'd been friends of Mr. Huey and that they'd rented his room for a month before leaving Vietnam several days earlier. What Tung didn't know, and what Huong had only been able to figure out piece by piece in the days that followed, was that the Chinese women had been traveling under fake passports. When they tried to leave the country, their passports had been confiscated and the women had been arrested. Because the women had been living at Tung's house, the police turned to Tung.

After a half hour or so, the policemen stood up and invited Tung to join them at their office for further questioning. In the four days since then, Huong had neither seen nor heard from her husband. All she knew was that the police could hold him as long as they liked.

Huong's face had grown thinner over the course of the last few weeks, and it seemed to be set in a permanent expression of worry. But her magnificent self-containment, that quality that made her seem lazy and indifferent to everything around her, had now evolved into an impulse toward self-preservation. Everything about her suggested competence and determination, and it gave a hint of the kind of internal strength people like Huong must have mustered in order to endure all those years of war. As the Vietnamese themselves liked to point out, they weren't victims, but survivors.

"Duyen," she nudged me, "will he take the room?"

I'd done everything I could to market the room as fabulous. I looked at Hugo. "What do you think?" I asked.

Hugo sighed and shrugged, as if defeated. But after a moment he looked over at Huong and smirked. "I like croissants from the French café down the road. And my coffee must be very, very hot," he said.

Huong must have understood that the news was good. She was already smiling as she waited for my translation.

⌒⌒⌒ Phai only asked me once where Tung had gone, and when I told him the Saigon story, he didn't question it. Phai's own life was in such a state of flux that he was in no position to notice inconsistencies in anyone else's. He'd found a new job on the other side of town, but he left it after only a few weeks because business had been just as bad as it was at his old job. All over the city were signs that Vietnam's economy had taken off. Modern luxury hotels were filling rooms that cost two hundred dollars a night. Importers did a brisk business in Rémy Martin, Heinz ketchup, and Snickers. A sports boutique around the corner from my house sold tennis racquets and exercise machines, products that could only attract consumers with significant disposable income. International business magazines forecast that Vietnam was fast becoming the next Asian dragon. And still, on a busy day as a mechanic, Phai could only hope to earn 10,000 dong, or roughly a dollar. That was barely enough for a bowl of beef noodle soup, much less a meal in one of the city's new restaurants. As the economy boomed, Vietnam's proletariat could only watch in wonder, poor cousins invited to a debutante ball, but not allowed to dance.

Phai wanted to dance. Unlike the farmers out in the fields, who only saw urban luxuries on their communes' TVs, Phai stood so close to all this glitter that he could feel the warmth of its glow. Since he'd become friends with Tung and, of course, with me, the wealth of the world had come to seem like a possibility to him. Even if fixing motorbikes had earned him a decent wage, which it didn't, he was sick of dirty hands, torn clothes, and low prestige.

As Phai struggled to change, he and I struggled with the differences between us. The economic gap between the two of us was so enormous that money issues were both extremely awkward and very simple. We had ridiculous races to see who'd be quicker to pay for a two-dollar dinner, although that expense, which set him back a week, wouldn't amount to the loose change I could find wadded up in a pocket. Still, I usually ended up letting him pay. To assert that I was rich and he was poor, especially in our neighborhood noodle shop, would only humiliate him. And so I let Phai make a show of reaching into the pocket of his pale yellow shirt and pulling out his small stash of bills.

When we were alone, we were more honest and practical. Phai never asked me for anything, but when I offered to help him embark on a new career, he accepted gratefully. That I had money and Phai didn't seemed like an obvious fact of life between us, intrinsically related to my being born in America and his being born in Vietnam. Late at night, we would sit talking in my room, visualizing all the possibilities for his future. If my financial capabilities seemed miraculous to him, they seemed no less so to me. With a simple investment of a few hundred dollars, I could help him change his life.

In his free time, Phai had been making bronze ornaments and Buddhas at the family kiln across the street from his house. Though he seemed to enjoy it, he considered the craft a sideline, nothing that could sustain him. For the long term, he thought he should learn English and computer skills. Although he'd learned some English words, he didn't know any grammar. As for computers, Phai had never used one, but his mechanical skills seemed to promise that he'd pick it up quite quickly. I had a different idea in mind. I imagined him opening a bike rental business to cater to the increasing numbers of foreign tourists visiting Hanoi. To both of us, it seemed reasonable that he embark on all three ventures at the same time. The English would help him communicate with tourists. Computer skills would give him entry into the world of the office or help in the bike-rental business. Using the $400 he got from me, Phai enrolled in an evening computer class, found space to rent near the tourist hotels, and bought six Chinese bikes.

He also found a way to improve his English. Along with the change of wardrobe, the shy motorbike mechanic had metamorphosed into an extrovert. Once, as we rode Tung's motorbike through the center of Hanoi, we saw a Western tourist pedaling a bike. Phai slowed down alongside him. "Can I help you?" he shouted, over the rush of the traffic. "Where you going?" His English was garbled, and I wondered if the foreigner could understand.

The scruffy, bearded man looked at us. "Hanoi Hilton," he said, using the nickname the Americans had employed to describe the famous Hoa Lo Prison, where POWs had been held captive during the war.

As we puttered along beside the Westerner, Phai launched into an enthusiastic, if not terribly effective, set of directions, complete with hand signals, that gave the foreigner enough information eventually to know when to turn right. We slowed to watch him pedal off down the street.

"Do you think he'll find it?" I asked, uncertainly.

"Maybe!" said Phai happily.

I was Phai's first foreign friend. Hugo was his second. On the evening that I told Phai that a Frenchman had moved into the second-floor room, he raced downstairs to say hello. He returned an hour later, his eyes gleaming and his face bright red from drinking beer. I was lying on the bed with a book in my hands, and he lay down beside me and closed his eyes. "Hugo's so *vui*," he said, and then he fell asleep. I had no idea how the two of them had managed to carry on a conversation, but before Hugo had been in the house for two nights, he and Phai had come up with a plan. Twice a week, Phai would teach Hugo Vietnamese and Hugo, the Frenchman, would teach Phai English.

Hugo's *vui*-ness became obvious to everyone else before me. I might have been the only one able to carry on an extensive conversation with him, but they appreciated him sooner. Huong liked to peek out at him from the kitchen and watch the ritualistic way he drank his morning coffee. Sa thought Hugo was such a funny guy that all he had to do was smile and she would dissolve into giggles.

One night, Huong invited Hugo, me, and Phai to have dinner with her, her mother, Sa, and Viet. After we'd cleared away the dishes. Huong passed around a big bowl of lychee fruit.

We talked for a while about Hugo's native Bordeaux, which, he explained, was famous for wines. Then the conversation drifted from a discussion of France to one of Vietnam. The Frenchman had only recently arrived here, and Huong and Phai were curious to hear what he thought of their country.

"Ffffft!" Hugo answered immediately. "The country is quite nice. But this government of yours, this Communist government. They talk about helping workers, but they don't care about anything except their own power." He paused and smiled in my direction, waiting for me to translate.

"Are you sure you want me to say that?" I asked. I'd never said anything so critical of the Vietnamese government.

Hugo looked at me and nodded as if his words were a dare. "Yes, I'm sure," he said.

"What?" Huong asked. Her mother had gone upstairs to lie down. Sa was in the kitchen doing dishes, intermittently peeking out to watch us talk. Among themselves, foreigners criticized the Vietnamese government all the time. I'd come to have plenty of complaints of my own, after finding out that my "friend" Harry was a member of the secret police, after learning that my neighbors were keeping tabs on me, and, worst of all, after Tung was jailed without trial or even the benefit of a lawyer. I had a lot of thoughts about Vietnam's government, but I would not have expressed them to my Vietnamese friends.

Huong and Phai were obviously curious to hear what Hugo had to say. I thought for a moment. "Well, he doesn't like Communists," I finally told them.

Phai and Huong looked at each other, their eyes wide with surprise. They began to chuckle, then their chuckles got louder until laughter filled the room, making Sa look out of the kitchen to see what was going on. It wasn't an easy laughter, like the reaction to a silly joke. Instead, it sounded shocked, like the inadvertent hilarity when a child utters a string of dirty words. "He doesn't like the Communists," Huong said, between breaths. Her eyes were glowing.

For a while, Hugo said nothing, although the glimmer in his eyes told me that he was pleased. He leaned forward, took a lychee out of the bowl on the table, peeled it and pulled out the seed, then slid the smooth white fruit into his mouth. "I don't know why the people don't rise up and overthrow the bastards," he said.

The words were barely out of his mouth before Huong, like a soap opera fan desperate for the next installment, yanked my sleeve for translation. I leaned back, giving up. "He wants to see a revolution," I said.

Huong and Phai went speechless with laughter then, leaving Hugo and me to sit there silently, watching them in wonder. Huong's laughter was something beautiful to behold. For those few minutes at least, it smoothed the tension from her face, as if erasing the many weeks of worry.

The next day, I asked Huong why she'd found Hugo's comments so hilarious. Perhaps the simplicity of Hugo's judgment had struck her and Phai as comically naïve. Or perhaps she felt exhilarated to hear someone declare, so emphatically and fearlessly, ideas that most Vietnamese would be afraid to utter, even to their closest friends. But Huong wouldn't say. Hugo, a foreigner, could say whatever he wanted, in English, about Vietnam. But Huong had a $5,000 debt to the government and a husband in jail. Speaking openly about politics was a luxury she could not afford. In answer to my question, she only replied, "Hugo's so *vui,*" and refused to say more.

I had a recurring dream in Vietnam, and each time I woke up I felt shaken. In the dream, I found myself back in America. Friends rushed over to see me. My family gushed with pleasure that I'd finally come home. My garden spontaneously bloomed with a dozen varieties of beautiful flowers. I couldn't tell anyone the truth: It was all a mistake. I wasn't supposed to be in the States. I was still supposed to be in Vietnam.

Somehow, and I never could figure out exactly how, I'd ended up back home *by accident.*

I always woke up relieved from that nightmare, grateful to hear the blaring noise of morning traffic and to see the dirty teacups and candy wrappers scattered across the glass coffee table by my bed. I had to lie there for a long time, thankful that I was still in Vietnam and that I hadn't even set a date to go home yet.

I was not hiding out in Hanoi, or afraid to go back to the States. Of course, there were things back home I didn't like. It was tiring, hustling for writing assignments from editors who didn't care if I wrote for them or not. But life there did have attractions. I had good friends in San Francisco and no language problems in communicating with them. Despite the aggravations of the career, I liked being a journalist—more, surely, than I liked teaching English in Hanoi. I missed my family. The noodle soup and rice I ate almost every day in Vietnam had gotten very boring. Still, I loved Hanoi. Despite the nearly intolerable summer heat, the fatigue I felt bargaining for every tomato, I was as consistently happy as I'd ever been in my life. I got an extraordinary sense of satisfaction out of simply managing to survive here. I didn't take a single thing for granted about being an American living in Vietnam: not the fact that the Vietnamese government had been willing to grant me a long-term visa to study here, not the fact that I could have a friendly conversation with a man who'd had his leg shot off by my countrymen, not the fact that I could fall in love with a man who had grown up being taught that I was the enemy.

Still, I knew I'd leave, and soon. While I remained in my third-floor bedroom, riding a wobbly borrowed bike and working at a low-paying job teaching English, other Americans I knew with no more skills than I had found lucrative permanent positions with international organizations. They rented apartments with kitchens and invested in powerful motorbikes. They were willing to settle down here, while I couldn't move beyond the early bloom of romance. On some level, I considered Vietnam, and my happiness there, a luxury that, if I stayed too long, I'd use up. I kept my life in Vietnam slightly temporary and considered it a sojourn that I'd eventually leave behind. Vietnam was the dream, I knew, not the States.

One morning late in August, my mother called from Memphis.

"When are you coming home?" she asked. The question caught me unprepared. Mom had never questioned my decision to come to Hanoi. In fact, she was so proud of me that she had developed a devious tendency, when speaking with friends, to drop apparently offhanded comments about her daughter living in Vietnam. While I was in Hanoi, most of our communication was through letters. Phone calls were harder. We'd speak for five or ten minutes, but neither of us enjoyed those conversations. She always seemed distracted during these trans-Pacific calls, as if half of her brain were occupied with the knowledge of how much money the call would cost.

This morning, her voice sounded not distracted, but sad. "I just think you've been away long enough," she said.

I closed my eyes. "It's hard," I said.

"Every month you say, 'Next month,'" she told me. "We miss you."

I could see my mother's face, my house, the dry heat of a San Francisco autumn. It would be liberating to walk down a city street unnoticed, to buy food that had a price tag on it, to feel absolutely comfortable in the language being spoken all around me. Getting back to real life might not be such a bad thing. "I'll come back in early September," I told my mother, surprising even myself with the certainty of the statement. "I'll be home for my birthday."

I set the phone down and looked around my beloved room, not quite sure how I'd happened to make a commitment, so suddenly, to leave it. I felt a little shaken, but also relieved. My birthday was only a month away, and I didn't want to turn thirty here. It would be impossible to exaggerate the number of times every day I was asked how old I was. As a foreigner who could speak Vietnamese, I was always getting into conversations with strangers, and they were always asking me my age. Partly, they needed to know what to call me—"older sister," "younger sister," "aunt," "niece." But they were also nosy. The most important single bit of information they seemed to learn from me was that an American woman could be twenty-nine years old and not married yet.

My approaching birthday loomed large in my consciousness. I imagined everyone I knew nagging me with their conviction that I was avoiding my destiny, that I needed to settle down. I was tired of defending myself, tired of asserting that I still valued my independence and freedom.

That afternoon, I pulled my plane ticket out of the back of a drawer, rode my bike over to the airline office, and set the date of my departure. I gave myself two weeks.

My other reason for leaving Vietnam was Phai. And the two were, of course, related. If I was going to marry, then, surely, the man I should marry would be him. But I couldn't see it. In the two months since we'd first become intimate, I hadn't fallen out of love, but I'd become increasingly sure that I couldn't spend my life with him. Differences of language and culture had always existed as a gap between us, but they'd once been part of the attraction as well. Ironically, as I got to know him better, as we communicated ever more easily, the factors that divided us became more overwhelming.

I had hit what linguists refer to as a "plateau" in my language acquisition, a brick wall, a point at which a language learner perfects old skills rather than obtaining new ones. I now felt extremely comfortable speaking simple Vietnamese, but, over the last few weeks, my vocabulary had started to frustrate me. I had to characterize everything in life, it seemed, as "interesting," "sad," "happy," "difficult," "complicated," or "*vui.*"

Huong had no qualms about teasing me when I forgot a word she'd taught me. She considered me ignorant, and perhaps a little bit slow, because I still couldn't communicate at a more expert level. Sometimes, in the midst of a serious conversation, she'd simply give up, shrug her shoulders, and, looking at me as if I were a seven-year-old, say, "It's just too complicated for you to understand." Huong's intelligence seemed boundless to me.

Phai, on the other hand, was kinder. Whenever I happened to come out with a new word, he would clap his hands and shower me with kisses. At the same time, he limited his own conversation to the capacities of mine, speaking so simply that I never had trouble understanding how "complicated" opening a bike rental business might be, how "sad" he was after his mother sold the family pig, or how "happy" he felt whenever the two of us were together. After a while, I became as impatient with him as I was with myself. Phai started to strike me as annoyingly simple.

The conversation we had after I'd set the date for my departure didn't help. Phai was sitting on my bed that night, watching me wander around the room, getting my things together before we went to Linh's house for dinner. I sat down beside him and picked up his hand. "I'm going home soon," I told him. "In two weeks."

The expression on Phai's face shifted, but only briefly, like the shadow of a cloud passing over, then moving on. "Well, it's good," he responded. "Your family needs you."

During dinner, Phai seemed as relaxed and content as ever, but when we got back to my room, he sat down on the bed and put his face in his hands. After being so "happy" with me, he now felt "sad" that I was leaving and he knew that his feelings would become even more "complicated" once I was gone. I sat down next to him and ran my fingers through his hair, explaining that I, too, would be "sad" to say good-bye, especially because he made me so "happy," but my reasons for leaving were "complicated," and so I hoped that he could understand. Of course, both of us were more distraught and confused than our words could express.

There was one thing I couldn't have told Phai, even if I had actually had the words to say it. Over the course of the past month, I had come to realize that, as much as I loved him, that love had bloomed, in part, because I had wanted a human object of my passion for Vietnam. I couldn't tell how much of my love was for Phai himself and how much was for this place he came from. Sometimes, when the two of us were together, I'd look into his eyes and try to separate my love for him from my sense of his country. Maybe Phai had similar trouble distinguishing me from America, but I couldn't know for sure. I never asked.

Leaving Vietnam seemed the simplest and least painful way out of this relationship. Let distance separate us, I thought. Let us miss each other across the span of the ocean, not across the streets of Hanoi.

• • •

In a practical sense, I had very few responsibilities in Hanoi, and it wasn't hard for me to extricate myself from any of them. None of my jobs demanded long-term commitments. My teacher and I planned my lessons week by week. All I had to do, really, was pack up and go.

Emotionally, of course, my situation was much more complicated. I knew that the more time I had to say good-bye, the harder it would be to do it. Two weeks was plenty of time to say good-bye to everyone. Except for Tung.

He was in still in jail. According to Huong, the authorities were holding him in some nondescript building behind a district police station on the other side of town. He shared a cell with two other men, and though he'd grown pale from lack of sunlight, he was otherwise still healthy. We knew these things because Huong was finally allowed to visit him once a week. Every Sunday, she filled plastic bags with bunches of rambutan fruit, a kilo of fresh *phở* noodles, packages of pork pâté, and several loaves of bread, then hung the bags on the handlebar of the Dream and drove off to the jail. She always came back late in the afternoon, tired but no sadder looking than when she had left. Now that she was running the household, raising her son, managing a guesthouse, and trying to get her husband out of jail, she didn't have time for extraneous emotions.

Tung's punishment seemed extreme. The police must have realized pretty quickly that Tung didn't know anything about the Chinese women's fake passports, but they continued to hold him nonetheless. The Vietnamese authorities, so wary of China, must have decided that Mr. Huey's colleagues were spies (and, judging from their association with Mr. Huey, they may well have been). Keeping Tung in jail would punish him for his involvement. Secondly, Tung had never been a stickler for following regulations, especially if he could save a little money by ignoring them. In his dealings with Mr. Huey, he'd probably bent the rules a little bit. The authorities wanted to demonstrate that nothing got past them. Still, Tung could have learned that lesson in a single night. The police didn't need to hold him indefinitely. These days, I could barely ride past a cop without stifling an impulse to spit at him.

But neither Huong, nor anyone in their family, showed any anger at all. Everyone treated Tung's incarceration as one more setback, like an illness, or a war, to be endured. One evening, when I asked Huong if she felt bitter about what had happened to her husband, she merely shook her head. "*Bình thường,*" she told me. This is normal. A volcano had erupted, and Tung, unfortunately, had gotten stuck in the path. His destiny, lately, just wasn't so great.

The weeks had dragged on. As time passed, we grew less and less optimistic about when he'd come home. The date of my departure, however, was fast approaching. I was becoming concerned that I would have to leave Vietnam without saying good-bye to him. About five days before I was scheduled to go, Huong had an idea. She would ask Tung's captors if she could bring me by the jail so that we could say good-bye to each other. When she left for her visit that morning, she gave me one of her rare smiles. "I think it will be okay," she said.

I was sitting in the living room with Nga when Huong pulled up on the motorbike late that afternoon. She remained on the bike for a moment, pulling off her sunglasses and putting them back in her purse. Then she looked up. As soon as she saw me walking toward her, she shook her head. "They said no?" I asked.

Huong got off the bike and pulled her purse out of the front basket. "They didn't even say no," she said. "They didn't take the question seriously enough to say no. They just laughed."

We walked inside. Nga had a glass of cold water waiting to offer her sister. Huong sat down on the couch, took a sip of water, then used the bottom of her shirt to wipe the sweat off her forehead. "Tung told me to tell you good-bye," she said, looking up at me. "He said that you should be careful and make sure to stay healthy. He'll miss you, so you have to come back soon."

I couldn't think of anything to say that could make him as happy as his message made me. "Tell Tung," I said, finally, "that as soon as he gets out of there, I'm going to send him a pair of Levi's."

I had been in Vietnam for six months, but in only a few hours my bags were packed and I was ready to leave. I'd like to be able to say that the speed had something to do with my own innate efficiency, or a desire to restrain myself from accumulating too many possessions. In fact, I planned to travel home with three times as much luggage as I'd brought to Hanoi. For one thing, as soon as I'd decided to go, I had to take whatever I could of Vietnam home with me, and so I began a mad rush for souvenirs. I'd bought every style of bowl, silk scarf, lacquer box, and tablecloth that the city had to offer. I became even more weighed down because of the Vietnamese tradition of offering good-bye gifts. During my last few days in Hanoi, I received, among other things, a large ceramic tea set from Huong, a kilo of jasmine tea from Nga, ten pairs of Chinese underpants (decorated with turtles and rabbits) from Linh, a hefty Vietnamese-English dictionary from my teacher, and an extremely fragile, foot-long handmade scale model of a wooden sailboat from one of my students, a mechanical engineer I called Frank. No one took into consideration the problem of how I would get their precious gifts back to the States, least of all Frank, who arrived at my house the evening before I left and handed me the sailboat as if it were something I could stick in my pocket.

The reason that my luggage got packed so efficiently was that I didn't pack it myself. Huong and Phai only had to see the way I sat in my room, panic-stricken, staring at the mountain of my belongings, before they grabbed the bags and some rope and shooed me off to the side. Within an hour, the job was finished. Somehow, they even managed to find room for the boat.

The night before I left, Phai showed up at my room holding a package. It was conical, thicker on the bottom and narrowing toward the top, and about the size of a small chicken. "This is for you," he said, holding it out to me.

I looked at him, suddenly feeling shy, but he pushed the package into my hands. It was heavy, tightly wrapped in newspaper and tied with twine. "Open it," he urged.

I sat down on the bed and lay the package on my lap. It took me a while to untie the twine and get my fingers beneath the paper, which was heavily taped. Then, with a little maneuvering, I was able to tear a small section of paper away from the bottom of the thing. Inside, I could see the ruffled edge of a dark metal surface. I looked up at Phai. "This is bronze," I said. "You made it."

Phai smiled and his face looked so proud and sad and beautiful that I had to stop what I was doing and hold my hand against his cheek. He pulled my hand down and held it, then looked back at the package on my lap. "Go ahead," he said. "Look at it."

It was a Buddha, sitting in lotus position, with its hands resting gently on its legs and its face looking straight ahead, as if gazing toward the truth and the future. The color of the

bronze was deep and rich, traced with hints of gold, like something alive, and old, and changing. It was so beautiful that nothing I could say seemed good enough, and so I sat there staring at
it, saying nothing.

"You're going to miss the pagodas, when you get back over
there," Phai said. "Now, even in California, you'll have a place to
pray."

I'd been shopping like a crazy person, collecting as much as
I could in hopes that, months from now, these objects would
help me remember my life in Vietnam. But Phai's little Buddha
was really all I needed.

The next morning, Phai woke up early and was
standing, wet from the shower, when I opened my eyes. I lay
there, staring at him, trying to remember if I'd ever, even once,
seen him sleep. "You've got to leave soon," I whispered. "I can't
bear it if you don't."

For a few minutes, we sat next to each other on the bed,
staring out at my mass of luggage. I could see the soft bulge of
the wooden boat at the top of one of my bags. My backpack sat
next to it, still open, with Huong's ceramic tea set well wrapped
and gently nudged into a corner of it. The Buddha, back in its
newspaper and twine, was at the bottom of my carry-on.

I turned and looked at Phai, wanting to memorize his face,
but it was so full of pain that I had to turn away again. The fact that
I was leaving hadn't, I realized, registered for me yet, and I found
myself wiping the tears from his eyes and telling him not to be sad.
Phai stood up. "I love you," he said, as he pulled me toward him. I
prepared to touch my lips to his. But the kiss he gave me wasn't the
kind of kiss I knew. His face came close to mine, his fingers slid
into my hair, and then he inhaled, very deeply, as if memorizing

my scent. He moved across my face, behind my ears, through my hair and over my neck, breathing in all of me in quick, short gasps. Then, suddenly, he pulled back, gazed into my eyes one more time, then let go of me and walked toward the door.

"I love you," I said, and Phai turned around and smiled at me one more time, then he opened the door and disappeared behind it.

I ran out to the balcony and stood for a long time, watching for a sign of him. But the sidewalk was empty except for two guys lackadaisically washing a motorbike. Grandmother Nhi sat at her empty tea stall, watching the traffic pass.

Huong and Linh had both offered to come with me to the airport, but they rode in cars so rarely that the experience nauseated them. I'd seen it happen. They threw up discreetly, rolling down the window and quietly thrusting their heads outside, then, afterwards, pulling themselves back in and using a handkerchief to wipe their faces, which were pale and trembling and beaded with sweat. I didn't want to put them through that. Tra's sister, Hoa, had volunteered to come along. She'd lived in Europe, so she was used to cars.

Huong and I stood on the steps in front of the house. Little Viet was standing beside us, leaning against his mother and hanging on to my hand as if I were a balloon he didn't want to fly away. Huong held my other hand, gently squeezing it. "Write," she said, biting her lip.

"You write, too," I told her.

She giggled, wringing my hand with both of hers. "You know me," she said. "I'm lazy." Her eyes were bright and sad, and looking into them I felt a sharp pain in my throat. I quickly leaned over and gave her a kiss on the cheek, then kissed Viet.

"Good-bye," I said.

Huong shook her head. "Don't say 'good-bye,'" she told me. Say, 'See you again.'"

I smiled. "See you again." As we pulled away from the curb, Huong stood watching us from the doorway, one arm folded against her chest, the other hand waving listlessly. I turned around in the seat and watched her through the back window as we drove up Dream Street.

The car headed north and west through the city, past the Ho Chi Minh mausoleum and then past Truc Bach Lake. We circled the perimeter of the West Lake, driving past the new-money villas, the farms that produced the city's flowers, and the restaurants that specialized in dog meat cuisine. We headed out of the city across the new Thang Long Bridge. In the countryside, the view beyond the window was little more than rice fields, scattered brick kilns, and women trudging down the road, leading water buffalo on long ropes behind them. The scene looked so normal to me now.

The bright summer sun beat down upon the green rice, infusing it with a yellow light. The fields were so beautiful that I couldn't blink, couldn't do anything but stare at them. I wanted to make the whole thing stop, to turn around and be back in my room on Dream Street, with Phai. Leaving had seemed the right thing to do, the practical way to get on with my life, to let Phai get on with his. But, still, leaving Vietnam felt like deliberately wrenching my arm out of its socket. I wanted leaving to be a dream from which I would simply wake up. But I'd started the thing and I couldn't turn back.

A large Vietnamese family took up an entire corner of the departure lounge. In contrast to the dozens of for-

eigners and ten or twelve Vietnamese businesspeople on this
flight, these people looked like farmers, hardly the sort one
would expect to find preparing to jet off to Bangkok. I watched
them for a while, then walked over and squatted down beside the
oldest person among them, an ancient woman with lacquer-
stained black teeth, black trousers, and a scarf wrapped around
her head. She looked like any Vietnamese tea-stall lady. "Where
are you going, Grandmother?" I asked.

She smiled, surprised that she could understand what I said.
"We're emigrating to London," she answered. "I've got a son
there."

It took a while for me to tell her how old I was, that I wasn't
married yet, and that I'd been living in Hanoi, studying Vietnamese and teaching English. While I answered her questions,
she listened carefully, nodding as I spoke. Then, when I'd finished, a look of worry crossed her face. "Miss, can you tell me
something?" she asked. "Do you think we'll like London?"

I thought of the London I knew, the rows and rows of flats,
crowded subways, pubs, closed doors. I hadn't been there for
years, but I was sure of one thing about the place. This old
woman wouldn't spend her days there in the manner of so many
Hanoi retirees, sitting on her doorstep and chatting with her
neighbors. At her age, she'd probably never learn English. And,
even surrounded by family, she'd be lonely. I thought of the millions of Vietnamese living in diaspora, growing old far from
home. It seemed a tragedy to spend one's life in exile, but it was
perhaps a greater tragedy, still, to die there.

She was looking at me expectantly, waiting for an answer.
"London's a beautiful city," I finally said. "Your family is there, so
I think you'll be happy."

The agent announced that my row was boarding, so I said
good-bye to the old woman and got in line. Outside the window,

I could just make out the smooth tail of the jet and, beyond that, the desolate tarmac of an airport that didn't see more than a dozen planes a day. Just past the tarmac, the rice fields began, stretching toward Ba Vi Mountain.

I was already in my seat when I saw the old grandmother standing at the head of the aisle, scanning the rows of seats in front of her, her eyes squinting in confusion. A flight attendant approached her from behind and pointed down the aisle toward some point beyond where I was sitting. The old woman nodded and hurried forward. Just as she was about to walk by my seat, she noticed me. She grabbed my hand, gave it a quick squeeze, and then disappeared down the aisle.

11 Shifting Positions

I DIDN'T LAST A YEAR AWAY from Vietnam. In fact, I'd only been in the States for two months when I began to think about going back again. I felt like someone who'd spent a huge amount of energy learning how to plant a garden, then abandoned the project just after I'd gotten the soil ready for planting. I'd never settled down there and now, back in the States, I couldn't settle back into my old life, either. Though I'd returned to my house in San Francisco and started working as a journalist again, I was distracted. My friends kept asking me about my "trip," but my time in Vietnam hadn't felt like a trip, even though I'd never allowed it to be real life, either. I had a sense that I was floating through my life, baffled over where to land. On the night before my birthday, I went to my sister's house, looking for some company, then proceeded to break down in tears before she even had a chance to open the door. Even if I was thirty, over the hill, and destined to be pestered about it, I wanted to be in Hanoi again. I'd left Hanoi in early September of 1992. By July of 1993, I was back.

No one met me at the airport. Last time, I'd taken a public

bus that dropped me off at the city center, and then a cyclo to Tra's house, proving to myself that I could handle it. Today, I could have hitchhiked into the city on the back of a motorbike if I'd set my mind to it. But why bother? For a couple of dollars, a tourist minivan would take me to my front door.

I climbed into the front seat of the minivan, beside the driver. A couple of German tourists hauled their backpacks into the rear seats and we drove away. It was mid-July and the air was a thick soup. At least that hadn't changed. I'd been afraid that something would happen to Hanoi that would make it either incomprehensible or unappealing to me now. Maybe I'd find a skyscraper in the spot where my favorite noodle shop used to be. Maybe too many cars would clog the roads and I'd find myself terrified, all over again, to ride a bike. Maybe, now that Vietnam had become the tourist destination of choice among wealthy Europeans, my white face would attract hordes of vendors and children hoping to sell me postcards. Maybe I simply wouldn't like it here anymore. Outside the dirty windows of the van, though, Vietnam looked pretty much the same. The just-planted rice fields lay baking in the midsummer sun. Young men drove by too fast on their Hondas. Ramshackle roadside restaurants advertised their menus with hand-painted signs. Vietnam looked familiar, like a friend who hadn't changed much.

I'd wanted to use this ride into the city to acclimate myself to being back. I needed time to focus on the sight of children playing flip-flop toss in their dusty front yards, on the men hauling baskets of live chicks on the backs of their bikes, on the musical cadences of Vietnamese, which was now blaring out of the tinny minivan radio. When I'd spoken to Huong on the phone from the States, I told her I didn't know when my plane would arrive. "Sometime in the afternoon," I'd said vaguely.

Arriving back in Vietnam was overwhelming enough, but I

felt very nervous about seeing Phai. When, a few weeks after I first returned to the States, I opened my mailbox and found a letter from him, I had stood for a long time, trembling, marveling over the fact that I was holding in my hand something he had so recently touched. It had seemed magical then, a rare jewel my letter carrier had not even known she was delivering. Phai and I wrote to each other regularly after that. We even had a few teary conversations on the phone.

Week by week, though, I became increasingly convinced that our relationship was impossible. One night, not long after I'd returned from Vietnam, I went to a party full of journalists. As I wandered through the rooms, sipping wine, eating peanuts, and trying to remember how to schmooze, I imagined what it would have been like if Phai had been at this party with me. While I chatted with a friend about the difficulty of sending stories by modem from Asia, I pictured him sitting alone on the couch across the room, making an effort to smile every time I glanced in his direction. Later, he would follow me into the kitchen and stand at my elbow while I listened to a litany of complaints about a magazine editor who didn't return phone calls. Phai wouldn't have understood a word of it. Even if the conversation had been in Vietnamese, he would not have understood much more. He was not an intellectual, or even a professional in the "white collar" sense of the word. The San Francisco journalists would regard him as one more curious souvenir I'd brought back from Asia. Phai would sit on the couch, studying the gestures, the way people laughed, as if partygoing in America were a test and he was destined to fail it. The thought of him in that context made me feel sorry for him in a way I didn't want to feel. That night, driving home, I felt something like relief—relief that he had not been at that party with me, relief that he was still in Vietnam.

Writing letters to Phai, and reading his letters, came to mean a tiresome afternoon with the dictionary. My Vietnamese grew labored, and I couldn't remember how to spell. And it wasn't just that my language skills had deteriorated. The simplest details of life didn't translate. Normal activities like "I drove out to Berkeley to see the house my friends just bought" or "My dad's flying in for the weekend" or "We ordered out for pizza" required paragraphs of explanation that I was too lazy to provide. Just as our conversations in Hanoi had become dull from the gaps in our ability to express ourselves, so, too, my letters grew generic and vague. "I'm seeing my friends and family often," I would write. "It's very *vui* here." At the same time, my feelings for Phai were growing generic and vague as well. To write "I miss you" or "I love you" required conjuring a feeling that would only last the time it took to write it down. These feelings could be vivid and intense, but I caught them like beautiful, slippery fish. Within moments, they wriggled free and disappeared.

As the months passed, I still held Phai's letters for long moments before opening them, but it was no longer to savor the fact that his fingers had touched them. Now, I needed time to make him real again, to connect the writing on the page to the photograph on my desk and then, with more difficulty, to the actual person back in Hanoi. Sometimes, I couldn't even conjure his face, and I had to let the return address invoke an image of that house by the Red River, of that courtyard where a young man would someday partition off a private room for himself and a wife. With an uncomfortable sense of having escaped, I opened Phai's letters and conscientiously read descriptions of the struggling bicycle-rental business, the nasty weather, his love for me. I was always aware of the care he had taken to write, using a clear script and simple vocabulary to make sure I could understand every word. But after a while, I stopped bothering to keep a dictionary next to me. I grew impatient to finish. If I didn't know a word or two, I'd guess.

Meanwhile, my friends had never understood what had drawn me to Phai to begin with. Then, as those feelings began to wane, to admit the change seemed to mean admitting that he had never meant much from the start. Even my closest friends saw him as little more than the sum of the adjectives I'd used to describe him: gentle, poor, loving, beautiful, uneducated, agile, dark, thin, a genius with a roll of duct tape or a wrench.

All of this change in my feelings for Phai caused me to reevaluate my life in Hanoi. During the time when I had fallen in love with him, I sometimes wondered if my happiness there had more to do with him or the city. Those long afternoons in the living room with Huong seemed mostly focused around the possibility of catching a glimpse of Phai. I'd come to think that maybe I was faking it, acting like I really cared about bike rides across the city or conversations with Huong when I was actually just structuring my life around opportunities to see him. But now, it was the thought of those bike rides, those placid afternoons with Huong—and not the prospect of seeing Phai—that made me desperate to return. The thing I missed most about Vietnam was not the man I'd loved there, but the life I'd lived.

Some things, of course, had changed. The Vietnamese authorities had finally released Tung from jail about six weeks after I went back to the States, three months after they arrested him. I'd spoken to him on the phone a couple of times from San Francisco, but hadn't been able to get much out of him. I knew that the family was still grappling with Mr. Huey's $5,000 phone bill, but Tung didn't want to discuss such things. He was more interested in telling me that Hugo had moved to Thailand and that they'd found a new tenant, an Australian named Max who loved to drink beer. Huong was a bit more forthcoming about the effects of Tung's incarceration, but she was uncharacteristically positive, assuring me that her husband was exactly the same, only thinner. It sounded, surprisingly, like things had returned to normal, and I felt relieved, not just for their family, but also for myself. I didn't just want my old room; I wanted my old life back. When I heard that Max the Australian had gone home to Sydney, I was pleased. My old life did not include another native English speaker living in the house.

The minivan crossed the Thang Long Bridge, and within a few minutes Hanoi surrounded us. Until now, we'd sped at a fairly brisk pace through rice fields and small suburban centers, but once we entered the more congested web of city streets, we stopped moving altogether. Trapped in a line of cars and trucks, we became as immobile as the shops and houses along the road. Bikes and motorbikes squeezed past us without stopping. We were stuck.

The cool air coming through the vents smelled dank and metallic, but when I tried to roll down a window, the driver motioned for me to stop. I glanced at his wristwatch. I'd been in Vietnam for two and a half hours, one of which I'd spent standing in a line with my passport and one of which I'd spent sitting in this minivan, failing to get home. On the street, a woman stepped out of her house, squatted in front of a meat vendor, picked through the slabs of flesh, bargained energetically, and carried her purchase back inside, all before we managed to move another inch down the road.

I leaned back against the seat of the van and listened to the guttural conversation of the Germans in the backseat. Though I couldn't understand what they were saying, I caught the familiar sounds of "Green Bamboo," "Especen," and "Darling Café," Hanoi's most well known hubs for low-budget travelers. For a moment, I felt envious. How easy it would be to rent a room in

one of those places, hang a camera around my neck, and wander
through the city anonymously. There would be nothing awkward
in that.

The minivan began to move again, then stop, then start.
After another fifteen minutes, we turned down Dream Street
and approached my house, which was no longer the tallest on the
block. Now, I couldn't even see the strange nautical trellis that
had seemed so noteworthy a year and a half before.

The muscles in my stomach tightened. Out in front of my
house, wearing a pale yellow shirt and crisp white pants, was
Phai, pacing back and forth.

~~~~~   Our hug lasted a quarter of a second before I
pulled away and let my hand drop from his clenched fingers. He
looked exactly the same. His hair was short on the sides and long
on top, a cut that had been stylish even before he had the clothes
to match. His body was lithe, his skin smooth and coppery, his
smile warm, his eyes wide, his expression unprotected.

He looked the same, but I felt different. I hadn't known for
sure how I would react to seeing him again. Perhaps all my love
for him would wash back over me as soon as I saw him. Perhaps
I'd feel confused about my feelings. But I was startled by the certainty of the emotions that flooded over me. I felt no joy, or desire, only a conviction that I didn't want Phai now. And shame
because of it.

"How are you?" I asked in Vietnamese, busying myself with
my pile of suitcases.

"Fine!" Phai answered in English. His laugh was loud and
somewhat hysterical. He grabbed the biggest bags and hauled
them into the house.

"How did you know when I would be arriving?" I yelled after

him, in Vietnamese. I picked up my smaller bags and followed him into the house.

"I wait," he said. "Ten o'clock morning, I here." He set my suitcases by the staircase and sat down on the couch, motioning for me to sit down beside him.

I sat down on a chair on the other side of the coffee table.

"Where are Tung and Huong?" I asked.

"Shopping!" he said, breaking the syllables into two distinct words—Shah-ping!

I smiled at him, then laughed, then smiled again. I couldn't speak. I was too dazed, in some way that I always am, to have moved, in less than two days, from my apartment in California to this living room in Hanoi. I wondered what Phai thought of my amazing ability to transport myself around the world, then back again. Phai had never traveled beyond Vietnam, though, and during this past year, he may never have imagined me in California. Maybe he thought of me only in Hanoi. Here. Then gone. Now, here again.

Phai reached down and unscrewed the hot water thermos that was sitting on the floor. He lifted it, pouring water into the teapot on the coffee table.

"I like your shirt," I told him.

Phai looked up at me and laughed. "Thank you, Duyen," he said. I'd given it to him the year before, for his twenty-ninth birthday. It had been the first birthday present he'd ever received. Like most Vietnamese, Phai and his family didn't follow the Western custom of celebrating birthdays, which demanded more disposable income than they ever had. To him, July 27 was just a date, a set of numbers that had no more effect on his life than the numbers on my Social Security card affected mine. But I had presented him with a pile of gifts when his birthday arrived. The sheer pleasure he got in receiving those presents had made me realize, more than ever, how few possessions he owned and how few gifts, for any occasion, anyone had ever given him. When he unwrapped that yellow shirt, he'd been so overcome that his embrace nearly toppled me.

More than a year later, the shirt still appeared brand new, although I had seen him wear it at least a dozen times myself. I pictured Phai, squatting in the courtyard of his house, washing that shirt with the kind of gentleness reserved for bathing infants. I could never treat an object with the reverence it would get from someone who had almost nothing else. Even the precious bronze Buddha had not enjoyed a pleasant transition to life in the States. When I first got back to San Francisco, I'd immediately set up a little altar for it. In front of the statue, I set a ceramic incense pot I'd carried back from Hanoi and filled, in Vietnamese tradition, with dry rice to hold the incense sticks upright. On one side of the Buddha, I'd placed a photograph of my mother's deceased parents, and on the other side one of my great uncle and aunt. For a while I had conscientiously lighted incense on the nights of the full and new moon. But in America, it gets hard to remember the phases of the moon. A month or so after I got back to San Francisco, my altar sat forgotten, and covered, not with a fine ash of incense, but with dust. I only noticed the moon, really, at those moments I happened to walk outside and glance at the sky.

Phai handed me a cup of tea. "How you mommy?" he asked.

I held the cup to my lips and took a sip, trying not to look at him. "She's fine," I answered. Following Vietnamese custom, Phai spent the next few minutes asking after every relative I'd ever mentioned to him, including all my siblings, my grandmother, and the housekeeper who had worked for my mother for twenty years. I couldn't even remember if Phai had one brother or two. "How's your family?" I asked.

"They fine." Phai's face wasn't as open and happy as it had been a few minutes before. He hadn't missed the fact that I was sitting across the room and that I was speaking to him as if he were a casual acquaintance. He was still smiling and chatting amiably, but his eyes had grown cloudy with hurt. Last month, I'd written him a careful letter, explaining that I still cared about him, but that I didn't want to marry him and therefore didn't think we should continue our romantic relationship when I got back to Hanoi. Phai had written back that he understood and he hadn't argued with my decision. Now, though, I could see that no matter what he'd said, he had still hoped. For the first time, I realized how big a mess I'd made.

I made a show of looking around the room. The house was exactly the same, except for a new wooden partition blocking off the loft space where Tung, Huong, and Viet slept. Then I noticed there weren't any dresses. "What happened to Nga's shop?" I asked.

Phai shrugged. "Closed," he said, then pointed out the doorway toward Dream Street. "The street's one-way now. Nga didn't get as many customers coming by as she did before."

I turned and looked outside. On the way here, I'd noticed that the driver had taken a circuitous route to my house, but so many things confused me in Vietnam that I hadn't bothered to figure that one out. Now I could see that all the motorbikes and trucks and cars were moving from right to left. Even when I was here a year before, the municipal authorities had been implementing changes to make traffic through Hanoi a bit less chaotic, and the shift on Dream Street had probably helped to make the busy intersection at the corner less of a nightmare. But I wondered if city planners considered the indirect consequences of these decisions, like the fact that they'd put one small dress shop out of business.

"That's sad," I said. My vocabulary in Vietnamese had shrunk badly. I glanced at Phai, but he was hardly listening. His eyes were on me, but his mind was somewhere else.

It would be hard to imagine a worse way to reunite than the way we chose, with me pulling back and Phai feeling hurt by it, with Phai speaking impossibly bad English and me having trouble remembering even the most basic Vietnamese. I looked around the room, up to the ceiling, out the door, back to the furniture, and down to my feet without once glancing at Phai. I longed for Tung and Huong to return home.

"Good see you, Duyen," he told me. "Happy very very."

Luckily, Phai and I had only been sitting in the living room for about fifteen minutes when Tung, Huong, and Viet finally drove up outside. Plastic shopping bags were dangling like pastel balloons from every handlebar and every hand. I leaped from my seat and rushed outside to meet them.

Phai had looked exactly the same, but everyone on the motorbike looked different. Little Viet had grown from a three-foot wild thing into a tall, skinny schoolkid with a sweet smile and a surprising eagerness to help carry several heavy suitcases up three flights of stairs. Huong was seven months pregnant, and, though I'd known about it, I'd had a hard time picturing her until she dislodged herself from the motorbike and tottered toward me, her full-moon belly pressing against the thin fabric of a summer shirt. Tung was altered as well, but not in ways I might have expected. Wearing the Levi's I'd sent him and a freshly pressed button-down shirt, he looked more like a slick, self-confident businessman than ever.

As soon as the motorbike pulled to a stop, I did what Americans do, rushing outside and hugging every one of them. Viet squirmed a bit, but didn't run away. Tung looked embarrassed but pleased. Huong dragged me by the hand into the house, forced me to sit down beside her on the couch, and then proceeded to examine me from head to toe.

I'd tried, I really had. On this trip, I'd packed a pair of nice trousers, which I could wear with a belt and either of a couple of pretty blouses. I had a dress and a few good wool sweaters to wear when the weather got cold. I'd brought jewelry and two different shades of lipstick. I didn't have any high heels, but I didn't only have sneakers, either. I even had new glasses, with smaller lenses this time.

Tung noticed the glasses first. "You don't look like an old grandmother anymore," he said with satisfaction.

Huong sat for a moment, still making her assessment. Finally, she said, "You're fatter," obviously impressed.

"Huong," Tung chided, "Americans don't like that."

"They hate that," said Phai, who was, like Tung, proud of his understanding of the Western psyche.

"No, really. I don't care," I argued, glancing in the mirror behind the couch. Maybe I did look fatter, I thought, despairing. Then, I turned toward Huong. "You look fatter, too," I said.

Huong's smile rippled into a laugh that sounded like a soft breeze. She squeezed my hand with both of hers. "I'm so happy you're back," she said, and I began to feel less anxious.

Over the next hour, I somehow managed to keep up my end of the conversation. Since leaving San Francisco, I'd hardly slept, and now the world around me seemed wobbly, as if I were looking out at it through a shimmer of heat. My Vietnamese felt thick and awkward in my mouth, like wet wads of cotton stuck between my cheeks and gums. In all the blur and nervousness of that afternoon, however, I was able to recognize one small miracle. They all were speaking rapidly to me in Vietnamese, and I had no difficulty understanding them.

Eventually, Huong ordered me to go upstairs to rest until she had finished preparing dinner. I tried to protest, but not very strenuously. As I got up and headed toward the stairs, Phai watched me uncertainly, as if he couldn't decide whether to follow me or not. He didn't.

Six people were crowded around the little coffee table in the living room. Each person held a bowl full of noodles in a rich broth of pork simmered with bamboo shoots. In addition to me, Phai, Tung, Huong, and Viet, there was a graduate student named Paula who was renting the room on the fourth floor. Paula, an American who'd been raised in Sweden, was tall and regal-looking, but her graying black T-shirt and ratty mustard-colored pants had the same worn-out quality that my clothes had developed after too many months of hand washing. Tung and Huong must have realized that I wasn't the only Westerner who had trouble maintaining a presentable wardrobe in Hanoi.

Even though she was obviously fatigued by the effort, Huong made the dinner herself. Sa had returned to the countryside. Her disappearance puzzled me. She'd always seemed so thrilled by the life of the city, and whenever she spoke to me about her village, she'd made it clear that she hadn't been happy there. Her mother had died and all her siblings had married and moved away. Her father drank too much and sometimes beat her. Sa had always viewed keeping house for Huong as an escape. When I brought the subject up with Huong, she just shook her head, unwilling to discuss it.

Tung pulled out his stash of Rémy Martin and held out a glass for me. "Rémy?" he asked, and the way he pronounced the word, "Ray-mee," reminded me of a night, long ago, when I'd gone out with my student John and some of his friends. They were a wealthy bunch, the kind of young people who wore expensive leather jackets and spent their Saturday nights dancing in discos or competing in dangerous motorbike races around Hoan Kiem Lake. One night, one of the women, a pretty young actress who had already made a name for herself in Vietnamese films, turned to me with a look of concern on her face. "What's the proper way to say it?" she'd needed to know, her expression so anxious that she might have been asking me to supply her with a vaccine for tuberculosis. "Is it Ray-mee Mar-tun or Ray-mee Mar-teen?" I hated to see the disappointment on her face when I'd told her, apologetically, that I didn't know the answer.

I looked at Tung and shook my head. I was so exhausted that alcohol might push me over the edge. He poured a glass for himself, one for Phai, and one for Paula. Then, after toasting to my return—One hundred percent! One hundred percent!—he told me he was planning to open a beer pub with Max, the Australian who had been living in my room. The two of them had found a nice spot across the street from Hanoi's cathedral, and they were going to turn it into the Kangaroo Pub. They'd already made T-shirts on which a kangaroo, decked out in tourist garb, stood waving a Vietnamese flag. As soon as Max returned from Sydney, they'd open for business.

I tried to push out of my mind thoughts of Tung's last foreign business partner, Mr. Huey. "Who's going to be the bartender?" I asked.

"G'day mate!" Tung beamed.

"G'day mate!" Huong, Phai, and even little Viet chimed in. They'd been practicing.

Sitting next to me, Paula was already plowing through a second bowl of noodles. "You're going to have to get some really good music," she said. Paula spoke Vietnamese so fluently that I could barely understand her. I told myself that her accent was off. But the truth was that her Vietnamese was better than mine had ever been. Now that I wasn't a major participant in it, the conversation raced along. After a while, I didn't even try to keep up.

"Duyen?" I must have fallen into a daze, because the voice startled me. I looked up at Phai. "Are you okay?" he asked.

His expression was so absolutely kind that I felt a sudden ache of love for him. "I'm fine," I said as brightly as I could.

Huong pulled my bowl from my hands and filled it with another mound of noodles and pork. "Eat or you'll get sick," she chided.

I held the steaming bowl close to my face, letting the pungent smell of pork and bamboo shoots float up to my nose. It was a fragrance that nothing in California could match.

Phai followed me upstairs after dinner, sat down next to me on the couch in my room, and took my hand. "So happy," he said in English.

The feeling of love for Phai had, like some fickle ghost, vanished as quickly as it had appeared. "Let's speak Vietnamese," I said, trying to figure out how to pull my hand from his.

"Thank you for coming back," Phai whispered. The expression of hurt I'd seen on his face this afternoon had shifted into something more steady and patient. He had waited ten months. He could wait longer.

I had once felt so confident in my love for Phai. Huong had warned me not to hurt him, and I'd hardly listened. I was convinced that I wasn't capable of hurting him. Now, less than a year after the last time I'd seen him, I looked at him and felt completely blank. Not only was I no longer in love with him, but I was having a hard time remembering why I had loved him to begin with. At other moments, when I didn't feel so besieged by guilt, I could have remembered, easily, how much delight and happiness I had gotten during those months that he and I had spent together. It had been easy to think that I had focused upon Phai all the love I felt for Vietnam, but, really, that was completely unfair to him. After all, I had met many men in Vietnam and he was the one with whom I fell in love. Phai had a soul that seemed richer, deeper, and more generous than the souls of other people.

Of course, I had idealized him, too, and there was no way that the real person could sustain an image of himself that was based, in many fundamental ways, on the fact that I just didn't know him very well. What I did know was that those qualities that made Phai seem so good were also ones that made him so vulnerable. I only had to look at the hope on his face. I felt a wave of nausea.

I dragged my hand out of Phai's and rubbed my eyes. Without looking at him again, I said quietly, "I am so tired. I have to go to sleep."

Phai stood up, ran his fingers across the top of my head, and said, "Sweet dreams, Duyen." It was the way he'd always said good night to me, as we lay together in that same dark room, hearing the sounds of the street sweepers brushing their brooms across the pavement down below. I gave a little wave of acknowledgement with my hand. I kept my eyes shut, listening to the soft sound of his footsteps cross the room and the click of the door as it opened, then shut, behind him. Only then did I look up.

❦   A young woman I knew named Yen had been
staying with Paula on the fourth floor. Early the next morning I
walked upstairs to say hello. Yen was a recent graduate in English
literature from Hanoi University. She spoke nearly perfect English and cultivated friendships with foreigners as if we were rare
flowers in her garden.

She was in trouble now. Several years earlier, she'd fallen in
love with an American graduate student named Nick, who had
been her teacher in Hanoi. Their love affair hadn't lasted long.
Nick returned to the States, and to his girlfriend there. Yen was
left in Vietnam with a broken heart. Then, a couple of years
later, just when Yen thought she'd finally gotten over him, Nick
returned to Vietnam. He asked her to translate the interviews
for a documentary he was making about contemporary Vietnamese writers. She agreed to do the job, but resolved to keep
her distance from him. He didn't let her. As soon as he saw her
again, he realized he'd been in love with her all along. He managed to wait twenty-four hours before asking her to marry him.
She waited a couple of more hours before she accepted.

It seemed like the happy, rather saccharine ending to a
bumpy romance, but then the Vietnamese government got involved. Nick didn't have permission to film anything in Vietnam, particularly not the country's politically controversial
writers. Mysterious men on motorbikes began following the
lovers around. Eventually, they were taken in for questioning,
which lasted days. Nick and his American colleagues on the film
were scared. Yen, who'd lived in Vietnam all her life and knew
the limits of her rights here, was terrified. As the only Vietnamese on the crew, she bore the brunt of the inquisition. After
a week of interrogations, Nick and his friends were expelled
from the country. Yen, of course, was not allowed to follow
them. It didn't make for a very promising engagement.

Yen was lying in bed with a Vietnamese translation of *Jane Eyre* on the pillow beside her. She was small, like Tra, but while Tra was muscular and energetic, Yen was round-faced and languid. When she saw me, she smiled like a screen heroine and weakly reached for my hand. She'd been hiding out in Paula's room for two days already, too afraid that her parents would be implicated if she ventured home, too weepy to get out of bed.

"Nick called," she said quietly. "He told me he saw you."

I'd run into Nick, whom I already knew from mutual friends in the States, at the hotel I'd stayed at in Bangkok. It was not as amazing a coincidence as it might sound. As a cheap hotel with basic amenities, it was frequented by English-teacher types like me and Nick. Yen and I talked for a while about Nick's health, Nick's emotional state, Nick's desire to see Yen again. Hearing his name seemed to revive her, and after a while the color flowed back into her pale face and she managed to sit up in bed and eat a banana.

"The interrogations must have been terrible," I said.

Yen shrugged. Nick, a fair-skinned, cynical Jewish historian, had complained that their story sounded like the script of a bad movie. But Yen took these circumstances as the normal course of events.

"What did they ask you?" I wanted to know.

Yen put the banana peel on the bedside table, then lay back down in bed. "They asked me about all my friends," she said. "They wanted to know everything I know about foreigners."

I got up and poured her a glass of water from a bottle sitting on the bureau, then sat back down and handed it to her. "They asked me about you, too," she added.

I looked at her. Through my mind flashed those things that could make me suspicious: living in the home of a guy who'd been jailed, having a Vietnamese man spend the night. Nothing very exciting. Even during the days when Phai left my bedroom by way of my neighbors' roofs, I'd never been afraid that the Vietnamese government would really care about what I was doing. I couldn't have been a very interesting subject. But the ominous quality in Yen's voice made me nervous. "What did they want to know?" I asked.

Yen laughed and pinched my arm. "Don't worry. They love you," she said. "They think you're so nice because you teach the children English. They just can't understand why you fell in love with that low-class man."

~~~~~ I'd resolved, before I even returned to Hanoi, that I would not teach English again. I'd never been very good at it, and it didn't pay the bills anyway. My friend Steve worked at the English-language *Vietnam Investment Review,* and his paper needed someone to write a column for prospective foreign investors. The editor didn't seem to mind that I knew nothing about foreign investment, or business in general. All I had to do was pick a topic every week that focused on some aspect of investing money in Vietnam. I could start immediately.

The column promised to pay more money every week than my English teaching had brought in a month. After only a few days back in the city, I was already feeling flush. Then, a few days later, just as I was beginning work on my first column— "How to Find an Investment Partner"—Steve called again. He gave me the number of an American named Scott Stein who was looking for a writer. The job had something to do with condoms.

Scott Stein was the Vietnam director of RSI Worldwide, an American nonprofit organization that specialized in birth control and AIDS education. Using a standard Western-style marketing strategy, RSI had launched Rely, the first international-quality

condom to enter the Vietnamese market. RSI's preliminary marketing efforts had focused on brand-name recognition, and, so
far, had enjoyed resounding success. After decades of socialism,
Vietnamese were hardly overloaded with corporate insignia and
so, through extensive television and print ad campaigns, as well
as a blitz of freebie T-shirts, baseball caps, key chains, and balloons, RSI succeeded in making the Rely logo, a romantic sil-
houette of two birds soaring across a pale blue sky, almost as well
known among Vietnamese as the swirling white-on-red cursive
of Coke.

Scott Stein was becoming well known, too. Westerners in
Hanoi were always noticeable, and the ones who lived there
eventually grew rather famous. My upstairs neighbor Paula had
achieved near star status when a Hanoi newspaper referred to
her as the "European beauty queen." My friend Jack had so
wide a reputation around town that people who'd never even
met him swore he spoke the best Vietnamese of any foreigner
in the country. Six or eight months into his Vietnam tenure,
Scott Stein had become nearly as famous as the others. Scott
drove around town on a motorbike with racing stripes. Plastered on the back of his chili-pepper red helmet was a sticker
bearing the now-familiar sky blue and black Rely logo. Vietnam was hardly a country that discussed its sexuality openly
and, now that Scott Stein had begun to market his condoms all
over Vietnam, a linguistic switch had taken place. Just as Americans hear the word "Vietnam" and think of war, Vietnamese
now heard the otherwise incomprehensible English word "rely"
and thought "sex." Scott quickly became known as Mr. Sex
around Hanoi.

As it turned out, Mr. Sex was actually a dark-haired,
bearded Jewish guy from Boston (along with me, Nick, and
Steve from the newspaper, Scott added to the already significant

number of Jews in Hanoi and supported the conclusion among some Hanoians that about half the U.S. population was Jewish). I followed him into his private office, its white walls decorated with safe-sex posters from across the developing world.

The RSI operation, he explained, was bare-bones, employing a small network of regional salespeople, but its goals were extensive: to get the Rely insignia into the window, and the condoms into the inventory, of every pharmacy in the country.

Scott walked over to a set of cabinets in a corner of the room and bent down. A moment later, he stood up and deposited a Rely baseball cap on the table in front of me.

"This is for you," he said.

I picked up the cap and turned it over. There was a small pocket under the bill, and when I reached inside the pocket I pulled out a silver-wrapped Rely condom.

Scott smiled proudly. "*Túi cao su,*" he said, obviously delighted with the cap's design. "That's what the Vietnamese call condoms—rubber pockets." It was strange to hear Vietnamese mixed with the broad vowels of a Boston accent.

I nodded, trying to look impressed. I didn't mention that I already had experience with *túi cao su* in Vietnam.

"I've never been a great language learner," Scott continued. "I can ask for a bowl of soup, buy gas for my motorbike, bargain at the market. Other than that, I focus on the vocabulary related to my job. And that's sex. I learn all the slang."

Learning how to talk about sex in Vietnamese was a serious challenge. Linh was the only person I knew in Hanoi who would talk openly on the subject. Even Phai hadn't been willing to go into the nitty-gritty of slang with me. Getting a Vietnamese to teach you the words for sex seemed like convincing the CIA to tell you their secrets.

"Who teaches you all this stuff?" I asked.

Scott smiled like the kid with the most Halloween candy. He motioned with his head to the door. "Mostly people in the office."

I'd only seen two people on my brief swing through the front room of RSI Worldwide. Both were women. The receptionist couldn't have been older than twenty. The other one, who'd been talking on the phone at a desk in the back, was primly dressed and middle-aged. I must have looked skeptical, because Scott called over his shoulder, "Mrs. Tuyet!"

After a moment, the older woman poked her head through the doorway. A haze of hair had escaped from the bun behind her ears and formed a gray cloud around her head, giving her the harried look of an overworked bureaucrat. But her face was full of happy anticipation, as if the part of her job she most enjoyed lay in joking around with her boss. "Yes, Scott?" she asked.

"What was that new word I learned a few days ago, Mrs. Tuyet?" he asked.

It took Mrs. Tuyet a few seconds to catch her boss's reference, and then she broke into a smile. "Oh, Scott!" she scolded, pretending to be embarrassed. "Not now," and then she escaped into the other room.

Scott leaned back in his chair, pleased with the exchange. "Mrs. Tuyet doesn't really teach me the words," he admitted. "I just tease her about them. Mostly, the guys who work here teach me, but she always makes sure I pronounce them exactly right. Can't miss a tone, you know. You could screw up your delivery."

I was beginning to wonder about Mr. Sex. He was looking for someone to write the script for a documentary about AIDS for Vietnamese TV, which was the reason for my appointment today. So far, however, he seemed more focused on collecting obscenities. I had to wonder if he was as committed to his work.

"The miracle of Mrs. Tuyet is that she's not embarrassed about this stuff at all," Scott chuckled, lacing his hands across his stomach. Then, his tone became, for the first time, quite serious. "I need a relaxed attitude from my staff, you see. If they're going to work for me, they have to be comfortable with words like "dick," "cunt," "whore"—or whatever the equivalents are in Vietnamese. It's not like I'm distributing farm implements here. We're talking about sex, condoms, and AIDS. Obscenity comes with the territory. Mrs. Tuyet is a grandmother, for god's sake, but I can say whatever I want around her and she won't even blink. I tell her she was a sailor in an earlier life."

Scott leaned forward in his chair and dropped his voice. "Phuong, my secretary, is different. Her first month here, she blushed so much she looked like she'd had a bad day at the beach. Now, if I ask her to find me some information about sexual practices among gay men, she'll just nod and do it. Success! I had to change her."

Scott reached out and picked up the baseball cap. "You see," he said, tossing it in the air, "people have to be ready to do this work. Even the uglier stuff—and sometimes it gets pretty ugly—helps us understand how this society approaches sex. I've seen how people are dying of AIDS in Thailand. I don't want it to hit Vietnam like that. But it might. People here know about AIDS and condoms, but they're doing damn little to protect themselves. The Ministry of Health is giving us this TV time to get the message out. If you're up for the project, I'd like you to do it."

Of course I wanted to do it. As a writer, I'd never had a chance to affect people's lives as directly as this TV show could, potentially, affect the way Vietnamese thought about AIDS. After a few seconds of consideration, I began to nod. Scott's face broke into a wide grin, which didn't seem so silly anymore.

Phai's bicycle rental business had gone under. His attempts to learn the computer had given him a couple of skills, but no foreseeable prospects for the future. And the results of his English classes were all too obvious. I was annoyed. The money I had given him, which had once seemed like a simple gift of love, now felt like my half of a contract we'd made for him to get his life together. The only changes I saw were that his wardrobe seemed bigger.

Rather than discuss such matters with him, I avoided him. This wasn't easy, because he was always at my house, trying to be helpful. Did I want to borrow one of his bikes? He had plenty. Did I need a ride to the bank? He could borrow Tung's motorbike and give me a lift. Anxious to keep our contact to a minimum, I borrowed a bike from Tra's family, who, even though she remained in the States, were still my friends. I took to leaving the house as early in the morning as possible, just to avoid seeing Phai. The irony of the situation wasn't lost on me. After spending so many months trying to get close to Phai, now I was constructing my days around trying to stay away from him.

It seemed like a blessing that I just wasn't home that much. My life in Hanoi was very different from the way it had been the year before. For one thing, I was working a lot. I still spent a good deal of time with Tung and Huong and Linh, but I was hanging out with other people, too. Paula, an art historian, invited me to gallery openings and introduced me to painters. And, after a week or so of lying in bed, crying over her boyfriend Nick, Yen got up, went home to her parents, and began to go out again. She and I roamed the city together, discovering new cafés, eating foods I'd never tried, going to films and the theater. She had grown up amid the small circle of Hanoi intellectuals, and she introduced me to some of Vietnam's best writers and critics, whom she'd known since she was a child. At about the same time, my teacher, Professor Mai, decided that it was time for me to delve into something more provocative than the "Dick and Jane"–style readers he and I had been using for my lessons. We began to read contemporary literature and, eventually, to translate it. My sense of the country became more complicated, and richer.

I was away from the house a lot, but I couldn't avoid Phai forever. A few weeks after I returned to Hanoi, he cornered me. Paula and I had just returned from a gallery opening downtown, and Phai was sitting in the living room, alone. A cigarette dangled between his fingers. Neither of us had mentioned the fact that he'd started smoking again. Paula started up the stairs, but I stopped and sat down beside Phai. "Do you want to go out?" he asked.

I shook my head. "I'm tired," I told him.

Phai's eyes roamed across the room, as if he were trying to find something he'd lost. "Let's go out," he said again, and his words sounded so desperate that I agreed.

We walked up to Dien Bien Phu Street, then across to the statue of Lenin, where we sat down on a concrete platform just beneath his feet. Phai put his head in his hands and said nothing. I stared out at the plaza in front of the statue, where three boys on bikes were riding back and forth, chasing the shadows cast by the floodlights. It was after nine at night, but so hot that the sweat rolled in streams down my face even as I sat still.

Without looking up at me, Phai took my hand. His skin was warm and smooth against mine. "Please, Duyen," he said.

I left my hand in his, but I said nothing. "Duyen" wasn't my name. How had I fallen in love with someone who didn't even use my name? At that moment, the whole thing seemed impossible, like a freak accident that should never have happened.

"I love you," Phai said. His breath smelled of alcohol and his words came out slowly, as if he were pulling each syllable straight from his gut.

The air was so heavy that I could hardly breathe. Leaning over, I lifted the hem of my shirt and wiped my face. "I can't," I said, and the words sounded hard, definite, as if I didn't care.

Phai looked up and stared straight into my eyes. "You have a new boyfriend?" he asked.

I shook my head.

"You have a new boyfriend."

"I don't."

He was wringing my hand with both of his. The boys on their bikes started closing in on us. I stood up. "Let's go home," I said. Phai remained seated. His lips were trembling.

We slowly walked back to my house. The street was empty, and the only open doorway was the one at my house, half a block ahead. "Why?" Phai kept asking. "We love each other." I didn't answer. He raised the heel of his hand and smacked it against his head. The sound echoed down the deserted street.

I stood still. "Stop it," I said.

Phai smacked his head again. Then again. I turned and continued walking toward the house. "Duyen!" he screamed. I didn't look back.

Tung was sitting on the couch watching the television news and smoking a cigarette. "Something's wrong with him," I said, pointing out the door. Tung stood up and walked outside. Phai was standing in front of the concrete electric pole by our neighbor's front door, a pillar that, late at night, he and I used to stand behind when we kissed. Now he was banging his head against it. Tung walked over and took him by the shoulder. "You've got to go home," he said gently. "You drank too much."

Phai pulled himself away. He walked unsteadily up the sidewalk, then reeled around and walked back. Tung put his arm around him and spoke so quietly I couldn't hear. After a minute, Tung turned around and looked at me. "Go upstairs and go to sleep," he said. I stepped into the doorway. The last thing I saw was the two of them, huddled together, walking slowly up the street.

12 New Arrivals

I LOVED BEING IN VIETNAM as much as I ever had, but my relationship with the country wasn't delicate in the way it once had been. I wasn't worried that if I spent the day with another foreigner I'd somehow lose touch with the real Vietnam. Now, I no longer thought of my friends in terms of who was a foreigner and who was Vietnamese, and I didn't worry about coming across as the Ugly American. My nationality no longer defined my identity here. If I did something stupid, it wasn't because I was American. It was because I was stupid. And I found myself for the first time getting into arguments.

One night, I went with two new friends, Van and Duc, to see the French film *Indochine*. Van and Duc were talented painters I'd met through Steve. Their work would have fetched high prices had they chosen to pursue the increasingly hot market in Vietnamese art. But rather than schmoozing with potential patrons, they spent most of their time hanging out in Duc's studio, a stilt house on the edge of the West Lake, where they painted, drank whiskey, and pontificated about the state of the world.

The screening of the film, which was playing at the August Cinema in the center of town, was a big event for Hanoi. *Indochine,* a film about the Vietnamese revolt against French colonialism, was one of the first Western films to arrive as the country slowly opened its door to the outside world. Everyone wanted to see it, and not just the starstruck Hanoians who had managed to capture a glimpse of the star, Catherine Deneuve, while she was filming on location. Outside the theater, ticket scalpers proved they knew a thing about capitalism by rushing back and forth across the sidewalks and jumping in front of passing motorists in a frenzied effort to secure their sales. Inside the theater, nearly every seat was filled, and the audience had to strain to see through a fog of cigarette smoke and to hear through the grinding crunch of sunflower seeds. But unlike the bemused, rather bored reactions I'd witnessed at *The Tower of the Screaming Virgins,* the audience at *Indochine* was clearly captivated. It represented most Hanoians' first chance to see a Western film projected on the big screen, and people's reactions to the production quality must have been similar to the way American audiences responded in 1939, when Dorothy stepped out of her black and white farmhouse and walked into Technicolor Oz. "Đẹp. Đẹp," I heard people whisper all around me: Beautiful.

After the film ended, the three of us went to get something to eat. It was nearly eleven already, past bedtime for most of Hanoi, and my favorite noodle shop had long ago pulled its metal doors shut for the night. A few establishments were still open, serving noodle soup and rice porridge to tipsy men trying to sober up on their way home. We sat down at a table on the sidewalk in the middle of the block, right next to a sewage drain that ran along the side of the road. The proprietor, a mustached man wearing a Tiger Beer T-shirt, was sitting on a stool next to his charcoal cooker.

"What do you want to eat?" he grumbled.

Duc and Van ordered fish porridge. I asked for a *Bảy Up*— Vietnamese for 7 Up.

Both of my friends were still feeling dazzled by the movie. They were used to the grainy black and white or washed-out color that characterized Vietnamese cinema. In contrast, the French film's luscious palette and perfectly defined contrasts of light and dark left them breathless. They didn't like the movie, though.

"The French!" Van said, with a dismissive wave of his hand. "They don't know anything about the war. It's worse than that movie, I'll tell you." Van, who was my age, was a thin, often grouchy man whose delight in the world only became evident in his gentle, romantic paintings. In contrast, Duc, who was nearly forty, was lumbering and cheerful, with a quiet voice and a shag of bushy hair.

Van lit a cigarette. During the movie, he'd smoked his way through half a dozen 555s. "Westerners will see that film and think they understand Vietnam," he said. "It's like me saying, because I've seen a few videos, that life is easy in America, that it's just Walt Disney over there."

Duc and I laughed. The proprietor came over and plopped the rice porridge and *Bảy Up* down in the center of the table. Van hardly noticed the food. Duc immediately took his bowl and spoon and began stirring sprigs of fresh dill into the thick mass of porridge.

I pulled open my drink and took a sip of the warm soda. "It's true," I said. I knew that Van and Duc had both seen Hollywood war movies. "The only thing most Americans know about the Vietnam War is what they've seen in *Apocalypse Now* or *Platoon*."

Instead of laughing, Van looked irritated, as if he found America's myopia more disturbing than Vietnam's. "Americans don't know anything about war," he told me. "You haven't had a war in your country in over one hundred years. You're lucky! But still, whenever a single American dies in battle, you're furious. You lost fifty-eight thousand Americans in Vietnam. We lost two million Vietnamese. You bombed us. We never bombed you. But still, it was the United States, not Vietnam, who held a grudge."

In another situation, I would probably have agreed with Van. After all, at that time, the United States was still maintaining its vituperative trade embargo against Vietnam, keeping the struggling nation from fully recovering from the double economic disasters of the war and several decades of communism. But the antagonism in Van's voice made me defensive. Not bothering to hide my sarcasm, I answered, "Oh, right. The Vietnamese would never, ever hold a grudge."

We looked at each other for a long moment, each of us trying to decide how far to let this conversation go. Finally, Van pulled back a little. "It's just sad, that's all," he said, his tone only slightly less caustic. "All over the world, people know about American hamburgers, American blue jeans, American cars. These are good things. They help to build a strong country. We Vietnamese beat the Americans and what are we famous for? War! In this century alone we've fought the French, Japanese, Americans, Cambodians, and Chinese. If we didn't have to fight all those wars, maybe we'd be rich now. We'd be the ones visiting Walt Disneyland and making blue jeans."

Van pulled his bowl of porridge closer, as if to signal that he'd had enough of this conversation. After only a couple of spoonfuls, though, he looked up again. This time he had a grin on his face, and I could see that he'd thought of a way to move the conversation toward friendlier ground. He leaned forward and poked Duc in the arm. "Remember the Gulf War?" he asked.

Duc laughed. "Yeah," he said. He kept eating his porridge.

Van turned to me. "We Vietnamese appreciated the Gulf War. For once, there was this huge international conflict going on and we didn't have to fight in it. We just sat around like everybody else in the world, watching it on TV."

Loud voices behind us made us turn around. The proprietor, back on his stool by the charcoal cookers, was yelling at a newspaper boy, one of the hundreds of often homeless children who spent their days walking the city streets, selling papers, cheap magazines, and horoscopes. The "boy" was at least twenty, with a slightly deranged look on his face. He wasn't arguing as much as whining, but the angry proprietor suddenly jumped up and boxed his ear. The newspaper boy raised his hand to his head and howled.

"I'm bleeding," he screamed.

The proprietor sat back down, pulled out a rag, and began to wipe the table in front of him.

"My ear! I'm bleeding," the newspaper boy screamed again. I had a momentary worry that he would pull out a gun and shoot us all, but this was not America. He cried for a few more seconds, then turned and wandered off down the street, holding his hand to his ear.

Street fights took place so regularly here that spectators watched them like fireworks, focusing for the instant of the flare and then losing interest as soon as it faded. I had more trouble forgetting such incidents. An American could hardly complain about the violence in Vietnam—after all, violent crime was relatively rare here—but the easy acceptance of petty brutality always bothered me. I watched the newspaper boy, who was peering into the rearview mirror of a parked motorbike, checking for signs of blood.

"Let's go," I said.

As we got up to leave, Duc pulled a pack of chewing gum out of his pocket and handed sticks to me and Van. Van tore the wrapper off his gum and tossed the paper onto the asphalt of the road.

"What's wrong with you?" I snapped. "How can you pollute your country?"

Van turned and looked at me. "Americans," he said calmly. "You think you can tell us how to keep our country clean after you dropped napalm and Agent Orange on us?"

I was so angry and humiliated that I couldn't look at him. But I no longer felt the guilt I'd always experienced when I thought about the war in Vietnam, as if, just by being an American, I was responsible for what my country had done. I regretted the war more than I ever had, having seen how it affected this city and the lives of the people I'd come to know. But over the past eighteen months, my sense of this place had changed dramatically. I'd once thought of Vietnam with the same stereotypes that one would use to describe a battered woman: miserable, victimized, helpless. Now, I would have used an entirely different set of adjectives: tough, resilient, passionate. As much as Vietnam had suffered, it didn't need my guilt. It might need my help—normalizing relations was a good start—but what Van had said was true. The only thing Vietnam was famous for were the wars. I'd come to see the place as more complex than that. If I could go for weeks at a time in Hanoi without even remembering the wars, perhaps Americans could forge a different kind of relationship with Vietnam and move beyond the past.

So I didn't break down when Van mentioned the napalm, and I didn't apologize either. And that was a good thing, too, because when I looked over at him, I saw that he was grinning, waiting to see how I'd react. I looked at him for a moment. "I don't know," I said. "Napalm or a Wrigley's wrapper. It's not an easy call."

In what might have been the clearest sign that the war was truly over, a Vietnamese and an American discovered that it wasn't that hard, actually, to joke about it.

Something happens in the last few weeks of a woman's pregnancy. Just when it seems impossible that her belly can grow any larger, it does. She totters under all the weight, can't bend over, needs help simply to stand up. Her body becomes the object of public fascination. Strangers stop to stare, as if they think she'll go into labor at that very moment. In Vietnam, the whole neighborhood becomes expectant.

Huong reached that point at the end of September, after I'd been back in Hanoi for about two months. Moving around became so difficult that she spent most of her time in bed, lying on her side reading magazines, or propped up on pillows like a Buddha. Huong had never been an energetic person, so she didn't complain about her sedentary lifestyle. Aside from the discomforts of heartburn and the muscle strains associated with carrying forty extra pounds, she seemed perfectly content. Often in the late afternoons I'd lie on the bed with her and watch her stomach. At that time of day, the baby pushed against her belly with such force and in so many places at the same time that it looked like little animals were scurrying beneath her shirt. It was a peaceful time in the house. Tung wasn't in jail. He and Huong weren't fighting. Another American graduate student, Whitney, had rented the last room in the house.

It was during one of those quiet afternoons that Huong finally told me what had happened to Sa. After I left Vietnam, Huong had rented my room out to a string of long-term travel-

ers, young Western backpackers who usually stayed a week or
two in Hanoi before moving on to Laos, or Thailand, or China.
Two Dutch women had stayed for three weeks. They were nice
women, friendly, and Huong liked having them around. Then
one day, one of the women discovered that $100 was missing
from the spot where she'd hidden it at the bottom of a drawer.
Huong was horrified. Nothing had ever been stolen from her
house and, with Tung still in jail, the last thing she needed was
more trouble with the police. The only person who'd been alone
in that room was Sa, and Huong confronted her.

At first, Sa had only laughed, denying the charge. Then she'd
gotten angry at Huong, declaring that she wasn't a thief. Huong
remembered that, in recent days, Sa had shown up in a new pair
of blue jeans. And she had a wristwatch that her wages would
never have enabled her to afford.

"Where did you get the watch?" Huong had asked.

Sa looked startled, but then she recovered. "I found it," she
declared.

"Where?"

"On the street!"

The chance of that was close to impossible. This was a country where scavengers competed for old newspapers and random
bits of string. One of them would have grabbed a fallen wristwatch before Sa's mind could even register that she'd seen it.

Sa finally broke down and confessed that she'd taken the
money. She still had most of it left, squirreled away with the rest
of her meager belongings, which hung in a plastic shopping bag
on a hook in the kitchen. Huong replaced what was missing and
gave the $100 back to the Dutch woman. Then she sent Sa, who
was now hysterical, back to her father in the countryside.

Huong was more sad than angry about the incident. "Sa
swore that she would never steal again, but I couldn't let her

stay," she said. "I have to have someone here that I trust. I couldn't keep a thief."

I nodded.

"I can guess what happened when she got back home," she continued. "Her father beat her, I'm sure. He was a mean man. She hates it there."

I'd never seen Huong so regretful, so uncertain about a decision she'd made. But her choice had been difficult. She cared about Sa, but her livelihood depended on the reputation of the guesthouse. She couldn't have people stealing from her guests. Still, both of us felt terrible. Here was a girl who had never seen anything but the desperate poverty of the countryside, suddenly confronted by more wealth than she could have possibly imagined. She'd seen foreigners spend more money on a cyclo ride than she could earn in a week. The temptation must have been unbearable, particularly to a girl like Sa, who'd only known the thinnest joys of life and ached for more.

"She's not a bad girl," Huong had sighed. "I just got a letter from her last week, apologizing all over again, and telling me how much she wished she hadn't done it."

The last days of Huong's pregnancy seemed to pass in slow motion. I'd never been so close to one before. Babies, in my experience, arrived prepackaged. A pregnant woman disappeared into the hospital and reappeared a day or two later, thinner, and with a newborn neatly swaddled in her arms. I'd never seen anyone go into labor. I'd never timed contractions or tried to ease the pain by massaging a lower back. The whole process was quite fascinating to me, but Vietnam wasn't like the States, where pregnant women could invite almost anyone they liked into the birthing room with them. When Huong went into labor, she would disappear until she had the baby.

These days, I had a hard time leaving the house because I was so afraid that she would go into labor while I was gone. Every morning, I rushed down the stairs to find out whether or not her contractions had started. Every night before I went to bed, I made Tung promise that if anything happened during the night he wouldn't forget to wake me. Tung started to joke that this was my pregnancy, not his wife's. Whenever I appeared in the doorway, Huong would simply smile and say, "Not yet, Duyen. Not yet."

Both of them assumed that my interest in the impending arrival was a result of how tardy I'd been in starting a family of my own. Though their assumptions were the same, their conclusions were different. Tung suspected that I had no intention of ever having children, and he took it as his mission to convince me that I should. Huong, on the other hand, believed I wanted children, and she assumed that my interest in her pregnancy was a sign that, at long last, I'd be getting down to business pretty soon myself.

Both of them were wrong, but Huong came closer to the truth. I did want a child, but I didn't want one immediately. For nearly two years, I'd been listening to Vietnamese tell me that if I didn't go ahead and have a family I'd be "*ê*," as they called it, rotten fruit. There was a gap between when Vietnamese considered a woman "on the shelf" (mid-twenties) and when Americans did (mid-thirties or even forties). I preferred to follow the American standard, which, supposedly, had more to do with biological clocks than with one's waning ability to catch a man. But now that I was over thirty, I was starting to take even the American schedule more seriously. I worried that I'd never find anyone I'd want to settle down with, and I also began to see my future as a choice: husband and family, or Vietnam.

The question of husband and family had begun to weigh on me even more of late. I hadn't told Phai, or anyone in Hanoi, the entire truth. I did have a new boyfriend. Sort of. It was one of those situations that I thought Vietnamese would not be able to understand. I had met Todd in San Francisco in February, eight months earlier. He was a tall, dark-haired graduate student from the English Department at U.C. Berkeley, miserably writing his dissertation. Todd's biological clock wasn't ticking quite as quickly as mine was and, after a couple of dates, he told me that he wanted to continue to go out with different people. After that, our relationship was determinedly casual. We agreed that we weren't monogamous, but he was the only one who actually wasn't. I kept meaning to call the whole thing off. Somehow, I never did. I loved going out to movies with him, eating pizza, debating the merits of Shakespeare's plays. When we fought, we ended up laughing. We grew to like each other more and more. Strangely, what seemed destined to fall apart didn't. Still, it was impossible to define what was happening, and after a while that became hard to take. The idea of marriage and family had started to loom over my life, and I had to know whether I wanted to be with him or not. After six months of not being able to decide how I felt, I had tabled it for both of us and gone back to Vietnam.

My flying halfway around the world had, not surprisingly, forced a change. Letters started arriving once, twice, sometimes three times a week. Consciously, I dismissed it, but, unconsciously, riding my bike through the crowded streets of Hanoi, I found myself composing long letters to Todd in my head. I couldn't figure it out at all, and I certainly wasn't going to tell Tung and Huong, much less Phai, about it.

With that strange prescience of hers, however, Huong had guessed. "You're in love with someone new," she said one day, not even bothering to pose it as a question.

I denied it. "Love" was a word that came easily to couples in Vietnam, as I, from experience, could attest. In the United States, people could have sex with each other for weeks, or months, or even years and never say they loved each other. When Todd and I were together, the word "love" came up to describe favored toppings for pizza, Martin Scorsese movies, two-year-old nieces and nephews, but never each other. "I am not," I told Huong, and I believed it.

⌇⌇⌇ Despite Huong's impending labor, I managed to leave the house long enough to earn some money. My column on foreign investment was taking me into the business community, the sphere of Vietnamese society that, these days, was getting all the attention in the national and international press. Riding from appointment to appointment on my rickety borrowed bicycle, I interviewed heads of banks, high-level government officials, directors of multinational companies, and international business consultants. Normally, business and finance didn't interest me, but I knew that economic development in Vietnam was having a transformative effect on topics that did interest me — the social, political, and cultural life of the country. In Vietnam, which traditionally placed so high a value on scholarship that it set aside a day every year to honor its teachers, money had taken on such importance that the country's best students were dropping out of school to become real estate developers and tour guides. The change was, of course, most transparent in the cities. I only had to remember the anxiety with which the young Hanoi actress had asked for the proper pronunciation of "Rémy Martin" to understand just how deeply the commodities of the international market were beginning to affect the once-insular life of this city.

One day, I went to the restored colonial-era mansion that now served as the Vietnam headquarters of the Korean conglomerate Bright Star. As part of my research on how foreign companies set up businesses in Vietnam, I was going to interview Mr. Choi, a high-level official there. Mr. Choi's secretary, Mrs. Lien, ushered me into Mr. Choi's office, which was more spacious than an entire floor of Huong and Tung's house and filled with solid, finely crafted furniture. As Mrs. Lien poured hot coffee into a porcelain cup for me, I looked at the framed photographs on the walls, most of which showed groups of Asian businessmen smiling widely and shaking hands. For the next fifteen or twenty minutes, I heard about Mrs. Lien's studies at Hanoi University, her husband and children, and how she'd managed to land this coveted job at Bright Star. "And you," she asked. "Please tell me how you feel about our country, Vietnam?"

The charming thing about Mrs. Lien was that she wasn't stalling at all. Western-style business practices were still new in Vietnam, and though a secretary like Mrs. Lien seemed capable of scheduling appointments, typing, filing, and taking messages as well as any secretary in New York, she didn't make the same distinctions between work life and home life, between the personal and professional as, I imagined, a New Yorker would. As I'd noticed so many times before, Vietnamese do not value personal space as much as Americans do. "*Càng đong càng vui*," Vietnamese like to say. The more crowded, the better. By the time Mr. Choi finally showed up for our meeting, I'd given Mrs. Lien advice on how to teach her children English, and she'd told me which shop on Hang Gai Street was the best place to buy silk and which market in the city sold the highest quality velvet. Then, as smoothly as she'd transformed herself into a mother and connoisseur of fine fabric, she reverted back into the demure and efficient secretary and installed herself silently behind her desk.

Mr. Choi was nearing middle age, a tall, robust bureaucrat who wore his dark business suit very naturally. He carried out the interview with the same professional ease and confidence as any executive in the States. But, in contrast to the frankness of his secretary, Mr. Choi displayed much more reserve than I would have expected from a typical American executive, who might, at least, have asked me how long I'd worked for the newspaper or where I grew up. He seemed convinced that the reputation of his company depended on erasing any hint of his own personality. Polite and formal, he answered my questions carefully, jumping up to check in his files for any additional information he thought might help him make his points. There was only one glitch. Though his English was better than Mrs. Lien's, his accent was much worse. I found myself in the embarrassing position of having to ask him to repeat such essential words as "authority," "electronics," and "Tuesday." Several times, we had to turn to Mrs. Lien and ask for her translation. Somehow, I managed to get several pages of information on Bright Star projects, at least enough that I could write, with confidence, that the company was building an $82 million refrigerator manufacturing plant on the outskirts of Hanoi.

At the end of the interview, I stood up and put my notebook and pen in my bag. Mr. Choi got up and, from what I was able to gather, told me to call if I had any questions. I nodded, shook his hand, and followed the secretary out the door. As soon as he was out of earshot, Mrs. Lien took my hand and walked me down the stairs. "Don't forget, buy the French velvet, not the Chinese, and definitely not the Vietnamese," she told me. "It's more expensive, of course, but it's worth it."

• • •

⌒〜〜〜✓   In the middle of October, Susie, a friend of
mine from California, came to visit. We decided to go to Ha
Long Bay and invited Linh to join us. Then, the day before our
departure, Huong went into labor. I came home from my Vietnamese lesson in the morning and found the front door to the
house closed. When I opened it, the living room was deserted.
Even the new servant who'd been hired to replace Sa wasn't in
the kitchen. I threw my bag on the floor and ran up the stairs to
Tung and Huong's loft. Huong was leaning against the pillows in
her Buddha position, and Tung was sitting beside her massaging
her legs. The new girl, Ly, was as reserved as Sa had been exu-
berant, as calm as Sa had been energetic. She was squatting in a
corner, folding clothes and packing them neatly into a bag. "Finally," Tung said, not bothering to hide the smirk on his face.
"We couldn't leave for the hospital before you got home."

I couldn't even joke about this moment. Stepping into the
room and squatting down next to the bed, I took Huong's hand.
"Are you okay?" I asked.

She nodded, but before she could say anything another contraction came on. She pushed her legs over the side of the bed
and doubled over, her eyes closed, her face frozen in a wince.
The contraction lasted about fifteen seconds, then she exhaled
loudly, opened her eyes, and sat back against the pillow. The
contractions had started at about eight that morning and they
were coming more frequently, every eight minutes. Despite
Tung's comment about leaving for the hospital, it was still too
early for them to go.

I quickly realized that my presence was more distracting
than helpful. I went upstairs, but came back down every hour or
so to see how things were going. As the day wore on, Huong's
contractions grew more painful, but didn't speed up. Her mother

and Nga came over. Everyone talked between contractions, then
fell silent, breathless, watching her face contort in pain. By early
evening, Tung was gathering up their things for the hospital. Nga
helped Huong down the stairs and over to the couch. I followed
Tung outside, watching him carefully hang their bags on the handlebars of the motorbike.

"Can't you take a taxi?" I asked.

He shook his head. A taxi would take every bump in the
road, he told me. At least on his motorbike he could avoid the
potholes, drive slowly, inflict on Huong the least possible pain.
Tung moved methodically through his tasks, with a seriousness
and confidence I never would have predicted. It reminded me of
how Huong had acted after Tung's arrest, how she had taken care
of the family and the guesthouse, made trips to the jail every
week to see him and bring him food. When things were good,
Tung and Huong complained so much about each other that you
would think only inertia kept them from divorce. Then, in a crisis, they seemed ready to sacrifice everything for each other.

Tung finished preparing the bike and we walked back inside.
He sat down next to Huong and said quietly, "We'll go after the
next one."

She nodded, looking straight ahead, then slipped into it.

A few minutes later, Ly and Nga helped Huong out the door
and onto the motorbike behind Tung. Huong was calm, but distant. She sat sidesaddle, with her right arm around her husband
and her left clutching the metal bar at the back of the seat. Her
stomach was so big that she had to lean backward just to keep
her balance. Tung started the engine and carefully maneuvered
the vehicle off the sidewalk and down into the street.

I walked slowly back upstairs. Susie, Linh, and I were scheduled to leave for Ha Long Bay the next morning. Now the trip

only seemed inconvenient, but I didn't want to disappoint them by canceling. I knew I wouldn't be helping Huong by remaining in Hanoi.

I was still ruminating over my predicament early the next morning when I heard a knock on my door. I opened it and found Phai standing on the landing. He was smiling slightly and his eyes were filled with concern. It was the first time he'd come up to my room in more than a month. My friend Kelly, the Hanoi representative for an environmental engineering firm, had hired Phai to deliver packages, make photocopies, and take mail to the post office. Sometimes, I ran into Phai at Kelly's and had no idea how to act. It was easier at my house, where he did the same things he'd always done: wrestled with Viet, drank beer with Tung, and spent afternoons squatting in the kitchen, fixing leaks. Occasionally, standing out on my balcony, I would see him down below, talking to Tung. He looked so normal. But as soon as I walked into a room where he was sitting, his grin would freeze, his laugh would get louder and his gestures more theatrical, and I somehow ended up responding with frozen grins, loud laughs, and theatrical gestures of my own. Someone might have guessed that we were two bad actors rehearsing for a play.

As soon as I saw Phai this morning, I forgot the awkwardness. I looked at him with genuine relief.

Phai said, "I've got my friend's motorbike. Do you want to go to the hospital?"

It was just after eight. I still had time to make a quick trip to the hospital before leaving for Ha Long Bay. I rushed down the stairs after Phai.

It had been more than a year since we'd ridden on a motorbike together. I gripped the metal bar behind my back, and when I had something to say I yelled instead of putting my chin on his shoulder and speaking into his ear. But Phai seemed relaxed, with none of the self-consciousness I'd witnessed in the past two months, and I eventually began to relax myself.

The hospital, not far from my house, contained the city's largest maternity facility. The building had large, airy corridors, high ceilings, and elegant archways, but mildew was creeping up its walls and it was dark, with the only light streaming in naturally through the door. We climbed a crowded stairway, where the air filled with voices and the clatter of rubber sandals against the stone floor. The stairway led up to a landing at the head of a hall. Light from large windows flooded the area, and a wrought iron barrier kept the crowd of people at the top of the stairs from continuing down the hall. It took Phai and me several seconds to work our way to the front of the crowd. Then we stood like visitors at a prison gazing through the metal bars.

The dark hallway stretched away in front of us. I could barely see its end. To the left, we could glimpse one section of a room full of simple wooden beds. A pregnant woman in a white hospital gown was sitting at the side of one bed, slipping her feet into a pair of sandals. Another woman sat beside her, massaging her neck. A man was standing next to them, with his back to us, his arms spread out, folding a blanket.

"That's Huong and Tung," Phai said, gesturing toward them.

The man turned around and I saw Tung's face. We raised our hands to wave, but his eyes were focused on his wife, who was trying to stand up. He bent over, put his arm under hers, and lifted her, while the other woman, whom I now recognized as Nga, did the same on the other side. Huong stood for a moment, breathing deeply. Suddenly, her legs gave out. Tung and Nga held her steady, keeping her from collapsing. Her face lifted toward the ceiling, her mouth opened, and she let out a wail that had no sound to it. Then her head sank down against her chest. Nga pulled a cloth from her pocket and gently wiped Huong's face.

They walked slowly from the room, turned down the hallway, and moved away from us, stopping every few seconds for another contraction. The back of Huong's hospital gown, I saw now, was stained with blood.

Late that night, I managed to get through a telephone call to Hanoi from the hotel where we were staying in Hon Gai City. The connection was worse than it would have been had I tried to telephone New York.

It took a long time before Ly answered the phone. "Is Huong okay?"

"Yes!" she said, giggling. Like her predecessor, Sa, Ly came from the countryside and didn't have much experience talking on the phone, particularly on long-distance calls with foreigners.

"Did she have the baby?"

"Yes!"

I waited for a moment, thinking she'd tell me more.

"Is it a boy or a girl?" I finally asked.

"Yes! It's a boy!"

I would have to wait two days before I learned that Huong had delivered by cesarean late that afternoon, that she was in a lot of pain, but doing well, and that the baby was a good-sized boy, and healthy.

I made it to the hospital the morning after we returned from Ha Long Bay. For five dollars—not cheap by Vietnamese standards—Tung had managed to secure the only private room the hospital had to offer. It was a dark, narrow space with just enough room for a long wooden bed, a couple of chairs, and the folding cot Tung had brought to sleep on. A single light bulb hung from the ceiling. A door at the far end led out to a tiny enclosed outdoor space that contained a squat toilet.

Right off the main corridor that led from outside the building to the large communal rooms shared by other patients, the room was full of the noise of people talking and shuffling by.

Huong was lying on the bed beneath a sheet. It was mid-October, and the summer heat was finally beginning to subside, but the room was hot and stuffy. She weakly waved a paper fan in front of her face. Dark circles ringed her eyes, and her skin was pale, almost bluish. She looked like someone who'd been ill for months. At the end of the bed, the baby lay, an egg-shaped swaddle of blankets squeezed between a pillow and the wall. When I leaned over to look, a tiny red face gazed up at me, then squeezed its eyes together and whimpered. His body was swaddled so tightly that I could see nothing but his face and the bright cotton cap that covered his head. His lips puckered as if he were eating. Tung picked him up and lay him down next to Huong, where he immediately latched on to her nipple and began to suck.

Huong motioned with her finger for me to come closer. I sat down beside her, picked up the paper fan, and began to fan her. "I've had all my babies," Huong said. "Now, it's your turn."

I laughed. Seeing Huong go through labor had made me feel uncertain, all over again, about what I was doing with my life. "I think I'll be a while," I told her.

The baby's jaws were moving gently as he sucked. Huong pulled off the cap, revealing thin strands of damp, dark hair. With her fingers, she stroked the top of his head.

"What's his name?" I asked.

Huong looked up at Tung, who shrugged. "It's still under discussion," he said.

Huong rolled her eyes. "Tung has a hard time making decisions like that," she said.

• • •

⌒⌒⌒⌒⌒   I stayed at the hospital until Huong fell asleep.
Then, planning to go home, I got on my bike. Instead of turning
left down Trang Thi Street, however, I impulsively turned to the
right toward the post office to make an international call.

Lately, I'd developed an odd habit. One day, when I'd telephoned my mother, her answering machine had picked up. I'd
listened for a second or two before hanging up. At that time, a
call to the States cost about seven dollars a minute, and even this
short call would set me back at least a dollar, the cost of a lunch
in Hanoi. When I went to pay my bill, however, the ladies behind
the counter didn't charge me. They didn't consider an answering
machine answer to constitute a real call. After that, I became a
junkie. I called anyone I could think of, just to hear their voices,
so long as I knew they wouldn't be home. It was like a trick of
magic to be able to cause a telephone to ring in California even
when I was thousands of miles away. I called my mother when
she was at work. I called my sister when she was out of town.
Mostly, however, I called Todd. I didn't feel ready to go back to
the States in order to see him, but I'd come to rely on his letters.
He was thousands of miles away, but he seemed to understand
me more fully than anyone in Hanoi. Some cultural gaps were
just impossible to bridge. Early in the morning in Hanoi, I would
often give his answering machine a call, knowing that he would
be teaching.

On that day, however, I must have called a little early.
"Hello?" a real voice answered.

I stared out at the bustling post office, unable to speak. A
meter box on the wall of the telephone booth started to tick the
passing time. Three seconds. Todd and I hadn't spoken to each
other since I'd left for Vietnam nearly three months earlier. It
was too expensive. Too serious. Maybe I should hang up.

Six seconds. "Hello?"

I could feel myself start shaking. "Hi," I finally said.

"Dana?" he finally asked, and then we both started to talk. "How are you?" and "I'm fine" took up more than fifteen seconds, and then, not knowing how to go on, we said it all again. There was too much time and not enough. I told him how much the phone call cost and, feeling like an idiot for calling, said I had to hang up.

"Wait," he said. Had I gotten the letter he sent me about two weeks earlier? I'd received lots of letters. I didn't know what he was talking about.

"I wrote you," he said. "Can I come visit?"

It took one second for that to sink in. Before I could respond, he explained that he had a break from school in December and, well, he'd never been to Vietnam.

"Yes," I said. "Come. Okay, bye."

"Bye," said Todd. I hung up.

Todd's letter arrived a few days later. He had frequent flyer miles that he could use to come to Vietnam. Would I take a few weeks off to travel around the country with him? Two weeks later, I received another letter, this one with a flight number and a date to meet him in Saigon.

The first person I told about Todd, as it turned out, was Mr. Choi. One morning, I got a call from his secretary, Mrs. Lien, asking if I could come by the office. My article about him had recently appeared, and I assumed he wanted to discuss it. Maybe he had more material that I could use for my next column.

Mrs. Lien greeted me with her trademark friendly chatter, asked me if I'd managed to find any good French velvet, then ushered me into Mr. Choi's office. He was already there, seated behind his desk, but when he saw me he immediately stood up. Something was different in his manner toward me, in the way he smiled when I walked into the room. He hurried around the side of his desk, zealously shook my hand, then touched a plush armchair, motioning for me to sit down. With his jacket gone and his tie loosened, he looked less like a bureaucrat, and less confident as well. He sat down in a chair near me, then immediately sprang back up. "Coffee?" he asked.

I nodded. I was always happy to have Western-style coffee in Vietnam. Mrs. Lien went outside and immediately returned with two hot cups. I opened my notebook and pulled the cap off my pen. "No, no," Mr. Choi said hurriedly. "This is not for an interview." He walked over to a drawer next to his desk and pulled out a heavy-duty plastic shopping bag emblazoned with the Bright Star label. He carried the bag over to where I was sitting and offered it to me. "You're a very nice person. I want to give this to you." He spoke very slowly this time, looking me in the eye.

I must have seemed uncertain, because Mr. Choi sat down in a chair next to me and gestured toward the bag. "Open it," he said, like he'd just given me my Christmas presents.

I'd hit the Bright Star freebie jackpot. Inside was a thick English-language hardback by the founder and chairman of the company, a handful of ballpoint pens, and a black velvet jewelry box, inside of which was a wristwatch with the words "Bright Star" on its face. There was also a large bottle of Rémy Martin enclosed in a gilded, embossed gift case. Of all the things in the bag, I was most interested in the watch. I needed a watch.

I couldn't accept any of it, though. As I carefully put it all back, I explained to Mr. Choi that I was happy he was satisfied with the article I'd written, but that journalistic ethics forbade the acceptance of gifts. It was my job to write about Bright Star, I told him. I didn't need to be thanked for it.

Mr. Choi shook his head and raised a hand as if to try to stop me from arguing. "No, this is for you. For you," he said, and the way he said "you" made me suddenly see this meeting in an entirely different light.

The dinner invitation followed a moment later. I told him I was busy. What about Saturday? I shook my head, then leaned over and took a sip of my coffee, wondering how I could extricate myself from this room. In another situation, perhaps in the States, I might have felt more flattered and less embarrassed. But in Vietnam I had a hard time taking such attention personally. They weren't interested in me, but in some "Western woman" they expected me to be.

"Do you have a boyfriend?" Mr. Choi asked.

I considered the question for a moment. "Yes," I said, still unsure if I was lying or not.

As I got up to leave, I tried to return the gifts, but he refused to take them. "For you. Please, enjoy the Rémy Martin with your boyfriend," he told me. He waved his hand impatiently, as if he had a closet full of corporate giveaways and more important things to do than worry about his inventory. With the slightest change of expression, Mr. Choi had already become a bureaucrat again. I didn't argue. I really wanted that watch.

The baby still didn't have a name when, four days after his birth, he left the hospital. Following Vietnamese tradition, Huong and Tung took him to her parents' house, where the whole family would spend the next few months. The house on Dream Street seemed very quiet. Ly spent every

day with Huong and the new baby, then she rode back every
night to keep an eye on the house. Tung showed up for a few
minutes every three or four days, just to check on things.
Other than that, there was so little activity that it felt like
Paula, Whitney, and I were living in a hotel that had shut down
for the winter.

I spent a lot of those weeks sitting on my bed surrounded by
piles of information on AIDS, sexually transmitted disease, and
sexual practices in the developing world. Before the birth of the
baby, Tung had been a fabulous source of information. I'd grilled
him on everything from prostitution to drug use to extramarital
affairs, and what he didn't know—or claimed not to know—
firsthand, he was more than willing to offer in the experiences of
his friends. From Tung, I'd learned that in the *cà phê ôm*—or
"hugging cafés"—on the West Lake, customers could pay wait-
resses to snuggle on their laps. Tung was also the one who first
told me that the imported used clothing sold near the Kim Lien
Hotel was known as *"aó quần si-đa"*—AIDS clothes—because
Vietnamese worried that one could get AIDS from wearing those
clothes. Most Vietnamese regarded AIDS as a scourge on foreigners, particularly loose-living Westerners, so it made sense
that all the worn denim and frayed wool blazers must be infec-
tious. After all, why else would someone give away perfectly
good clothing?

As much as I rolled my eyes over the things I heard from
Tung, I found much more upsetting what I read in the books
and pamphlets I'd borrowed from Scott Stein. One glossy
booklet, a study by CARE International in Vietnam titled
"The Risk of AIDS in Vietnam," examined sexual practices and
attitudes among urban men and "sex workers" (their less judg-
mental term for prostitutes). Ninety-seven percent of the peo-

ple interviewed in the study knew about AIDS, and most knew something about its transmittal as well. That statistic seemed to prove that the Vietnamese government, which had plastered the country with frightening "do it and die"–style AIDS posters, had actually had some success in educating people about the threat. But aside from generally understanding that AIDS could be transmitted sexually, Vietnamese had a fuzzy knowledge of everything else related to the epidemic. Many believed, for example, that HIV carriers looked sick and could therefore easily be avoided as sex partners. Some claimed that AIDS hadn't arrived in Vietnam and that they couldn't get the virus unless they had sex with a foreigner. It was, of course, possible to combat such ignorance with education. But there was something more disturbing that the study had uncovered. A significant number of Vietnamese believed that destiny, not their own behavior, would determine whether or not they got AIDS. As one sex worker, who wouldn't argue when her clients refused to wear condoms, put it, "I have to accept my fate."

Vietnamese women were willing to use condoms, but they wouldn't use them unless their partners agreed. Because of that, Scott and I decided to focus the documentary on convincing men to protect themselves and their families. We'd have to expose the myths surrounding AIDS, but that wasn't enough. We decided to present a set of options: Celibacy was the safest way to protect yourself from AIDS. If you couldn't be celibate, we'd say, you should be monogamous. If you couldn't be monogamous, well, at least wear a condom. We took the practical approach.

I knew, from my own experience, that these were racy topics for Vietnam. The government had put considerable effort into family planning programs, but, from what I'd seen, they hadn't put much energy at all into simply teaching the birds and the bees. One unmarried friend had asked if she could get pregnant from kissing. And I remembered all the time I'd spent with Phai, explaining the connection between sexual inter-course and the birth of babies. As an American, I still found such ignorance astonishing, but people simply did not discuss sex in Vietnam.

By the end of October, the script was ready. All we needed was to find someone to translate my English draft into Viet-namese. I suggested to Scott that he hire Yen. These days, she was much happier than she'd been after the government had kicked Nick out of Vietnam. Nick had spent most of the au-tumn trying to secure a visa to come back for a visit. His chances had seemed slim. But the Vietnamese government, al-ways unpredictable, had suddenly decided to grant it. Nick would arrive in Vietnam a few days before Todd. Yen was elated.

Still, the trauma of the previous summer had taken a toll on her. Before her troubles with the police began, she'd en-joyed a lucrative and highly respected position with an Ameri-can consulting firm. Yen's political problems, however, had alarmed her boss, a Yale grad named Edward who took pride in his good relations with the Hanoi government. Rather than de-fending Yen's civil rights, Edward responded to the news of her troubles by firing her. Now she spent most of her time lying in bed at her parents' house, reading novels. She seemed like a perfect candidate for translating our script. And she had excel-lent English skills (she'd translated *Peter Pan* into Vietnamese as her senior thesis).

My only qualm about Yen translating the script had to do with its content. Yen was as sophisticated about the world as anyone I knew here, but she was still Vietnamese, and so un-comfortable talking about anything related to sex that she couldn't even say the word "menstruation" without lowering her eyes and starting to blush. I didn't know how she'd cope with the explicit dialogue in the script, not to mention Scott Stein himself. When I tried to warn her about him, though, she shrugged it off. "I'm going to be translating for you, not him," she said.

I found myself seated once more at the big conference table, facing Mr. Sex. This time, Yen was sitting beside me.

Scott began the meeting by dropping a handful of Rely souvenirs—condoms, key chains, a T-shirt, and a baseball cap—onto the table right in front of Yen. Then he pulled up a chair and sat down, facing her. He had a friendly look on his face, but his gaze was focused on Yen as if he were a carnivore examining his prey. She began to shift in her seat.

"So, Yen," Scott began, "tell me something about yourself."

As Yen spoke, Scott reached his hand over to the pile of con-doms among the freebies on the table. He tore one open. At first, Yen watched him, but as he slowly began to stretch the condom between his fingers, her face grew tense and she dropped her gaze. She didn't stop talking, however. Barely miss-ing a beat, she said that she was in the midst of searching for a Vietnamese publisher for her *Peter Pan* translation.

Scott's eyes widened at the mention of the children's clas-sic, then he asked, "Have you seen our commercials?" He didn't look up. He was stretching the condom like a balloon between his fingers.

"Yes," Yen said quietly. She was rubbing the bridge of her nose with one hand, a gesture that served to shield her eyes.

Scott must have wanted a more emphatic answer. "You have seen them?" he asked again.

"I have seen them," Yen answered, still refusing to look at him.

Scott put the opening of the condom up to his mouth and began to blow. I didn't move. Yen, hearing the sound of air expanding into latex, shrank into her seat. The condom expanded until it approached the size of a basketball, and then Scott tied off the end. "I want to make sure that you're comfortable with all the subjects you'll have to translate," he said. "I can't have anyone embarrassed around here." With that, he lifted the condom balloon into the air, aimed, and bounced it like a free throw off Yen's head.

As soon as it hit her, Yen looked up. Her face was white, but she stared at Scott without flinching. "Are you looking for a translator or a foil for your comedy act, Mr. Stein?" she asked.

Scott leaned closer to Yen. "I'm looking for a translator," he told her.

"Then I'll do it," she said. And then she added, "But you had better not tell anyone that I work for you."

Hanoi in autumn turned out to be lovely, golden, worth the wait. The cafés beside the West Lake were crowded day and night. People strolled, took meandering bike rides, rented paddleboats, fished. The air was cool and dry and breezy. The city seemed perfect.

The documentary was the last bit of work I had to finish before Todd arrived in Vietnam. On top of that, I'd been rushing to write three columns in advance for my *Vietnam Investment Review* assignment so that I could take a vacation. For the first time since I'd lived in Vietnam, I was working the kind of schedule I might have worked in the States. It was a good thing

Huong was at her mother's house, because I wouldn't have had time anymore to sit around in the living room, watching traffic. I hardly even had time to go by and visit her. I missed the freedom I'd once had to sit around and absorb everything around me, and I knew that I no longer paid attention to the world as diligently as I had in the past. In a sense, I took Hanoi for granted now, but feeling comfortable made me love the city as much as ever, perhaps more.

I rarely saw Phai these days. I was hardly home, and he didn't stop by the house much either. The tension of those first few weeks had eased, and sometimes when we saw each other we were even able to talk a little bit. On the afternoon I got my bag of gifts from Mr. Choi at Bright Star, Phai and I had examined it all together, like pirates going through their loot. Another day, we managed to have a serious conversation about his prospects for a wife, although the only thing he had to say on the subject was that he didn't have any. Huong had explained Phai's predicament to me already. Phai wanted a woman who was sophisticated, educated, and pretty, but no woman like that would be attracted to a guy like him. One of the most interesting cultural differences I'd discovered between Westerners and Vietnamese centered on our varying concepts of beauty. Huong and I never tired of discussing who was good-looking and who wasn't, and we disagreed a lot. Although, to me, Phai's dark skin made him beautiful, Vietnamese valued pale complexions and, according to Huong, women here would not consider him attractive. Worse, he was poor and unskilled in anything that could provide a decent wage. The girls he liked weren't interested. And the ones who might like him, country girls like Ly or Sa, he wouldn't even look at.

I kept meaning to discuss Todd with Phai, but put it off. Of course, he eventually found out anyway. One afternoon, he came by the house and asked if I wanted to go for a walk. It was a crisp, sunny day, and, with anyone else, I would have agreed immediately. But, with Phai, the prospect of an open-ended outing made me uncomfortable. Too many awkward topics could come up.

"I'm sorry. I'm just so busy," I told him.

We were standing in the living room. Phai looked away, and, for a moment, stood gazing out the door. His expression wasn't angry, just thoughtful, and I waited to hear what he would say. After a while, he turned around. "Your boyfriend's coming for a visit?" he asked.

My first impulse was to say no. I'd been denying that Todd was a boyfriend to myself for so long that I could certainly deny it to Phai a little longer. But he deserved frankness. "Who told you?" I asked.

Huong, predictably, had taken matters into her own hands, telling Phai everything she knew, and then some. She'd even said that Todd and I had been planning this visit for months.

"That's not true," I said. I hadn't been entirely truthful with Phai, but I hadn't lied to him, either.

There must have been something desperate in my voice, because Phai smiled at me with such warmth that I felt ashamed at my efforts to protect myself at his expense. "Don't worry," he said. "It's good. That's what you want. He'll make you happy." He didn't look upset. He looked relieved.

Phai's worry, I saw now, was not so much that I'd met someone new in the States, but that I would meet someone new in Vietnam. I'd always told him, truthfully, that I felt the cultural differences between us were too great for us to be happy together forever. Now I saw how deeply Phai wanted to believe that.

"Do you think you'll marry him?" Phai asked.

"I don't know," I said.

Though Phai didn't look upset, I must have, because he said to me, very gently, "This is good. You'll be happy with him," as if it were me, not him, who needed consolation. I only felt worse. No matter how much I ever gave him, Phai always wanted to give me more.

He left a few minutes later. I spent the rest of the afternoon trying to avoid thinking about what a jerk I'd been. I might have ruminated over it all evening, had something not come up that took my mind off my own problems. About six o'clock, Ly came by the house to pick up a bag of clothes for Tung and Huong. The baby, she told me, was running a high fever and showed signs of lung infection. He was back in the hospital.

13   *Firecrackers on Dream Street*

THE MATERNITY HOSPITAL WHERE HUONG had delivered her baby had been rudimentary and rather run-down, but it came to seem positively high-tech in comparison to the pediatric hospital where I visited the baby the next morning. Tung brought me with him on his motorbike, which we parked in a lot at one side of an empty courtyard covered in weeds and rubble. Simply negotiating the cracked and broken sidewalk that led into the building felt like crossing a rocky river. The building was small and unadorned, the kind of ugly, no-nonsense structure that went up quickly and cheaply in the Socialist bloc. Inside, the floors were covered with dust, the windows cracked or missing panes. In the empty hallways, the sounds of coughing, machinery, and crying babies swept along the corridors, bouncing back and forth against the hard, bare walls.

We didn't see anybody until we'd walked down one corridor, through a set of doors, around a corner, up another hall, and then into a large room filled with ten wooden mat-covered beds, none of which was wider than a narrow cot. Two or three people sat on each bed. Another couple of people squatted on the spaces on the floor between the beds. Every other available space was taken up by suitcases, water bottles, dirty dishes, blankets, pillows, newspapers, and plastic bags full of dry rice, oranges, and loaves of bread. The place reminded me of a cramped, crowded compartment on a Vietnamese passenger train, where whole families and piles of belongings shared the narrow confines of a single berth. Babies were everywhere, sleeping, crying, coughing, nursing, or lying on tiny specks of blanket, staring up at the spiderwebs that stretched like lace across the ceiling. No one spoke loudly, but the simple presence of so many people made the room throb with noise.

Huong was sitting up on a bed near the far end of the room, her back against the wall, the baby, wrapped in a white blanket, sleeping in her arms. Ly sat cross-legged at the bottom of the bed, paging through the morning paper. When Tung and I appeared, Ly scooted over on the bed, making room for me to sit down. I sat closest to Huong and looked down at the baby. His skin was a rosy pink, but his breaths were thick and wheezy, like the slurpy sound of the last drops of liquid drawn up through a straw.

"How is he?" I asked.

Huong shrugged. They'd had a hard night, she said. The baby's lungs were congested, and he was so exhausted from the simple effort of breathing that he didn't even have energy to cry. He'd stayed awake the entire night, lying in Huong's arms, desperately wheezing. Because he was breathing out of his mouth, he couldn't nurse, and they'd brought him to the hospital because they were afraid he'd become dehydrated. The doctors had immediately put him on antibiotics, a series of injections that had made him scream in panic. When he finally slept, the sound of other babies screaming inevitably woke him up again.

Huong's face was pale and her eyes looked old and tired. "Are you okay?" I asked.

She reached over, picked up a cup of water that was sitting next to her on the bed, and took a sip. "This is normal," she said. "The same thing happened with Viet. Only with Viet it was even worse." She spoke matter-of-factly, as if sojourns in the hospital were part of every woman's childbearing experience.

Tung was squatting on the floor, unpacking a metal canister filled with hot noodle soup. Huong gingerly handed Ly the sleeping baby, then picked up the soup and some chopsticks and began to eat. Tung pulled some oranges and hard-boiled eggs out of a plastic bag and set them on the bed. "We're supposed to see the doctor again in a few minutes," he said.

Huong nodded. The two of them went through the simple tasks in front of them with serious concentration, as if they weren't willing to think beyond whatever required attention at that particular moment. Huong silently ate her breakfast. Ly held the baby on her lap, swaying back and forth. I looked around the room. A few men wore jeans like Tung's. A few women had on gold bracelets and sported stylish haircuts, but almost everyone else wore the simple garments of the countryside: faded cotton pants, shirts with patches on them, plastic sandals. To our right, a woman was dozing, her body curled into a ball at the top of the bed. Beside her, a little boy was singing to an infant who lay motionless on the bed, staring at the wall. At the other end of the bed, three runny-nosed little girls played peekaboo with an old pink shirt. To our left, a young girl was holding a medicine dropper full of red liquid over the mouth of a sallow-skinned baby. A teenage boy sat next to her, talking her through the procedure, holding the baby's legs to keep them from thrashing.

In comparison to these two infants, Huong's son, with his pink skin and plump body, looked fairly healthy. Still, every few minutes loud coughs wracked his tiny body, forcing his parents to stop what they were doing and stare at him in silent agony. After one such moment, Huong turned to me. "Last night a baby died in here," she said. The family had come from a village very far away in the countryside and by the time they got to the hospital, the baby was already nearly dead. The family stayed at the hospital for two days, just waiting for the infant to die.

"What was the problem?" I asked.

Huong shrugged. "A cough," she said, reaching over to take her own infant away from Ly. Feeling his body pass from one pair of hands to another, the baby's eyelids opened slightly, then fluttered closed again. His open mouth rounded into a perfect circle and he drifted back to sleep. His breath softened into the purring of a cat. Huong stared down at him, her fingers gently smoothing his dark hair down across his forehead. I tried to imagine how I would feel holding my sick child in my arms, helpless to do anything to cure him or even to relieve his pain. Had Huong and Tung lived in a more affluent country, they would have had access to advanced medical technology. The baby from the countryside might have survived, had it lived in the States. Here was something worse than losing a child, I realized: losing a child and knowing that it didn't have to happen. But maybe those parents didn't know that health care could be more effective somewhere else.

The teenage boy on the bed next to ours asked Huong something, then motioned in my direction. I was so used to being pointed at and discussed that I didn't even pay attention until Huong began to laugh. I looked at her.

"He thinks you want to adopt a baby," she said.

It was hard to tell if he was asking out of curiosity, or if he was interested in finding a home for his child. I looked at him and shook my head. Of course, I had no intention of doing such a thing, but I looked much more closely at the baby on the bed beside us. It was a scrawny little thing, only a few days old, but I had seen it kicking and screaming with an energy that belied its health and age. Calm now, it let out a sigh, then turned its head and, from beneath a shag of jet black hair, looked in my direction. My stomach clinched. I could imagine signing some papers and, in the not-too-distant future, having that baby lying on my bed back on Dream Street, then sleeping in my lap on an airplane headed to the States. Years from now, I'd tell my daughter —or son?— about that first moment when our eyes had met in that crowded hospital in Hanoi. The child would be big by then, an American Vietnamese, still scrawny and tough. A survivor. A kid in Adidas sneakers and Gap jeans, an Asian Jew who only knew what I could teach about Vietnam. Destiny, I would tell my child, had drawn us together.

The teenage father was still looking at me, as if he expected more. I knew what to say but I couldn't say it. Finally, Huong said it for me. "She's my friend," she said. "She's not even married yet."

Huong and the baby stayed in the hospital for three days before going home. A week later, they were back in the hospital for another two days, with another lung infection. Whenever I wanted to visit, I had to ask Ly where they were that day—at Huong's parent's house, or back in the hospital. The baby never seemed desperately ill, but he never seemed healthy, either. Finally, it was age that saved him. As he grew, his lungs got stronger. When he was a week away from his two month birthday, he left the hospital for the last time. And so, Tung and Huong were finally ready to make the decision they'd been putting off all these weeks. They'd give their son a name. Although they'd claimed they'd postponed the choice because they couldn't agree on what to call him, I suspected another reason as well.

Names are important in Vietnam. Introducing themselves to foreigners, English-speaking Vietnamese will often translate the meaning of their names. "I'm Orchid (Lan)," one might say. Or "Shining Jade (Ngoc Minh)" or "Spring Rice (Lua Xuan)." Some names sounded like poetry. I knew three brothers named "Mountain (Son)," "River (Giang)," and "Ocean (Hai)." I had a friend named "Moon Lute (Nguyet Cam)" in honor of a traditional Vietnamese stringed instrument. Another couple had named their three boys, all born during the years of the American War, Linh (after Abe Lincoln), Red (for the Communists), and Binh (which means "peaceful"). Binh must have been a popular name during the years of war, because I knew a lot of Binhs who were born at that time. When I told people that "Dana" doesn't mean anything in English, they were often baffled. If it doesn't have a meaning, they would ask, then why bother?

In Vietnam, names also carry a powerful force. Tradition claims that evil spirits like to steal babies, particularly the attractive ones. In the countryside, where old customs linger longer, new parents would go to lengths to make their children seem unappealing. They would never compliment their newborns. Instead, they'd call them "ugly," or "rat," or even "shit," in order to trick the spirits into staying away. Ironically, even such hideous names would come to sound like the sweetest of endearments when they were uttered by adoring parents. Urban Vietnamese, like Tung and Huong, liked to scoff at superstitions, but even they would cringe when I forgot the custom and cooed over how beautiful the baby was. "*Trọm vía,*" they'd hiss, reminding me to say that phrase before the compliment. As one friend later translated it, *trọm vía* meant "to sneakily talk behind a spirit"—in other words, to keep evil away. Although Tung and Huong claimed that it was indecision that made them wait so long to name the baby, it seemed to me that superstition and ancient tradition had more to do with it than they cared to admit. The supposedly irrational concern over "evil spirits" actually spoke to very real, and widespread, dangers that newborns in Vietnam had faced forever: poor hygiene, inadequate nutrition, and lack of medical care. Because infant mortality was such a risk, tradition dictated that only close family members would visit a new baby before its one-month birthday, the time at which its chance of survival was thought to be more secure and the moment at which it could be brought into society and openly named. In that context, Tung and Huong's so-called indecision made more sense. Rationally, they probably knew that their child's health would not be affected by whether or not they named it. But, in the same way that I avoid walking under ladders, they refused to take any chances.

Once the baby finally came home from the hospital for the last time, his parents settled on a name quite easily. They'd call him "Đức." It was a common name among Vietnamese, meaning "virtue" or "righteousness," but it also had a special meaning for Tung. "Đức" was the Vietnamese word for "Germany." Now Tung and Huong had a Viet and a Duc. A Vietnam and a Germany.

Hanoi had changed quite a bit since my first visit back in 1990. These days, there were so many Dreams on the streets that it seemed like only the poor people rode bicycles. Old buildings had been torn down, and new office buildings and hotels were rising in their places. In a city where it had once been difficult to find anything to eat other than rice and noodle soup, you could now dine, if you had the money, on pizza and pasta. French wines were sold in the Hang Da Market. Tung could buy his own Levi's right near our house.

But in mid-December, I flew down to Saigon to meet Todd, and Saigon was changing even faster. When I first arrived, I walked around in a daze, staring at all the fancy cars, the sushi restaurants, the Louis Vuitton purses. Flying from North Vietnam to the South in December meant that I'd moved from autumn to summer in the course of a few hours. The heat was oppressive and, to make it worse, Saigon seemed like nothing but concrete—roads and sidewalks and buildings running up against one another, all hard, only varying in texture. It was hard to find a tree or bush, and when I did, it looked like an exotic animal, caged by more concrete. Saigon seemed less like Vietnam and more like some in-between place, with one foot in this country and one foot out the door already, moving west.

Although I'd been counting the days until I saw Todd again, now that he was almost here I panicked. The two of us had never spent more than a day or two together at one time. Now we planned to spend the next four weeks together, without a break. But what if he bugged me? He might want to skip breakfast, while I'd want to eat it. He might insist on bargaining over every cyclo ride, while I'd want to agree to the price and get on our way. Maybe he'd talk too much. Or not enough. Maybe he wouldn't want to visit a single museum. Maybe he'd insist on going to every one. I hadn't even seen him yet, and he was already beginning to drive me nuts.

The airport was full of people, most of whom were waiting to meet the plane from Bangkok. Everyone surged against the railing at the main terminal exit, straining to get closer to the door that would eventually spit out arriving passengers. Out of several hundred people, there were three Westerners, including me. Right in the middle of the crowd, a gaunt, sandy-haired young man towered above the rest, hanging on to the railing like a rock fan determined to maintain his position near the stage. Over by the snack bar, a bearded guy in a summer suit sat sipping a Tiger Beer and reading the *International Herald Tribune.* He was the only person who seemed oblivious to the tension of the moment. The rest of us wore the same expression of disbelief. For me, the doubt stemmed from a fairly simple issue of physics. Just as I always felt stunned by my own ability to travel around the world in the course of a few hours, I had a hard time believing that Todd would actually show up.

My doubts had to do with logistics, but, looking at the expressions on the faces around me, I guessed that theirs had more to do with the passage of time. Many of these people were waiting for loved ones who had emigrated to countries far away, people they hadn't seen in years, decades even. One elderly woman stood next to me, her lips trembling, her eyes fixed on the terminal doors. One hand gripped the railing separating the surging crowd from the doors of the building. The other ran up and down the front of her silk *áo dài,* as if to use these last few seconds to smooth unsightly wrinkles. No one from the plane had even appeared yet. We knew, however, that the flight had landed. A video monitor hanging above our heads indicated as much.

I pushed my way out of the crowd and walked over to a window overlooking the arrival hall. At the far end of the hall, a number of foreigners stood picking through incoming luggage. I squinted my eyes and looked at the men. A short, bald-headed guy. A Nordic-looking fellow with a backpack. Three businessmen who looked Japanese. An elderly woman wearing a baseball cap. No Todd.

"Buy flowers, madame?" A young girl stood next to me, holding an armful of roses up to my nose.

I already had flowers. Early that morning, I'd strolled through the narrow aisles of the Ben Thanh Market, which overflowed with goods I'd never seen in Hanoi: durian fruit, fresh coffee beans, Pampers, tortoiseshell sunglasses. The flower stalls offered such a variety of blossoms that nature might have developed whole new species since I'd gone to Hanoi. Squatting on the pavement, choosy as a Vietnamese mother, I'd picked out three perfect lilies, then haggled a good price for them. Back at my guesthouse, the proprietor had, of course, asked me the price I'd paid. When I told him, he'd nodded approvingly.

Still tied in their neat purple bow, the flowers were now drooping like tourists after too much sightseeing. I pulled out some money and bought the roses, then turned and put my face to the window one more time. A tall Westerner was walking toward me on the other side of the glass. He had on a wide-brimmed hat and a tired smile. He waved at me. I used the flowers to wave back. Todd was in my time zone.

It took us a while to get used to each other. I felt like one part of my life had mysteriously superimposed itself upon another. Here was that guy I knew from Oakland, asking me how to say "good morning" in Vietnamese. It wasn't just having Todd around that felt odd. Having anybody around was a change. I suddenly had to check with somebody else every time I wanted to sit down, turn a corner, or get something to eat.

Todd was a scholar, but he wasn't bookish. He liked Bob Dylan as much as Shakespeare, and he liked movies even better.

Between college and graduate school, he'd spent a year back-packing through Asia. He'd been injured when a horse kicked him in Tibet, then managed to recover and hike from there to Nepal. In India, he'd lived on an ashram, traveled up and down the country, and, like so many Westerners in India, gotten very sick.

Todd was two years younger than me, born in 1964. Be-cause he'd spent so much time traveling in the region, he asso-ciated Vietnam with Asia, not with war. Buddhist temples reminded him of China, not the monk who had immolated him-self on a Saigon street corner in 1963. In the guidebook he'd brought with him from the States, he'd underlined the entries for various historical sites of the war, but he'd starred the places that looked beautiful or seemed like good places to eat. He wanted to visit Buon Ma Thuot because it was supposed to have a spectacular waterfall, not because it had been the scene of a spectacular battle.

For the first few days, we wandered through Saigon, and it quickly became apparent that he and I were traveling through two very different cities. He walked wide-eyed through a teem-ing third-world metropolis, while I was busy gaping at all the Western luxuries I hadn't seen in months. Where Todd saw open sewers, I saw sidewalk vendors pushing Rolex knockoffs. He was drawn toward street stalls hawking noodle soup and rice pan-cakes, while I hovered near the entrances to the Apocalypse Now Bar and the California Hamburger Restaurant. He noticed the stink of dried fish reeking in the markets, and I noticed the per-fume floating off the wrist of a waitress in the rooftop bar of the Rex Hotel. I giggled over his first awkward climb onto a cyclo, and he rolled his eyes when I stopped to peer through the tinted glass of a Mercedes. We both tried to be patient. I didn't mind the time it took him to take a photo of a street choked with motorbikes, and he, in turn, never complained about the hour I spent at the Ben Thanh Market, picking out lipstick, sunglasses, and barrettes.

On our last night in Saigon, I told Todd I wanted to go to Maxim's, a famous restaurant and nightclub that was known for its onion soup and filet mignon. Todd loved the food we'd been eating out on the streets every day, and he would have been happy enough with noodle soup for a month, but, like an urbanite anxious to please his country cousin, he agreed to go because I was so determined. Once we'd made the plan, we tried to make an event of it. I slipped on my sundress, wiped the dust off my leather sandals, and put on my brand new Cherry Red lipstick. We wanted to look nice because this was going to be an expensive night for us. We figured dinner would cost at least ten dollars. Each.

After four months eating in the noodle and rice shops of Hanoi, I felt like I was on my way to the Ritz. I wanted Maxim's to be both glittery and dangerous. Waiters would listen to orders and, like spies, write nothing down. (I'd read too much Graham Greene.) Todd had lower expectations, and it quickly became apparent that his were closer to reality. At first glance, Maxim's looked like the great hall of the Emerald City, redone in ruby red. Unfortunately, decades of cigarette smoke had given the decor the brownish tint of pork blood drying on a busy market floor. A heavy, balding maître'd led us past tables full of gray-suited Asian businessmen who were huddled together building towers out of empty beer cans. We sat down at a table in front of the stage, unfolded cloth napkins dotted with stains, and opened our menus, the heavy pages soft as cotton and yellow from so many years of use. Within five seconds, a scowling middle-aged waitress was standing in front of us. She pulled the stub of a pencil from her pocket, pointed at the menu, and said. "Eat. You want eat. What?"

I ordered macaroni and cheese. The waitress looked at Todd, her pencil hovering over her order book. He was squinting at the menu. Finally, he muttered, "They don't have any Vietnamese food. And it's so expensive."

I'd lived in Vietnam for almost a year already. I was used to the disappointment of things being less than I'd hoped for, and so I recovered faster. But Todd looked completely disgusted by the place. "Don't worry," I told him. "We'll find Vietnamese food tomorrow."

He pointed at a line on the menu and looked up at the waitress. "What kind of fish is this?" he asked.

"Fish," said the waitress, nodding. She scrawled into the order book.

"What kind of fish?" I asked her in Vietnamese.

The waitress looked even more annoyed. She reached over and poked a finger into Todd's menu. "Fish. It says 'fish,'" she snapped in Vietnamese.

"River fish? Lake fish? Ocean fish?" I asked.

"Ocean fish," said the waitress.

"It's fish from the ocean," I told Todd, forgetting that "ocean fish" means very little in English. Todd wanted a word—sole, halibut, tuna—that would convey information about taste and texture. In America, one could expect such information when dining. After more discussion that went nowhere, he gave up and ordered the fish.

The waitress left and Todd took a sip of his lemonade while he looked around the room. I could tell he was frustrated, and I felt irritated that he'd had to ask so many questions. Forgetting that my own expectations had, just a few minutes earlier, been very high, I felt like reminding him that we were in Vietnam, not Paris. Why couldn't he have just ordered a steak? He didn't know the trick I'd learned to preserve my sanity in Vietnam. At a certain point, you just stop trying. Okay, you tell yourself. Whatever.

The floor show started, and we turned to watch, trying to get some space from each other for a minute. Women in denim hotpants and baby blue leotard tops attempted a cancan on dangerously high heels. A man wearing a James Dean black leather jacket sang "I Left my Heart in San Francisco," while rear-projected slides covered the back of the stage with shots of Big Ben, the Eiffel Tower, and the Sydney Opera House. At the table next to us, a Tiger Beer pyramid had grown to eight beers across and eight rows high. Thirty-six cans of beer, divided among four Asian businessmen, all of whom were smoking cigars and downing shots of Johnnie Walker Black. The youngest of these men stood up, turned a beer can upside down to prove its emptiness, then placed it at the top of the pyramid. Even James Dean up on stage paused to look. The structure held.

"Are they Vietnamese?" Todd asked. He knew that I was annoyed with him, and now, with his head cocked to the side and a look of curiosity on his face, he was trying to smooth things out between us.

I looked at the drinking buddies at the next table and shook my head. Vietnamese didn't dress that well. "They might be *Việt kiều,* though," I said, referring to Vietnamese émigrés living abroad.

I told Todd about the time my student John and I had met a *Việt kiều* man at the Shrimp Cake Restaurant on the West Lake in Hanoi. The *Việt kiều* was wearing a loud Hawaiian shirt, Wrangler jeans, and sunglasses so heavily tinted we couldn't see his eyes. He told us he lived in Los Angeles—he called it "Los" for short. He'd escaped Vietnam by boat, leaving his wife and a couple of babies behind. After a few years in a refugee camp in Malaysia, he made it to the United States, where he managed to put himself through engineering school at night by working as a high school janitor during the day. For ten years now, he'd worked for a defense contractor in Southern "Cal." He told us he came back to Vietnam every couple of years now, to see his family. When I asked him why he didn't bring his wife to the States, he said he had a new American wife in Los already. "New life, new wife, man," he'd laughed. "Do you want to see her pic?"

John had nodded immediately, and the *Việt kiều* pulled a picture out of his wallet. "That's my wife. Isn't she a babe?" he asked. The photo showed a woman lying on a beach with the sun setting behind her. She was beautiful. Blond. Long legs. Breasts popping out of a bright red bikini. She had a classic model's physique, which was why it was such a weird picture. She really was a model. The guy had simply clipped the photo of a swimsuit model out of a magazine. I looked up at him to see if he was joking, but he was staring down at the picture, saying, "I love my wife."

John couldn't take his eyes off the picture. "She's so beautiful," he gushed.

At the next table, the Tiger Beer pyramid suddenly toppled in a thundering crash. The businessmen howled with laughter. Up on stage, James Dean paused to clap, while our waitress squatted to pick the cans off the floor.

"Why would that *Việt kiều* go to such an effort to lie?" Todd asked.

"A lot of *Việt kiều* want to show the folks in Vietnam how well they're doing," I explained. I had heard of people getting their pictures taken in front of expensive sports cars they found parked on the street, then sending the photos back to Vietnam.

The lies disguised the less glamorous truth that many, if not most, Vietnamese immigrants worked ten- and twelve-hour days as janitors and dishwashers just to survive in the West. People remaining in Vietnam, however, expected that every *Việt kiều* was rich. When the emigrants finally saved enough money to return to Vietnam for a visit, they had to spend hundreds, or thousands, of dollars on extra gifts and cash to dole out to their huge extended families. They had to take the whole neighborhood to eat at Maxim's. Plus, Mom needed a new house. Little Brother wanted a motorbike. Sis wanted to start a new business. A simple trip to Vietnam could set a person back for years.

Todd wasn't sympathetic. "It's their own fault. They're raising expectations by telling everyone they're rich," he said.

I shook my head. "You don't understand," I said. "They *are* rich. Even if they wash dishes in the States, they're rich compared to people in Vietnam. There's nothing they can do to ease the expectations."

Our dinner arrived, and it looked like Denny's food, down to the wilted parsley. My macaroni and cheese contained more cream, butter, and cheese than I had eaten in a month. I was ecstatic. Breaking a piece of crusty cheese off the edge of the dish, I put it in my mouth and let my tongue absorb its sharp saltiness. Todd looked less delighted with his fish, but he gamely picked up a fork and scraped the thick blanket of tartar sauce off the top.

He took a bite and chewed pensively. "*Ngon,*" he said, doing his best to pronounce the word for "delicious." "Really, really *ngon.*"

There was something about the way Todd and I dealt with each other that I'd never quite managed with anyone else. Even when we were so irritated with each other that we didn't even want to talk, we always managed, eventually, to pull ourselves back out of it. No one had ever told me that being able to be annoyed with your partner could be such a necessary quality in romance.

That night, I dreamed I was sitting on the couch in the living room in Hanoi. Phai sat next to me. He was talking, but I couldn't understand what he was saying. After a long time, the walls and ceiling began to change colors, like sky growing dark at dusk. Phai touched me on the shoulder and I shivered.

I sat up in bed, forcing myself awake, and remembering that I was in a guesthouse in Saigon. Next to me, Todd turned over onto his stomach. I got up and went to the bathroom. When I came back, he asked, "Are you okay?"

"I'm okay," I said. I ran my hand down his arm to his fingers, which closed around mine. He was already breathing heavily again, in sleep.

For the next two and a half weeks, Todd and I made our way north through Vietnam. In the southern coastal city of Nha Trang, we spent Christmas Eve with the family of a bus driver we'd met on the road. We were delighted by their invitation to join them, though we explained that we were Jewish and would be going to mass with them out of curiosity and not devotion. On that tropical night, the huge French-era cathedral overflowed with thousands of worshipers, many of whom, like us, were not Christian, but were drawn by the festive spectacle. The bus driver didn't understand the meaning of "Jewish"— người Do Thái in Vietnamese—but that only mattered when, after mass, he set a bowl of pork in front of Todd, who wouldn't eat it. That led to a serious confrontation between Todd and me, as his religious beliefs conflicted with my sense of good manners. I demanded that he eat the pork, and he refused to touch it.

But neither of us held grudges. When Todd came down with an ailment we labeled "the mysterious exhaustion disease," I brought him food, rubbed his back, and played cards with him during the brief intervals when he wasn't sleeping. In the highland town of Buon Ma Thuot, we rented a motorbike that broke down as soon as we got far enough out of town for it to be a problem. Todd pushed the bike all the way to the repair shop, while I walked along beside him, entertaining him with Helen Reddy songs and watching him sweat.

For better and worse, we got to know each other very well. Todd was willing to wait while I told our life stories to every meat-seller and cyclo driver in Vietnam. I was willing to listen to every masterful plot twist from the movie *The Abyss*. I got used to the fact that he sometimes liked to wait an hour or two after waking up in the morning before he'd say a single word. He got used to the fact that I wanted to translate everything from Vietnamese for him, even the most boring conversations with the most boring people. I didn't complain when he became addicted to sunflower seeds and cracked his way through a bag of them every day. He didn't complain when I insisted he sing the same Bob Dylan song to me every few hours. I discovered that if I wasn't bossy about what I wanted to do he would follow me anywhere.

We spent a week in Hanoi and, though Todd met most of my friends there, he didn't meet Phai. They saw each other once, but only accidentally. Phai had told me that he wished me well with Todd, but he didn't want to meet him. Then, on the day we arrived in Hanoi, our train got in earlier than anyone had expected, and Phai was sitting in the living room, talking with two of Huong's brothers, when we pulled up in front of the house.

I saw him first, from the sidewalk, as we were getting our bags out of the cyclo. I rushed into the room before Todd and said hello, hoping to give Phai a chance to prepare. As soon as he saw me, Phai sucked in his breath, then glanced toward the door. Todd, the tall, dark-haired American, was carrying our backpacks up the steps. In the briefest moment, a flash of panic swept across Phai's face, and then, just as quickly, it disappeared. He smiled then. It wasn't a broad smile, and it certainly lacked the *vui*-ness that Phai had learned to offer foreigners. It was a flat smile, and pleasant, one that would make him blend in, unnoticed, among the three Vietnamese that Todd would see before him in the living room. "Hi," he whispered.

Todd looked around. Every face was new, and he was unable to focus on any of them. "Let's go upstairs," I told him. Todd gave a wave to the men on the couch, then turned and started up the stairs. I looked at Phai and Huong's brothers. "We're just so exhausted from the train ride," I explained.

"Welcome home," Phai said. I smiled at him, then followed Todd up the stairs. A few minutes later, after we'd put down our bags in my room, I told Todd that Phai had been one of the men in the room downstairs. Todd stared at the ceiling, trying to pull the faces from his memory, but he couldn't. "It doesn't matter," he told me. "I'd rather not know what he looks like anyway."

Tung and Huong both decided that Todd was acceptable. Huong declared him "*đẹp*"—handsome—which came as a relief; if she had found him "*xấu*"—ugly—she would have pestered me about it for weeks. She and Todd couldn't carry on any kind of conversation, but whenever they had a chance they traded words. Eating a bowl of Huong's noodles, Todd would say "*ngon*" and Huong would giggle and respond with "tayn," which was her version of the word "thanks." Todd played so many games with Viet that Huong upgraded "*đẹp*" to "*vui*." Tung and Todd discovered a mutual passion for sunflower seeds, and the two of them spent many hours sitting on the couch, cracking seeds, and discussing everything from pop music to politics, while I acted as translator.

Of all my friends, Todd got along best with Tra. Like him,

she'd taken advantage of her university's December break and flown to Vietnam for a few weeks. She and Tuyen were still married, but their relationship had shifted to a new stage in the two years since her last visit. Tra no longer hosted large family dinners, and when Todd and I came to visit, Tuyen was always absent. It seemed that, though their marriage continued on paper, in spirit they'd already divorced. Tra was clearly suffering, and hanging around with two Americans seemed to lighten her mood. She delighted in showing us out-of-the-way spots in Hanoi, whether it be a hidden pagoda or a shop selling traditional rice candy. Whether because Tra was so Americanized, or simply because she had such an engaging spirit, Todd liked her best of all my friends. The admiration was mutual. When Tra and I had a moment alone, she said, "He's a good guy. A very good guy." Then she added, "You marry him!"

Even though I would have told anyone who asked that it didn't matter whether my friends liked Todd or not, deep down I cared a lot. In a sense, they were like beloved relatives whose ideas about the world were rather different from mine. I wanted them to approve of the choices I made. So I was happy to hear Huong, like Tra, insist that I should marry Todd, and to see Tung nod his head in agreement. It didn't even seem to matter to them that I was two years older than Todd. "*Gái hơn hai, trai hơn một,*" Huong told me, using the old axiom with a satisfied smile: If the girl's older, she should be two years older; if the boy's older, he should be one.

Todd went back to the States after a week in Hanoi. Though Huong might have liked the idea, he and I had never even spoken of marriage. Far from it, in fact. We still shied away from words like "love," but our relationship didn't seem casual anymore, either. For the first time, my consideration of how long I'd stay in Vietnam had quite a bit to do with him.

When I took him to the airport and said good-bye, I had trouble letting go of him. And I knew that, whenever I did return to the States, he'd be waiting.

          Tung, Huong, Viet, and the new baby finally returned to Dream Street about a week before Tet. For the first time in months, the place didn't seem like a boardinghouse anymore. When I left for my Vietnamese class in the morning, I could hear Duc crying in their loft. When I came home in the afternoon, the smell of frying fish or simmering chicken wafted out from the kitchen and through the front door. I decided we had to have a party to celebrate their return.

Todd had brought me a package of treats from the States. I'd finished the bag of Doritos before we ever left Saigon. We'd gone through every single Three Musketeers on the train ride to Nha Trang. I still had ten or twenty Oreos, though, as well as some wintergreen Life Savers, a box of Lipton Earl Gray tea bags, and two cans of anchovies. I hadn't known what to do with cans of anchovies in Vietnam. Now I had an idea.

Pasta puttanesca was one of the only dishes I knew how to make by heart, and so, when I took off for one of Hanoi's new imported food shops, I knew exactly what I needed. The little food stalls ringing the outer walls of the Hang Da Market had once carried almost the only selection of imported items you could find in Hanoi. These days, however, there were small specialty stores springing up all over the place. Items that would have been considered dull staples in the grocery chains of America —corn flakes, jars of pickles, mustard—were luxury items, and expensive, here. But now you could find them easily in Hanoi. Within just a few blocks of my house, I managed to get Italian linguine, French olive oil, and even jars of olives and capers to round out my sauce. After all these months in Hanoi, I got an inordinate amount of pleasure simply from spotting familiar brand names. I'd lived in Vietnam long enough to understand why people from former Communist countries often turn into the greatest capitalists of all.

I came home that afternoon with my arms full of packages. Huong was curious, but, after the hamburger evening, skeptical about my ability to cook. She believed that burgers and fries were something American women learned to make when they were toddlers. What I'd proven to her of my cooking skills was less about what I knew than about what I didn't know. And, I was planning to cook a dish that wasn't even American. It was Italian. She was even more skeptical when I explained that pasta puttanesca meant "streetwalker's pasta." What did I know about Italy, and prostitutes? Besides, she believed that I knew almost nothing about cooking in general. When I'd returned to Vietnam, I'd brought her a carrot peeler as a gift, thinking it would ease the chore of making dinner. Huong had merely laughed and looked at me with pity. What kind of a cook, she'd wanted to know, couldn't even peel a carrot?

This time, I was determined to make the meal myself. Rather than looking uncertainly around the kitchen, I started my preparations purposefully, chopping garlic, then sautéing it with the anchovies in olive oil, explaining every step to Huong as if I were Julia Child.

"That's weird," Huong told me, eyeing the pan full of garlic and salted fish. A few minutes later, when I dumped an entire jar of olives into the concoction on the stove, she gasped, then shook her head. "Well," she told me, "we can always go out for noodle soup."

Huong lurked in the doorway the whole time I was in the kitchen, watching me cook. I only had to glance around the

room and she would jump to find me exactly the right knife. As
soon as my fingers touched the chili sauce, she hurriedly opened
it and helped me measure out a spoonful. She might have been
doubtful of my ability to cook, but she was also determined to
make sure I didn't flop.

By the time dinner was ready, Huong was heavily invested
in the meal's success. While Tung set the table and opened his
cache of Johnnie Walker for us to drink, she stood in front of
the kitchen shelves, trying to figure out how to make Vietnamese dishware work for an Italian dinner. Although both
cultures eat noodles, it was actually quite an awkward fit.
Vietnamese rice-based noodles are light, and slurped, with the
help of chopsticks, out of deep bowls. Italian pasta, on the
other hand, is heavy, and eaten in small quantities out of shallow bowls. If we gave each person enough pasta to fit in a Vietnamese noodle bowl, we'd either end up throwing away a lot
of uneaten pasta, or we'd all get sick. In the end, we abandoned the noodle bowl idea and decided to eat out of tiny rice
bowls.

Tung, who'd eaten Italian before, was almost finished with
his first bowl before Huong even started. She ladled a small
spoonful of sauce over her pasta, explaining, "I don't want to put
too much on it. If I don't like this, I'm going to take the noodles
into the kitchen and stir fry the whole thing." Then, she took a
bite. I sat without moving, watching her chew, then swallow. She
paused for a long time, like a judge contemplating the texture of
pie at the state fair. Then she looked at me and shrugged. "Not
bad," she said.

Tung was already having thirds. Viet was ladling sauce into
his bowl and drinking it straight. Ly held a piece of garlic bread
in her hand, tearing off tiny pieces and nibbling on them, as if she
wanted to eat it slow and savor it. But it was Huong who pleased

me most. "Not bad" was the only verbal compliment she offered, but she ate the sauce like soup, with a spoon. I was more pleased than I cared to admit.

By early February, I had lived in Hanoi for over a year altogether. I'd experienced every season, from the coldest days of winter to the most sweltering summer heat. I'd witnessed all the holidays, from International Women's Day and Teacher's Day to the Mid-Autumn Festival and the birthday of Ho Chi Minh. I'd experienced every holiday—that is, except for Tet. Most Americans hear the word "Tet" and immediately combine it with "Offensive." But for Vietnamese, the word conjured entirely different ideas. Tet, Vietnam's Lunar New Year, was the most important time on the Vietnamese calendar. For Vietnamese, it was like Thanksgiving, Christmas, New Year's, and everybody's birthday combined.

I decided to stay in Hanoi through Tet and then return to the States. Certainly, Todd had a good deal to do with the comparative ease with which I decided to go home. But, more than that, after living for more than a year in Vietnam, and over a span of two, I finally had confidence in the durability of my relationship with this country, and with the strength of my friendships here. When Huong talked about me coming back to visit her again when we were old, I no longer worried that I would never see her again. I fully expected to grow old with her, even if the gaps between my visits lasted years. Huong was like a family member who lived far away, whom I wouldn't see very often, but with whom I managed to feel just as close, and happy, when we did.

Now that Tet was fast approaching, everyone I knew, and even people I didn't know—shopkeepers, friends of friends, the guy who fixed my bike—asked the question that seemed foremost in all their minds: *"Ăn Tết Việt Nam?"* Translated literally, it meant, "Are you going to eat Vietnamese Tet?" but, more roughly, they were anxious to find out if I was going to celebrate Tet here. For Vietnamese, Tet was so fundamental that they seemed to take it as a sign of my commitment to their country.

It did take commitment, really, to spend a Tet in Vietnam. It might have been the *vui*-est holiday of them all, to Vietnamese, but many foreigners considered it a chore. After all, we didn't have the spiritual and traditional connections to it that would make all the more grueling aspects of the holiday worthwhile. For one thing, when people talked of "eating Tet in Viet Nam," they meant it. According to an old Vietnamese adage, "You can go hungry even on the anniversary of your father's death, but you must be full for the three days of Tet." Just as revelers at Mardi Gras consider it their duty to drink, in a country as familiar with hunger as Vietnam, tradition demanded that people stuff themselves at Tet. The eating was intimately connected with the other central activity of Tet, going from house to house to *"chúc Tết"*—wish one another a happy New Year. More and more people were getting lazy and deciding to *chúc Tết* by phone these days, but most people still spent the holiday visiting—and eating. A host would feel insulted if the guest didn't eat something, and though the eating could be as inconsequential as a couple of pieces of candy sampled from the Tet candy dish, just as often it involved sitting down to a feast. Every household I visited had virtually the same menu: five different varieties of fresh fruit, spring rolls, pork sausage, pork-stuffed mushrooms in broth, and *bánh chưng,* a lard- and egg-filled steamed rice cake. Dense and tasteless, *bánh chưng* was the fruitcake of Tet. Vietnamese liked to have it around, but they wouldn't necessarily eat it. They ate everything else, though. American Thanksgiving was like a midnight snack compared to Tet. Rather than one enormous Thursday afternoon feast, Vietnamese would eat this meal twice, sometimes three times a day for at least three days. Vietnamese believed that the way you spent the days of Tet would set the tone of the entire year. Eating a lot at Tet was a way to help insure that you'd have plenty to eat for the next twelve months as well.

Many foreigners who lived in Hanoi celebrated Tet by leaving the country. Why not avoid the *chúc Tết* duties, and the heavy eating, by spending the Vietnamese New Year lounging on a beach in Thailand? The weather was getting colder just as the Vietnamese holiday season erupted in full force, and I could certainly understand the attractions of the beach. But I'd been hearing about Tet for two years. I wasn't going to miss it.

"You can never understand Vietnam," Yen told me, "unless you've experienced Tet." She began to point out things I never would have noticed, things that, for someone who'd grown up in Hanoi, were unmistakable signs of Tet's approach. The stores selling children's clothes, for example, were crowded with parents buying new outfits for their sons and daughters. And sunflower seeds had become, by the end of January, nearly as omnipresent as rice. Vietnamese munched seeds all year, but now they began to consume as if the *crack-crack-crack* of teeth on seeds marked some kind of drumroll for the season. Seeds did, I saw now, demand conviviality. No one sat alone in a room munching seeds. No one ate them for dinner. Seeds were sitting-around-with-friends snacks, *chúc Tết* snacks. In my earliest attempts at Vietnamese, I'd learned a verb for this sort of activity: *ăn nhậu lai rai,* which meant to eat and drink in a leisurely manner, keeping the mouth and fingers happy, while the mind is busy socializing. I thought I'd known what *ăn nhậu lai rai* meant, but it wasn't until I watched Tung and three of his friends sit in our living room one afternoon and consume an entire kilo of sunflower seeds that I finally began to understand the true meaning of the term.

Other signs of the approaching New Year began to appear as well. According to tradition, in the days before Tet, people bring delicacies to others they want to impress. To keep up with the demand for these items, temporary specialty shops opened all over town, their bright red banners wishing everyone a happy Tet and proclaiming the delectability of their particular products. Yen and I went shopping at one of the biggest markets, where shopkeepers stood in front of dozens of glass jars full of sugar-coated dried fruits, the holiday treats known as *mứt*. A saleswoman weighed out half a kilo of apricot *mứt* for Yen to give to her aunt, a mixture of cherry and ginger *mứt* for her mother, and tomato *mứt* she'd give to her favorite professor from the university. All around us, shoppers were stocking up on jars of imported pickles, apricot wine, Russian vodka, dried sausages, and tins of golden Danish sugar cookies. In a country where most diets were limited to whatever local farms and factories produced, a jar of French mustard meant real luxury and could serve as the perfect holiday gift. Foods that foreigners bought in Hanoi all year were now being swept up by the locals.

Vendors began to appear on the city streets selling miniature orange trees and *hoa đào,* the small blossoming peach trees that were as much a requisite part of Tet as Christmas trees at Christmas. The vendors roamed the city with trees slung to the frames of their bikes, and prospective buyers checked the trees carefully, looking for just the right mix of branch, bud, and flower. One afternoon, I took Viet to the Tet flower market, in the center of the city's Old Quarter. With Viet balanced on the back of my bike, I rode right into the center of the market, stopping in what seemed like a forest of trees. The tree-sellers were bundled up against the winter cold, and as the wind picked up, I buttoned all the buttons on Viet's coat. The lacy pink veil of peach blossoms couldn't keep out the chill, but it promised the coming of spring.

Viet, who normally had a hard time interrupting his play long enough to eat or go to the bathroom, was motionless now. "It's beautiful," he whispered. Then he put his face into a mass of blossoms and let the soft petals touch his skin.

I spent a lot of time thinking about what Yen had told me about the days of Tet setting the stage for the entire year. If your Tet was happy, she'd told me, you'd have a happy year. If it was sad, you'd have a sad one. Even Tung and Huong took this concept very seriously, though they were not at all religious. They had a little ancestral altar, but they often seemed to forget that it was there. As Tet approached, though, they both sprang into action. Huong cut Viet's hair and bought new outfits for both him and the baby. Tung had the Dream washed and buffed until it glistened as much as anything could glisten on those sunless winter days. Ly stood on a ladder and pulled year-old spiderwebs off the ceiling with the handle of a broom. One afternoon, a few days before New Year's, Tung brought home a peach tree and moved the TV out of the way so that the plant would occupy the most prominent position in our house.

Hanoi's wealthy weren't the only ones preparing. The street children who lived on Cam Chi Street, where I ate noodle soup, were getting ready as well. All year, they slept in a half-hidden corner of the alley; at first glance, their bodies, curled around one another, looked like piles of discarded rags. Over the past few months, I had gotten to know a few of them. One afternoon, I invited an adolescent girl and a boy of about ten to eat with me. They were shy, and, at first, they couldn't even look at me. Only after the food arrived, and we all had something to

focus on, did they begin to relax. I asked them about their lives.
Both had left home in the countryside because their families
were too poor to take care of them. They lived in Hanoi and returned home once a year, at Tet, bringing with them whatever
money they'd been able to save over the past twelve months. It
seemed ironic that homeless children sleeping on the streets of
the city would end up being breadwinners for their families back
home, but that's how the economy was shaping up in Vietnam.
They could earn more than farmers out in the countryside. The
girl had managed to save ten thousand dong, about ten dollars.
The boy, who was younger, cuter, and therefore more successful at begging, had earned fifteen. They would have had more,
they told me, but they'd both been robbed. They explained all
this to me as if they were telling me what grades they got in
school, and not describing the circumstances of urban homeless-
ness. We were just three people having lunch together who happened to be discussing poverty. After lunch, I gave them some
money, but, later, after I'd gone home, I decided to give them
more. By the time I went back to the food stall alley, however, all
of the street children were gone. They'd already returned to the
countryside.

By then, the firecrackers were beginning to explode. Children treated them as toys and shot them like missiles into the
rush-hour traffic. Foreigners were easy targets, a fact that added
a whole new challenge to my rides through the city. The Vietnamese authorities had begun to criticize firecrackers as a social
problem, and thus, in the fluid way that official opinion came to
dominate the pages of the press, newspapers ran prominent stories about fireworks-related deaths. In one incident I heard
about, a bus exploded because a reveler had set off a firecracker
inside it. By the next year, in fact, the government, citing danger
and expense, would ban firecrackers entirely, which meant that

my first Tet was the last explosive one in Vietnam. For now, though, Hanoians were still setting them off with abandon.

Hanoi became strange and dreamlike then. Even time changed. As if following some subtle shift designated by the heavens, just as the holiday began, Vietnamese returned to their ancient tradition of marking days. Throughout the rest of the year, they follow the solar-based calendar that's used in the West. At Tet, they switch to the lunar one. If, for example, Tet began at midnight on February 9, then February 10 was the first day of the Lunar New Year. Suddenly, Vietnamese began to follow the moon. No matter what the Western calendar might call the date on which the Lunar New Year's Eve fell, Vietnamese called it "the thirtieth of Tet," and, according to the logic of the season, New Year's Day itself was known as "the first of Tet," followed by the second, the third, fourth, etc. The rest of the world continued racing through the same old year, while Vietnam stepped off for a week and then, reluctantly, stepped back on.

Because the holiday set the tone for the coming year, Vietnamese gave a great deal of thought to whom they would invite to be the first person to walk through their front door in the first minutes after the new year began. It must be a person whose previous year has been prosperous, or a person with a reputation for bringing luck. As a foreigner, I was considered both prosperous and lucky. Thus, almost everyone I knew wanted me to come visit them on Tet. The competition for my presence was so great that I had to settle my schedule weeks in advance, filling every day like a dance card to accommodate all the people anxious to have me visit.

My first appointment was at Yen's house, where I'd committed myself to helping cook, then eat, the feast for New Year's Eve. The family had made their *bánh chưng* well in advance (also like fruitcake, *bánh chưng* has a long shelf life), but there was much more to do before the new year arrived. I sat on the kitchen floor, wrapping spring rolls, while Yen, her mother, and her younger sister hurried to complete the dozen or so dishes they would prepare as an offering to their ancestors. Only after the ancestors have had their share of the food could the living family members eat. As we completed each dish, Yen or her sister would climb the three flights of stairs to the family altar, then set the dish there. For hours, the two sisters ran back and forth between the kitchen and the altar, while their mother and I kept working in the kitchen.

It was after dusk already, and the firecrackers were exploding constantly on the streets outside. I looked out the window, excited but nervous about the increasing onslaught of noise. I'd grown up watching firecrackers from a cozy distance on the Fourth of July. These explosives were closer, constant, and more dangerous.

Yen's mother, a successful businesswoman who ran a number of beer halls in Hanoi, could see that I was edgy. "Don't you have firecrackers in the States?" she asked.

"Yes, but mostly for public displays," I said. "In many states, people are forbidden to buy or sell them."

"Forbidden!" She found the idea incredible. "Why?"

"Because they're so dangerous," I said.

Yen's mother was silent for a while, slicing beef and considering what I'd told her. When she looked up at me again, she had a smirk on her face. "So you Americans aren't allowed to shoot off firecrackers," she said, "but it's quite all right for you to carry guns around and shoot each other?"

A huge bang went off in what must have been a neighbor's yard. It was followed by a string of tiny pops that sounded like machine-gun fire. Yen's mother looked back down at her cutting board, chuckling, neither expecting a response nor wanting one. I stopped what I was doing and gazed outside, but the night was dark and I couldn't see a thing. Even though Yen's mother seemed satisfied with her knowledge of my country, part of me felt that she should know that her information wasn't accurate, that it wasn't "quite all right" for Americans to shoot one another. In the end, though, I kept silent, reaching my fingers into the bowl full of spring roll filling and continuing to wrap. There was no point, really, in correcting her. And, in some ways, she wasn't all wrong.

By the time we finally sat down for the first feast of Tet, we were too exhausted even to talk, and we ate almost silently. The women in Yen's family had spent the last weeks cleaning and cooking without respite. For them, the holiday was no vacation. Still, their tired faces showed content, even joy. Afterward, we went out to the front porch, and Yen's father and sister lit firecrackers.

Midnight on New Year's Eve, known as *giao thừa,* is the most significant moment of the Vietnamese year, and I wanted to experience it at the very center of the city. At around ten that night, Yen drove me over to my friend Van's, who lived near Hoan Kiem Lake. After all the exploding firecrackers of the past few weeks, now, only hours before the new year arrived, the streets were eerily quiet. Almost everyone was inside their homes, setting offerings before their altars and praying. On every doorway hung a long strand holding hundreds of bright red firecrackers, ready to be lit at precisely the instant when the new year arrived. At Van's house, five or six of us sat drinking rice wine. We didn't look so different from a group of friends hanging out on New Year's Eve in the States, but it didn't feel like an American New Year's Eve at all. The evening seemed hushed and somber, as if something enormous were about to happen. We kept glancing at the clock.

And then, as the clock struck twelve, the firecrackers began to pop, slowly at first, but with increasing frequency. We walked out of Van's house and made our way up Ba Trieu Street toward Hoan Kiem Lake. For so many weeks, I had braced myself for this moment when the world would explode, and now it was happening.

I couldn't see anything except the black of the sky, the white flash of exploding firecrackers, and the rusty fog of smoke. But the noise was a demon in the air. For the first time in my life I could imagine the sound of war. And that, perhaps, was one of the main reasons foreigners had such a problem with Tet. Given Vietnam's history of war, *giao thừa* could have given outsiders an uncomfortable suspicion that there were inherently violent tendencies within Vietnamese culture. On the surface, it seemed true. Any culture that would willingly put itself through something as aurally painful and potentially destructive as the simultaneous explosion of millions of firecrackers seemed, at the very least, masochistic. But standing in the middle of Hanoi at the moment of *giao thừa*, I realized that something entirely different was going on. All around me people were joyous, not reveling in the danger, but reveling in their happiness. At that moment, I began to understand the truth about Tet. Vietnamese didn't love firecrackers because of their violence. They loved them because of their noise. Firecrackers were Vietnam's call to the heavens: "Here we are! Don't forget us! Let the new year be better!" Clutching my hands to my ears to protect them from the sound, I knew that what Yen had said was true. Tet revealed the essential nature of Vietnam. This place was complicated, yes, and full of pain as well, but beneath the hardship lay a sense of joy, a recognition of change, and, perhaps most significantly, a pervasive hope for the future.

My head ached from all the explosions, but my whole body

felt alive and strangely grateful to have a head that could ache, lungs that could fill with smoky air, ears that could ring, and, most importantly, a mind that could sense the power of what was happening all around me. Holding my fingers in my ears, I rotated in slow circles, bracing myself for each new flash of light. Vietnam changed then. For a few brief moments at least, it floated between reality and dream, between heaven and earth. As an outsider, I might never fully understand the meaning of Tet, but I knew that I was witnessing something spectacular and precious. A whole nation, through the force of firecrackers and collective will, was transforming itself into something utterly different, to herald the future, and welcome it.

For days after *giao thừa,* every street and sidewalk was covered with the paper fragments of exploded firecrackers, which Hanoians considered a blanket of lucky red covering the city and all of Vietnam. I spent the days of Tet in a whirl of feast after feast, visit after visit. Most of my visits were also good-byes, because I planned to leave for the States on the fifth day. I wasn't the only one going away. My friend Linh was also leaving Vietnam. Son had managed to secure a coveted position at the Vietnamese embassy in France, and the family was about to move to Paris. On the evening I went by their house, they were packing up the last of their belongings. It was an ironic time for them to leave. After living for years in a bare, one-room house, they'd finally saved enough money to complete an extensive renovation, enlarging their space into a three-room home with a tile floor, a comfortable loft, and, most thrilling of all, a sparkling new Western-style bathroom. The place wasn't big, but, for a family that had quite recently used a tin pail for a toilet, it was like a palace. Their fortunes had improved so much that Linh was able to quit her job at the Metropole Hotel in order to go be a housewife in Paris. Despite all that, she wasn't completely happy about the idea of leaving Vietnam. She'd never been overseas before, had never even ridden in an airplane. The flight to Europe would take an entire day, she told me. She was worried that they wouldn't have enough food to eat on board. That they wouldn't be able to sleep. And, up in the air, a plane can't stop. What if one of her little sons had to pee? As she walked me to the door that night to say good-bye, she held my hand tightly. "Write letter to me," she whispered fiercely. "Over there in Paris, I will be very lonely."

I gripped her hand, telling her not to worry. I'd been lonely when I first arrived in Vietnam, I said, but, slowly, I'd managed to build a life for myself and make friends here. "You'll have a good life in Paris," I said. "You'll be happy there."

Linh didn't look convinced. "I don't love Paris," she told me. "You love Vietnam."

No one ever seemed puzzled by the fact that an American woman would abandon the United States, with all its glitzy cities, modern conveniences, and wealth, in order to come live in a country as poor and troubled as Vietnam. I'd often had to explain my actions to people in America, but the Vietnamese didn't even ask. They could understand why I loved their country, because, despite their grudges and gripes about things as fundamental and disparate as the weather, the government, and the economy, they loved it, too.

I left Vietnam on the fifth of Tet. After five days, which all of Hanoi spent eating, drinking, and racing all over town, the holiday spirit was finally beginning to diminish. Huong didn't make as much of an effort anymore to keep her

Tet dish full of sunflower seeds and candied ginger. Tung, who had visited aunts and uncles, old school friends, and former teachers, now began to draw the line, telling himself that it just wasn't that important to go visit one more distant cousin and one more former neighbor. He settled down on the couch and began to *chúc Tết* by phone instead. Out on Dream Street, some of the shops were open again, conducting business as usual. For the past few days, it had been impossible to find any food in the city, other than what people were serving in their homes. Now, a couple of the stalls on Cam Chi Street were, once again, ladling out steaming bowls of noodle soup. With the waning of the holiday, the wedding season was officially beginning again, and the fifth of Tet must have been deemed, by those who read the calendars, an auspicious day for nuptials, because busloads of wedding revelers kept zooming past our house. Sometimes, I could spot the bride and groom, riding by in a rented car covered in garlands of silk flowers. Some couples wore the traditional Vietnamese *áo dài*. Others wore garb so Western that they could have posed for the figures on the top of an American wedding cake. Many couples did both, spending the first half of the day in traditional Vietnamese costume and the second half in black tux and silky white dress.

Tung rode in the car with me to the airport. We talked for a while about his plan to open the Kangaroo Pub with Max, a dream for him that had never materialized, but in which he still believed. Tung's dreams were as grand as ever, but, these days, he seemed more content with what he had, less desperate to make every new dream come true. Sitting in the car with him, I wondered if it was age or experience that had mellowed him, but I didn't have a chance to ask. Tung was so worn out from Tet that when I turned to look at him again, just after we'd crossed the bridge out of the city, his eyes were closed and his breathing was already heavy in sleep. I turned again and looked out the window. I didn't mind the silence at all.

The night before I left, I'd invited friends over. Phai came, but he didn't stay long. When he got up to go, I walked outside and stood on the steps with him. The night was quiet, with only the occasional rumble of a motorbike passing by on Dream Street. Behind us, I could hear Tung and Paula laughing. Duc, lying in Huong's arms, began to cry. A cassette tape of Vietnamese pop music, which my former student John had brought, formed a sugary, synthetic backdrop to the murmur of people's voices. Phai seemed distracted, but anxious to say something before he left. Just as he was about to speak, however, Tung's mother arrived on her bicycle. After a minute, she went into the house. I waited to see if Phai would speak, but I didn't press him. Whatever it was he wanted to say, I wasn't anxious to hear it. I wanted this good-bye to be kind to both of us. These days, I felt grateful to him in a way that, even in my most articulate moments, I couldn't have expressed.

I lunged forward and hugged him. When I pulled back, he was looking at me. He was smiling, but I could see the hurt, again, in his eyes. He took my hand and squeezed it, then he turned and walked down the steps. I watched him pass the building that had once housed the motorbike shop, the spot where he'd squatted on the sidewalk taking apart a carburetor while I stood on my balcony, gazing down at him. The two of us had walked along that sidewalk together so many times, heading off for a bowl of noodle soup after spending hours in bed. All of that seemed long ago now, years in the past, but not impossible.

"Duyen!" Huong called to me from inside the house.

In the gray morning, the road that led to the airport passed along rice fields and was dotted with puddles from a predawn rain. We drove past a man carrying a bride on the back of his motorbike. The woman sat sidesaddle, her white dress hiked up to keep the ruffles from dragging through the mud. Her arm was around his waist, and her face was impassive as she stared ahead, up the road. Looking at them through the car window, I remembered a photograph I'd seen once of an image like this one, published in some magazine somewhere in the States. It was supposed to reveal the quintessence of modern Vietnam: the fascination with Western style, the contrast between the novelty of technology and the timelessness of the rice fields, a bride's hope for the future competing against the hopelessness of keeping her wedding gown clean as she passed along this muddy road. The image was perfect, really, but I didn't like the thought of it. Looking out through the window, I could already feel the growing distance between myself and this place I had come to love. It was so easy, from far away, to turn people into symbols, a bride into "Vietnam," the indefinable into apparent truth.

When we arrived at the airport, I nudged Tung awake, and he helped me with my bags. He wasn't allowed into the terminal, but, since I had two hours before my flight took off, he suggested that I check in, then come back outside and drink a cup of coffee with him. Tung was getting a free ride back in my taxi, but that wasn't until after the next international flight arrived, in several hours. I knew how much he hated to wait.

It only took me half an hour to put my luggage through the X-ray machines set up to make sure tourists weren't taking any antiquities (or seditious videotapes or books) out of the country, then to check my luggage, pick up my boarding pass, and pay my airport tax to leave Vietnam. By the time I got back outside, Tung was talking to a man I didn't recognize. "This is my friend, Minh. He drives a taxi," Tung explained.

I nodded at Minh, then turned to Tung. "Do you want to go for coffee now?" I asked.

Tung looked at me, then glanced nervously at his friend, who was peering out across the parking lot and twirling a key chain on his finger. "Minh's on his way back to the city now," Tung said. He left it at that, looking embarrassed.

I understood immediately. "Go with him," I said, emphasizing more satisfaction in my words than I actually felt inside.

Tung looked at me, his face uncertain. Minh had already started off across the pavement, headed toward the parking lot.

"Go on," I urged.

Tung stood there, hesitating, and I imagined that he was trying to figure out what Huong would say he should do. I could tell by the look on his face that the lure of the ride was too much for him. He grinned at me, embarrassed, then we hugged each other, American style. A moment later, he was jogging off across the parking lot, getting into the little gray car, and driving away. And that was it. I turned around then, went into the airport, and prepared to return to America. During all my time in Vietnam, I'd never wanted anything more than to see these people as people, not as the enemy, not as poverty, not as a focus for America's anger or guilt. The image of Tung dozing off in a car heading back toward the city didn't say as much about modern Vietnam as a bride on a motorbike might have done. But it was the Vietnam I knew. It was true. And it was what I'd always wanted.

$\mathcal{W}$hen I returned to Vietnam in May of 1998, the house on Dream Street wasn't a house anymore. Tung had managed to lease it out, long-term, to a Vietnamese company that had converted the whole building into an office. I felt a bit sad knowing that I wouldn't get to sleep in my sweet bedroom anymore, but I wasn't surprised by the news. I had known about their move for months already. These days, Tung had e-mail. We didn't communicate very often, because we were still pretty lazy correspondents, but we managed to exchange all the important information nonetheless.

Tung and Huong knew that Todd and I had married in 1995, that Todd had been hired as an English professor at the University of North Carolina at Wilmington, and that we had moved there from San Francisco in 1996. They also knew that in 1997 our son Jesse was born. Of course, Huong had been ready for me to have a baby for years, and she'd even managed to send, through mutual friends, two packages of baby clothes: the first as a wedding present (a not-too-subtle hint) and the second after Jesse actually arrived.

Now that they'd leased their house, they were living, again, with Huong's parents, where they'd spent those first few months after Duc was born. Tung had never opened the Kangaroo Pub; now he was putting his energy into arranging tours for foreigners traveling through Vietnam. He'd introduced Sa, the young woman who'd stolen the $100, to a German man looking for a Vietnamese wife. But Sa's strong spirit didn't appeal to a Westerner who wanted a demure Asian bride, and the German ended up marrying Ly instead. Now, Ly was living somewhere in Germany. Sa was back in the countryside, working in the rice fields with her father again.

I also knew about Phai. Sort of. In one e-mail, after telling me the news about Ly's marriage, Tung had added, "Phai also got married last year, his wife already five months gone." I spent a long time trying to decipher that one. Had Tung's English gotten so good that he knew that "gone," in this context, could be taken to mean "pregnant"? Or, when he wrote "gone" did he mean *gone?*

The telephone in our guesthouse room rang just a few minutes after we arrived. Todd was holding Jesse down on the bed, changing a diaper. I'd been unpacking our suitcases, and I walked over to the phone and picked it up. "Hello?" I said. Except for a few intermittent conversations with friends in San Francisco, I hadn't spoken Vietnamese in more than two years. Luckily, except for a slight difference in pronunciation— "allo" instead of "hello"—Vietnamese answer the phone just like Americans do.

"Duyen? Dana?" It was a man's voice, and vaguely familiar.

"Yes?" I said in English.

"I am Phai!"

My mind raced around like a nearsighted person trying to find her glasses. Finally, I was able to stutter a ridiculous-sounding, "*Có khỏe không?*" I remembered that it was the wrong thing to say, that Vietnamese reserved "How are you?" for people who'd been sick, but I was out of practice.

"*Rất khỏe,*" Phai answered. "*Có con gái rồi!*" I'm just fine— I've got a baby girl!

"Really?" I was so thrilled that I dropped the Vietnamese entirely, and I was grateful, for once, that Phai had enough English to keep the conversation going.

"My family. Party. Wednesday. You come?" he asked.

"Yes!" I said.

⌒⌒⌒⌒⌒ Because I returned to Vietnam with a husband and a child (and a male child at that), my friends treated my arrival like the homecoming of a hero. Finally, after all these years, I'd fulfilled those womanly duties about which they'd been needling me all along. "Now you are a happy lady!" cooed Linh. "You have every dream come true in life." Huong, who was less given to hyperbole, said, "It's about time. You're old already." And Tra, who was more skeptical about the institution of marriage, and more taken by the West, told me, "I'm happy you found a good American. Vietnamese guys are too much bother."

Linh called herself a happy lady, too. She and Son and their boys had recently returned to Vietnam from France. In addition to his job at the Vietnamese embassy, Son had moonlighted by translating legal documents for French families adopting Vietnamese babies. He'd amassed a considerable fortune that way, and their house in Hanoi, which they'd renovated once already, was now a four-story palace. They had two bedrooms, two kitchens, two bathrooms, an exercise machine, a washer and dryer, an aquarium full of tropical fish, and a life-size sculpture of a tiger.

Much more than Linh and Son's material life had improved. Their experience showed that money could solve an awful lot of problems. Of course, Linh still complained to me that she didn't believe her husband loved her enough. She had yearnings he couldn't satisfy, and those desires would probably never fade away. But she was a stay-at-home mom now. She had her own motorbike and no longer had to argue with her husband over transportation. For a couple that had struggled, daily, over such issues, being rich was no small thing. I would never forget the envy in Linh's eyes, years back, when she came over to my house in Hanoi and saw the expensive furniture and frivolous knickknacks with which Tung and Huong had furnished their home. Now, she was a woman of leisure herself, spending her days taking Japanese classes, visiting friends, and cooking. She spoke of the changes in her life with such joy and relief that it seemed she would never take a single luxury for granted.

Linh's life had improved, but Tung and Huong's appeared to have gotten worse, at least in terms of material convenience. They were living in a cramped two-room house in Huong's parents' compound, some distance from the center of town. Compared to the average living conditions in the West, compared, even, to what they had enjoyed on Dream Street, their new conditions were almost squalid. Tung and Huong slept in the main room, which contained, in addition to their bed, as much of the furniture from their old place as they could squeeze in: a couch, chairs, bureaus, a wardrobe, desk, television, and computer. Off the main room, Huong's "kitchen" was a cold-water sink with a bit of floor space underneath it. Beyond that was a tiny toilet and the boys' bedroom, which didn't have much more space than a closet.

Given such an obvious change, I wouldn't have been surprised to hear Huong and Tung complaining, but I didn't. Like Linh and Son, they had achieved a degree of contentment with their lives that I couldn't have imagined a few years before. It wasn't that either of these couples had solved all their marital problems, or even that they now communicated better than they had before. But, as Huong explained to me when the two of us had a moment alone, she and Tung had finally learned "to understand each other better, without having to talk." She seemed more content than I'd ever seen her, and she took better care of herself, too. She wore makeup, jewelry, pretty dresses, and even high heels. In another woman, such attention to fashion might not have meant a thing, but with Huong it demonstrated that she'd started to care. She wanted to do more than sit around her house all day and watch TV. The two of us zoomed around on her motorbike, ate in restaurants, and went shopping. When she heard Todd and I worrying about whether or not restaurant food would be hygienic enough for Jesse, she offered to make him rice porridge to eat instead. For the remainder of our visit, she cooked a batch of it every morning, then brought it over to our guesthouse on her motorbike.

Not all of my friends were happier now than they'd been when I met them. In the summer of 1997, Thailand's economy had collapsed, sparking the beginning of the Asian economic crisis. Vietnam's excessive bureaucracy and rampant corruption had already helped to dim the once-glowing forecasts about foreign investment and the country's economy, and this new regional crisis didn't help. Fewer multinational corporations were willing to invest in Vietnam, and some that had already invested were pulling out. Among all of my friends, Tra had suffered the most. Armed with her American M.B.A., she had returned to Vietnam in 1996 and, at first, been offered a number of jobs. None had thrilled her, and she'd decided to take her time before settling on anything permanent. Then, as the economy declined, the offers started to dry up. Now, Tra had the exact same job at a Vietnamese government institute that she'd had before she ever left for the States. Her salary amounted to something like thirty dollars a month, hardly the income she'd struggled all those years in Michigan to earn.

As expected, Tra's personal life had changed as well. Her marriage to Tuyen had finally ended in divorce, and their son Minh, a teenager now, preferred to spend most of his time with his father. Tra lived alone, renting out the spare rooms in her big house to boarders. She was philosophical about her bad luck, and tried to joke about it, but she couldn't hide her sadness. "You've got to find me a good American husband," she told me and Todd, as if a perfect spouse were as easy to come by as the jars of Oil of Olay I'd brought her from the States. "I've had enough of these Vietnamese men. I want someone *progressive!*" Tra was forty years old and as attractive and resilient as ever. But it was hard to say that her future looked bright.

Before coming to Vietnam, I'd traveled quite a bit. I kept moving, however, and almost never returned to a place I'd already seen. The Scotland I know is from 1983. India, for me, is frozen in 1989. After coming here over the course of nearly a decade, I had enjoyed the luxury of watching it change. I remembered when there were twice as many bicycles as motorbikes in Hanoi. These days, it seemed like just the opposite. I remembered when the typical summertime outfit for a Hanoi woman would be a thin cotton pajama set and plastic slip-on sandals. Now, she'd be as likely to have on hot pants and platform shoes. I remembered when red banners hung over the streets, proclaiming the wisdom of Ho Chi Minh. You could still see the banners these days, but it was hard to spot them among all the billboards for Coca-Cola and Toshiba. I felt grateful to have witnessed this country's transformation over all these years. But it was the more intimate changes that moved me most. Tung had gray hairs now. Linh's son Giang had grown into a shy and gangly teenager. Grandmother Nhi had taken ill and passed away.

And after all this time, I could see how much I'd changed as well. Living in Vietnam had caused a shift in the way I saw the world. When I read about the war in Bosnia, the genocide in Rwanda, or our bombing of Iraq, the people of those countries no longer seemed so far away, or impossible to comprehend. They could have been Huong, or Linh, or Tra, or me. I had learned, finally, that I am not so different from all the other people in this world. The idea seems simple, and obvious, and I'm sure that my teachers tried, again and again, to teach it to me years ago in school. But it is one thing to hear something and another to figure it out for oneself. I had to spend some time in Vietnam to learn it.

On the night of Phai's party, Todd, Jesse, and I took a taxi to the Nghia Dung neighborhood. Phai was waiting for us in front of his house. As soon as we appeared, a huge smile spread across his face and he hurried toward us, both arms outstretched. "Allo!" he said, immediately grabbing Todd's hand and shaking it vigorously. Then his eyes swept over to me. "Duyen!" he said. He'd changed a bit. He sported a sparse mustache, and his skin, older now, had grown less smooth and fresh. His body was as small and wiry as ever, but his face had filled out enough that a Vietnamese would have clucked approvingly, "*Béo hơn!*"— You've fattened up! What struck me most deeply, and what stayed with me longest, was the change in his expression. Tonight, he emitted confidence and satisfaction. His eyes showed none of that too-familiar pain, or the failed attempts to hide it. "Baby!" he exclaimed, and, with one scoop, he lifted Jesse out of my arms and carried him like a tiny prince into the house.

I followed Phai back to the private bedroom he now shared with his wife and child, the room he'd talked of building so many years before. It was narrow and plain, furnished with a stand-up electric fan, a wooden bureau, and the bed, which filled an entire end of the room. Bare as it was, however, a fresh coat of pale blue paint and a new linoleum floor gave it a clean, cheerful look. On one wall hung a day-by-day calendar with tear-off pages. Against another wall sat a small case full of books. For an instant, I remembered that I could have been the one to live here with him, but then something pulled my attention away. On the bed sat Phai's bride, Thuy, with their daughter.

Thuy was curled up on the pink sheet, cross-legged and barefoot, with the little bundle of baby in her lap. As soon as she spotted me, she leapt off the bed and, baby in her arms, rushed in my direction. "Miss Duyen!" she gasped, pushing the infant into my arms. "Here's our child." Thuy was small-framed and delicate. She had bright eyes, full lips, and a braid that fell like a rope down her back. A new mother's cloud of exhaustion hung over her face, but her expression was very *vui*. The two of us sat down on the bed together and I held Ngan, Phai's daughter, who was still so new to the world that she couldn't even hold up her head.

Thuy gazed at me. "I'm so happy to meet you," she said in Vietnamese, her hand gripping mine. "As soon as I met Phai, he told me about his American friend Duyen, and about how precious you are to him."

Thuy had used the word "*qúy*," which translates as "precious" or "esteemed." One could use the word to describe one's feelings toward one's grandparents, but I could also remember how Phai would whisper it into my ear while he and I were lying in bed.

"Phai is *quý* to me, too," I stuttered, wondering what she knew.

Voices drifted in from outside the door, and within a few moments the room was crowded with women cooing over the baby. Huong and Linh arrived, then an American named Kyra, an expatriate whom I'd introduced to Phai years before. The one-month birthday of his daughter turned into a reunion, and we moved into the main room of the house, where a feast of a dozen dishes had been laid out on straw mats spread across the floor. Down at one end of the room, the men ate, smoked cigarettes, and drank their beer. Jesse played on the floor, alternating his attention between Todd and Phai's father, who knew how to whistle like a bird. Thuy sat down at my end, holding Ngan in her arms, gently caressing her. Linh and Huong admired each other's clothes and gossiped. Phai's mother, debilitated now by illness, sat on a bed eating rice with a spoon.

Seeing Phai's mother reminded me that his life still had its sorrows. None of his enterprising job ideas had evolved into a successful career. And according to Huong, he had no work at all. Because he and Thuy lived with his parents, their expenses would be low. But now they had a child to raise. Phai could no longer get by on only a few thousand dong for a week. Whenever I looked at him, though, he was smiling. Even when he and I had been intimate, he had never allowed me to fret about his future. He certainly wouldn't do so now.

We'd finished eating. Son, Tung, and Todd were laughing, telling jokes. Phai got up and walked over to where I was sitting. "Duyen," he said, squatting beside me. Thuy had taken baby Ngan into the bedroom to nurse her to sleep. Jesse, worn out from so much play, was curled up in my lap, sucking his thumb. It was almost time for us to leave. "Are you happy?" Phai asked, in Vietnamese.

For years now, I had considered my life and Phai's as two lines that had intersected briefly, then veered off in opposite directions. But now we seemed quite similar. We were the same age, both recently married, and each of us had a child. In the most fundamental ways, our lives were running parallel after all. I looked at Phai and nodded. "I'm happy," I told him. "And you?"

His face eased into a wide grin, and he shifted into English. "Happy very very," he said, and he had a look in his eyes that told me he meant it.

Acknowledgments

The verb *acknowledge* sounds too unenthusiastic to express the gratitude that I feel for the support I've received while writing this book.

First, and most importantly, I'd like to thank the people whose stories I told here. In order to protect their privacy, I changed their names and certain biographical details, but I struggled to capture the truths of their lives in a way that I hope will satisfy them.

I have learned about Vietnam from many sources, but I especially wish to thank Robert Brigham, Nguyen Ba Chung, Nguyen Nguyet Cam, Barbara Cohen, Lou Dematteis, Dan Duffy, Wayne Karlin, Le Minh Khue, Natasha Kraevskaia, Bui Hoai Mai, T. T. Nhu, Peter Saidel, Lisa Spivey, Vu Dan Tan, Nguyen Huy Thiep, Bac Hoai Tran, and Peter Zinoman. Thanks to Kyanh Tonnu for her astute analysis of Vietnamese attitudes toward illness and to Neil Jamieson, whose *Understanding Vietnam* helped me do just that.

Nell Bernstein, Bill Clegg, Linzy Emery, Sara Frankel, Laura Fraser, Randy Frisch, Sherry Goodman, Carolyn Jones, Eileen Kelly, Hope Mitnick, Kathryn Olney, Kathy Steuer, and Kathryn Winogura all either read pieces of this book or offered other forms of valuable advice along the way. I don't know that I could have finished this manuscript without the unfailing guidance and unwavering support of Paul Wilkes. Thanks also to the community of writers at the University of North Carolina at Wilmington, particularly Wendy Brenner, Stanley Colbert, Rebecca Lee, Lindsay Pentolfe-Aegerter, and Bob Reiss. Thanks to my agent, Sarah Lazin, and her associate, Cory Halaby, for all of their efforts, and to my editor, Kathy Pories, whose wisdom and precision added immeasurably to this book.

Finally, I wish to thank everyone in my large and loving family, especially Diane Sachs, Ira Sachs, Lynne Sachs, Ira Sachs, Jr., Rose Sachs, Todd Berliner, and Jesse Berliner-Sachs. I've had many blessings in my life, and I can trace every one of them back to you.